SOCIOLOGICAL THEORY
AND
SURVEY RESEARCH

*Institutional Change and Social Policy
in Great Britain*

Edited by *Timothy Leggatt*

 SAGE Publications

For information address:

SAGE PUBLICATIONS Ltd.
44 Hatton Garden
London EC1N 8ER

SAGE PUBLICATIONS Inc.
275 South Beverly Drive
Beverly Hills, California 90212

International Standard Book Number 0-8039-9902-X

Library of Congress Catalog Card Number 74-76326

FIRST PRINTING

Printed and Bound in Great Britain by BURGESS & SON (Abingdon) Ltd., Abingdon, Berkshire.

CONTENTS

iii

JACK BARNES of the Centre for Studies in Social Policy, worked in the Research and Statistics Group of the Inner London Education Authority, 1968-1972. His current interests are in urban problems, income distribution and the analysis of trends in public expenditure.

JAY G. BLUMLER is Reader in Mass Communication at the University of Leeds and Director of its Centre for Television Research. He has written about the influence of broadcasting on industrial relations, the mass communication of images of British royalty, and the different roles available to audience members in the political communication process.

RICHARD BROWN is Senior Lecturer in Sociology at the University of Durham. His research interests are in the sociology of work, industry and organizations.

GEOFFREY HAWTHORN, Lecturer in Sociology at the University of Cambridge, was Visiting Professor of Sociology and Demography at Harvard University in 1973. His research interests include the social and economic determinants of fertility.

MORRIS JANOWITZ Professor of Sociology at the University of Chicago, was Pitt Professor of American History and Institutions at the University of Cambridge, 1972-73. He is currently engaged in preparing a theoretical analysis of social control in the United States.

JOHN D. KASARDA is Assistant Professor of Sociology at the University of Chicago and Book Review Editor of the American Journal of Sociology. His current research interest is in the ecological basis of the urban crisis in the U.S.A. and the changing structure of suburban America.

TIMOTHY LEGGATT Fellow of King's College, Cambridge, was formerly Lecturer in Sociology at the University of Sussex. His current research interests are managerial careers, systems of education and the development of the social sciences.

HENRY LUCAS now working for the Institute of Development Studies and the Centre of Social Research at the University of Sussex, was in the Research and Statistics Group of the Inner London Education Authority, 1971-73. He is mainly interested in the impact of social statistics on policy formulation.

JACK M. McLEOD is Professor of Journalism and Mass Communication, and Chairman of the Mass Communications Research Center, at the University of Wisconsin (Madison). His research focus over the last decade has been on co-orientation and interpersonal communication process, socialization, and professionalization in the mass media.

RICHARD T. SCHAEFER is Assistant Professor of Sociology and Anthropology at Western Illinois University. He is currently engaged in research concerning American Indians and changes in occupational prestige as evaluated by college students in the United States.

JAMES SPENCE now at Social and Community Planning Research, was formerly in charge of the political opinion poll at National Opinion Polls, 1968-73. His current research is into new town planning, public participation in planning, and political behaviour.

MICHAEL WHITE of Ashridge Management College, has held research appointments at the Oxford Centre for Management Studies and the Ashridge Management Research Unit. His research interests currently include the methodology of organizational surveys, and managerial ideology.

PREFACE

This volume presents a series of research papers on contemporary Britain which grew out of an ongoing seminar on "Sociological Theory and Survey Research" sponsored by the Survey Unit of the Social Science Research Council. The twin aims of the seminar were to stimulate the application of sociological theory to the analysis of survey research and to examine specific contributions of survey research to sociological theory. The explicit assumption which led to the organization of the seminar was that more extensive application of sociological theory to survey research results could and would increase the relevance of survey research findings to issues of social policy.

It is a commonplace that survey research groups collect more data than they are able to analyze effectively. The pressures of immediate policy problems help to account for the increasing volume of data collected by survey research methodology. Budgetary restrictions and the mechanics of managing the day-to-day machinery of a social survey reduce the capacity of staff members to develop their analyses so as to relate them to wider theoretical frameworks. On the other hand, it remains difficult to understand why sociologists in universities fail to exploit extensively these sources of data. The goal of the seminar, therefore, was to make a contribution toward narrowing the gap between survey research and sociological theory, and to serve as a bridge between independent research groups and university-based sociologists.

The format of the seminar was a year-long series of meetings in London, 1972-73, which brought together a number of social scientists who in varying degrees were engaged in survey research in Great Britain and/or were concerned with the development of operational sociological theory. Each of the core members of the seminar had at his disposal an existing body of survey research data. He presented to the seminar periodically his plan for reanalysis and the emerging results of his efforts. The other members of the seminar served as discussants and critics and thereby produced an active and critical forum reflecting differing approaches and expertise.

The seminar was organized and chaired by Morris Janowitz, Department of Sociology, University of Chicago, who at the time was Pitt Professor, University of Cambridge and Fellow of Peterhouse. In the course of the proceedings, Timothy Leggatt, King's College, University of Cambridge (who was a member of the faculty of the University of Sussex at the time of the seminar), became involved in editing the papers for publication. The members of the seminar were:

Mark Abrams (Survey Unit, Social Science Research Council)
Philip Abrams (University of Durham)
Barbara Adams (Centre for Environmental Studies)
Jack Barnes (Centre for Studies in Social Policy)
Jay Blumler (University of Leeds)
E. Brostoff (London)
Richard Brown (University of Durham)
Elizabeth Gittus (University of Newcastle upon Tyne)
Jack Goody (St. John's College, University of Cambridge)
Julius Gould (University of Nottingham)
John Gray (University of Sussex)
John Hall (Survey Unit, Social Science Research Council)
Geoffrey Hawthorn (Churchill College, University of Cambridge)
Morris Janowitz (Peterhouse, University of Cambridge)
Aidan Kelly (Imperial College, University of London)
Timothy Leggatt (King's College, University of Cambridge)
Alan Little (Centre for Studies in Social Policy, now at Community Relations Commission)
Martin Lowe (Inner London Education Authority)
Henry Lucas (Institute of Development Studies, University of Sussex).
Alan Marsh (Survey Unit, Social Science Research Council)
Louis Moss (Government Social Survey)
Margaret Peil (University of Birmingham)
Norman Perry (Survey Unit, Social Science Research Council)
Richard Schaefer (Western Illinois University)
James Spence (Social & Community Planning Research, London, formerly at NOP Market Research Ltd.)
John Utting (Survey Unit, Social Science Research Council)

Eric Van Hove (University of Antwerp, formerly at the
   University of Surrey)
John Warder (University Department of Psychiatry, Royal
   Edinburgh Hospital)
Michael White (Ashridge Management College)
Peter Willmott (Institute of Community Studies)
Sy Yasin (Social Science Research Council)

The seminar was supported by a grant from the Social Science
Research Council which we would like to acknowledge gratefully. Dr.
Mark Abrams and Dr. Sy Yasin of the Social Science Research
Council both actively assisted in the formulation and direction of the
seminar. Without their intellectual stimulation and skillful
management the seminar would not have been possible.

M. Janowitz
T.W. Leggatt

Chapter 1

SOCIOLOGICAL THEORY, SURVEY RESEARCH AND SOCIAL POLICY

Morris Janowitz

INTRODUCTION

In the development of sociology and social research in Great Britain, the social survey holds a central and esteemed position. The intellectual history of British sociology reflects the dominance accorded to the social survey tradition rather than to the continental approach by way of "grand theory". Moreover, it is impossible to think of the history of social reform movements in Great Britain without reference to the consistent and continuous efforts to buttress these movements with empirical findings from social survey research. Survey research in the contemporary period has continued to reflect the aspirations of organized interests, public and private, to initiate or to respond to social and political change.

The record of past accomplishments and limitations, however, must not allow one to overlook the new ferment in social research. There is now increased concern by the more direct application of sociological theory to guide empirical research. By sociological theory more is implied than an interest in single ideal type concepts. At a minimum, a sociological theory requires a number of assumptions and two or more concepts in order to generate some testable hypotheses. From this perspective the claim is also being put forward that a more theoretical analysis of survey research findings will improve the reliability of survey findings for social policy purposes.

The reasons for the growth of interplay between survey research

and sociological theory are varied. First is the concern to strengthen
the conclusions drawn from empirical research. While the data
collection procedures of survey research have not undergone drastic
development, the capacity to analyze available findings by new
computer and statistical techniques has been immensely enlarged.
Much more elaborate analysis is now possible, and at the same time
there is increased need for intellectual and theoretical guidance of
these procedures so as to avoid "mindless" empiricism.

Second is the desire to substantiate and develop theory. It is
generally recognized that social science theory, including sociology,
is and must be grounded in classic philosophical issues: in questions
of values and the pursuit of particular values. However, among those
sociologists who indicate their interest in sociological theory, there is
an important minority — small though it may be — who believe that the
findings of empirical research should contribute to the refashioning
of sociological theory. The idea that theory is concerned primarily
with grand ideas which have their own life cycle is being tempered by
a stream of empirical criticism.

Third is the aspiration to contribute to social policy formation.
There is a persistent sentiment among some sociologists that if the
methodology of survey research is to produce results which will have
increased impact on social policy, the design and analysis of such
research must be more closely articulated with sociological theory.
This assertion is not to deny that the descriptive results of survey
research are of central importance for social policy or that the full
strength of survey research rests on its ability to describe and chart
social and political trends through time. It is to emphasize that the
issues of social policy involve assessing alternative strategies of
intervention and resource allocation. To evaluate the relevance of
alternative strategies some notion of cause and effect, implicit and
explicit in sociological theory, is certainly relevant and, it is hoped,
clarifying.

It must be remembered that sociologists have diversified interests.
The range of styles of theory construction in sociology is indeed
great; methodological approaches are equally varied. Thus, in
pursuing the issues involved in applying sociological theory to survey
research data, there is little danger of narrow unity or premature
closure. However, there is an important element of agreement or at
least convergence, which is to be found in each of the papers
presented in this volume. In each case, the sharp distinction between
basic and applied research developed by the physical and biological

sciences was not felt to be applicable to the analysis of survey research data. (This assertion can indeed be applied to empirical research more generally in sociology.) This outlook of course maintains a long-standing tradition in sociology.

Particular examples of contemporary research naturally differ greatly as a result of sponsorship, time schedules, explicitness of theoretical orientations and concern with "practical results." But even in the most descriptive survey there are implicit general considerations. If these general considerations were made more explicit and related to other research efforts, each particular social survey would possibly have greater social impact and certainly more enduring intellectual consequence. At the same time, the investigator who would claim that he is engaging in basic research is not relieved of the necessity of collecting detailed empirical data, of making use of the criteria of formal proof and validation and of examining his findings in the context of the social and political processes of the period.

Much of the debate between basic and applied research in sociology reflects differing estimates of the actual and potential impact of knowledge on the social and political process. Those who argue for applied sociology think in terms of an "engineering concept" of sociology and stress its capacity to solve particular social issues. Those who de-emphasize the distinction stress that sociology supplies both descriptive data and analytical research results. These findings serve to stimulate men and women to think more realistically and more creatively about alternative solutions to the problems they face.

Social policy-making is enriched by such an admixture of the search for broad hypotheses and a recognition of the concrete and specific context. The assessment of the causal patterns and sequences in a particular social setting investigated by survey research supplies no mechanical guidelines to other circumstances; each application must involve reasoned judgements beyond the findings of social research. In fact, to isolate patterns of influence does not necessarily indicate the likeliest and most legitimate approach for social intervention and social policy, which requries political imagination, moral conviction and the ability to create new solutions and build institutions without being confined to the patterns of influence which have operated in the past. But the essential component of survey research findings, grounded in some elements of sociological theory, is that they offer alternative explanations as a basis for estimating the consequences of various social policies.

In any case, the social scientists who participated in the seminar and prepared the papers in this volume have all shared the assumption in their varying fashions that sociological theory should serve to clarify their data and thereby to enhance the relevance of their results for social policy. They have all also sought for some degree of explanation – not explanation in general – in terms of the particular social, economic and political circumstances under consideration. For example, what are the trends in racial prejudice and which factors are their main determinants; how extensive is local community participation and how are local social networks influenced by urban density and population size? For each problematic issue, generalized hypotheses are insufficient. Survey research findings because of their concreteness highlight the limitations of the generalized formulations.

In the course of the seminar it was possible to identify and develop considerable agreement about those elements of sociological theory, those assumptions, concepts, variables and hypotheses, relevant to specific bodies of survey data. This is not to assert that in each case a fully elaborated set of hypotheses was formulated, but rather that in each case the reanalysis could proceed further than had the original analysis before the more systematic framework was employed.

Three central problems come to focus and are reflected in varying degrees in each of the research papers. First, it was of course recognized that in the reanalysis of bodies of survey data collected for administrative purposes and with little regard for theoretical consideration the limitations of the original research design appeared and reappeared. In a few cases the original survey was academically based and had the benefit of an initial theoretical orientation. There can be no doubt that the latter approach had certain important advantages over the former. Yet even the reanalysis of these bodies of data encountered particular difficulties. There were the problems of crucial omissions in the original formulation; likewise, to make use of a refined conceptual approach was to go beyond the original goal and thus to encounter defects in the data. But on the basis of this seminar, and the resulting papers, it is indeed interesting to note that no clear-cut advantage could be given to the academic studies. In part, this was due to the fact that the administrative studies had to confront basic empirical issues and collect highly relevant data. In some cases, the administratively inspired studies were based on very extensive samples beyond the resources of an academic investigation. To state the issue in other words, purely academic purposes might not have been able to justify the financial costs involved. These social policy studies were also often based on excellent access to survey respondents and other data sources and were able to innovate in the operationalization of key variables. It is hoped that future studies, both academic and policy-sponsored, will be able to take into consideration the results of the theoretically based reanalysis, both in the formulation of hypotheses to be tested and in the corresponding collection of data.

Second, a central issue facing those concerned with the fusion of sociological theory and survey research is the task of converting or making use of data collected from individuals into a basis for understanding social groups and group processes. There can be no doubt that the emphasis of sample surveys on social psychological variables of attitudes and motives reflects the fact that the survey approach centres on an individual respondent; a single individual is the central actor in the interview situation.

Survey research specialists have developed considerable expertise in making use of the respondent as a source of data about group structure, about his family, his work and his community – the respondent serves in effect as an informant. However, one central thrust of survey research analysis in the past has been to aggregate by different means the characteristics of individuals into group properties. One approach has been by the use of ecological and areal units; while there are inherent dangers, the procedures for such a strategy have continued to develop. Refined statistical procedures also assist in the guiding of this process of transformation; for example, multiple regression analysis in its alternative form contributes to the identification of relevant and meaningful group processes.

It is hoped that these papers will help to demonstrate that the use of survey data for the analysis of social structure and group processes rests on the formulation of suggestive theoretical models and applicable testable hypotheses. It is not statistical procedures which will transpose data from a collection of aggregate measures into meaningful elements reflecting the social process but penetrating sociological questions.

Third, it can be said that much of sociological theory is concerned with the institutions by which social groups seek to adjust means to particular ends. This is to say that it focuses on rationality in the sociological sense. In this sense, rationality implies that men are motivated not only by self-interest but act in terms of their social attachments and in terms of the limitations on their knowledge. The outcome is that collective purposes and collective goals fall short of desired objectives and develop a natural history of limited and unanticipated consequences.

Thus it is striking to note that many of the surveys which formed the substance of this seminar dealt with purposive and conscious efforts at social intervention. In short, the findings which dealt with "practical" objectives articulated directly with core issues in sociological theory. In these studies the empirical reality was often the failure to achieve desired objectives — in family planning or in education. It is striking that such studies centrally concerned with "evaluation" could be directly fitted into theoretical frameworks because of the inherent sociological issues involved.

Of the various converging themes in the papers presented in this volume, one dominant element is that of the limits of "rationality": whether rationality should be thought of as calculated self-interest or as institutional efforts at premeditated social intervention. In essence, the findings of contemporary survey research articulate with the very notions which led to the emergence of sociology as a separate discipline, the presumed limitations of "economic man" to account for the persistence and discontinuitites in the social order. The implications carry no particular philosophical or ideological conclusions *per se*. They rather give meaning to the sociological phrase, "the unanticipated consequences" of social action, and therefore place the process of adjusting means to achieve specific ends in sharper perspective.

Thus Geoffrey Hawthorn's paper on "Family Size and Spacing in Recent English Cohorts" explicitly seeks to assess the extent to which family formation — family planning — can be analyzed in terms of a model of rational considerations, rational in the sense of calculation of economic self-interest. He is, of course, fully aware that self-interest can be thought of in broader terms of prestige and psychic income. His panel data collected by survey research methodology lead him to reject — or at least to question fundamentally — the limitations of a rational interpretation of the decisions about the number and spacing of children. The alternative model is that of a more sociological orientation — the notion of a normative explanation — with strong overtones of unreflective behaviour. Such a model is most difficult to operationalize by means of survey analysis, but appears to be as "powerful" or more so in explaining practices in family planning.

If the adaptation of family formation to the conditions of an advanced industrial society involves the diffuse decisions and behaviour of individual families, efforts at the transformation of mass education centre on a highly centralised process of intervention. With the goal of equalizing educational opportunity and overcoming deep-seated social deprivation, educational authorities have been pursuing policies of positive discrimination in education. Although it can be argued that many more years are required to assess both the individual and institutional consequences, Jack Barnes and Henry Lucas have made use of survey data on pupil reading performance in order to examine the short-term impact. Their analytical focus proceeds by means of steps that follow from revealing an "ecological fallacy." By allocating extra funds to designated Educational Priority Areas, the government sought to assist schools with high concentration of youngsters from socially deprived backgrounds.

However, Barnes and Lucas are able to demonstrate that in terms of numbers, there were more youngsters from deprived backgrounds outside of the schools in the Educational Priority Areas than within their boundaries. Moreover, to speak of students with educational deprivation runs the danger of excessive "reification" since there are a variety of sources and types of disabilities. While the success resulting from these compensatory programmes in improving educational performance is hardly impressive, from these data there is no reason to dismiss the effects of school characteristics as an important dimension which can be modified so as to improve educational performance.

Richard Brown explores another segment of mass education in an advanced industrial society, namely apprenticeship training, in this instance in the shipbuilding industry. As the technology and organization of shipbuilding are transformed into a more complex division of labour and into larger and more consolidated units of production, the older system of highly personalized and individualized apprenticeship training gives way to a more formalized and centrally managed enterprise. The purpose of Richard Brown's study is to examine both the success of the emerging system of apprentice training in supplying manpower needs and to probe the process of socialization and the resulting personal and social values of the new young worker.

While survey research methods collect information from individual respondents, they supply a central source of data on selected aspects of organizational processes. Thus Michael White in "Organizational Factors in White-Collar Unionism " presents a reanalysis of a large scale survey of white collar employees' orientations toward unionization. His approach makes use of two alternative models, as is so often the case in the reanalysis of existing bodies of survey data. On the one hand, he casts his findings into the traditional theory of bureaucracy in which the development of management procedures and impersonal relations produce an interest in unionisation. Alternatively, or rather as a supplement, he makes use of the notion of rational pluralism — a modified notion of self-interest — which is pursued via trade union membership. Both of the models have explanatory power, in part because they are not mutually exclusive but reflect differing emphases in the analysis of the environment of large scale organizations. As a result, white collar unionism is not seen as a result of the deterioration of internal relations or the essential outgrowth of worker dissatisfaction; in White's case study, there is greater impetus for unionism among satisfied workers. The expansion of unionism is a consequence of the emergence of large-scale managerial institutions and the desire to pursue goals of modified self-interest. The implication of these research findings for social policy requires a concern with assessing the impact of specific management and union policies on productivity and social responsibility.

The second paper starting out from traditional bureaucratic theory is Timothy Leggatt's paper "Management Style and Economic Success in Industry." Leggatt examines his data, derived from a survey of the management educational policies and practices of industrial firms, to see whether the pervasive "mechanistic" and "organic" models of management are exemplified in practice. He identifies the two models; and then specifies some of the dimensions of these management styles together with certain of their correlates. Further, he looks for relationships between the dimensions of management style and economic success; and finds none. The paper, by virtue of its basis in survey data, carries the development of bureaucratic theory away from the organization case-study out into the search for relevant industrial sector characteristics. On the policy front it sounds a cautionary note for those looking for easy recipes for economic health and success.

The issues of social research and social policy are not only defined in terms of bureaucratic organizations but also on the basis of the community setting in which the citizenry of an advanced industrial society pursue their daily existence. The Royal Commission on Local Government in England collected a unique and detailed body of data on patterns of community participation in order to assist the formulation of plans for the restructuring of local administration and elected bodies. These materials supply the basis for an exploration of the "Social Construction of Local Communities" by Morris Janowitz and John D. Kasarda. The underlying focus of this reanalysis is on the underlying patterns of local communal life. In sociological terms, this is but a restatement of the classic issues of urban sociology. Does the growth of the urban metropolis reflect the linear model of the *Gemeinschaft-Gesellschaft* outlook which postulates that with increased size and population concentration the social fabric of the local community, that is, interpersonal networks and localistic attachments, attenuate?

These data join a growing body of material which calls into question such a formulation. Instead, a more systemic outlook explains the patterns of social networks and community involvements. There is no straight line linkage between population size or concentration and a decline of social networks and localistic attachments. Instead, community attachments are substantially influenced by participation in local social networks and in voluntary associations. Participation in these local social networks, in turn, are found to be influenced primarily by length of residence in the community, and not by population size. In terms of social policy, the citizenry in varying degrees are able to construct for themselves a local "community," and the essential problematic issue is the extent to which economic and social policy operates to facilitate such involvements.

The growth of the non-white population in Great Britain as a result of immigration and natural birth increase serves to complicate and heighten the tensions asssociated with local community life. The extensive survey of race relations in Great Britain completed in 1966, both with its national sample and with its additional focus on particular selected communities, supplies the most comprehensive body of base-line data against which to measure and assess trends in prejudice and intergroup contacts. Richard Schaefer's strategy in "Correlates of Racial Prejudice" is first to identify the linkages between position in the social structure and level of expressed prejudice toward the non-white population. His findings confirm and amplify those of previous studies that age, social position, and education are key variables since young, middle class and better educated persons displayed lower levels of hostility. While these variables are key manifestations of basic changes in an advanced industrial society, they hardly imply an inevitable decrease in level of prejudice. Therefore Schaefer is also concerned with situational variables — the extent and patterns of interpersonal contact between the "native" population and the new social elements. The overall finding is that contact does not necessarily reduce intergroup hostility nor does prejudice invariably mean avoidance of contact. For example, while contact with immigrants in work situations appeared to decrease hostility, residential proximity is associated with higher levels of prejudice.

In addition, Schaefer makes use of a multiple regression model which indicates that the key variables of age, social position, education, and measures of contact account for only ten percent of the variance in levels of prejudice. In essence, for a deeper understanding of prejudice levels, an interplay of psychological and sociological variables is required. Likewise, the phenomenon of intergroup hostility reflects historical and cultural processes which develop a common mental set and produce the operative "definition of the situation." From the point of view of social policy, the implications which must be examined are that while the long-term social structural changes create a potential for a decline in the level of prejudice, social policy will have to face the realities of the situational variables — the interpersonal contacts which are as often as not operating in the opposite direction.

There has been a special emphasis in survey research on the study of political participation. This concern reflects the interest of political leaders and political groups in the information generated by survey research. It also reflects the fact that survey research imposes a sense of order on the very highly complex and diffuse political processes in a parliamentary system by focusing on the voting decision. In particular, survey research has the advantage of making it possible to probe the impact of the electoral campaign, including especially the role of the mass media. In their paper, "Communication and Voter Turnout in Britain," Jay Blumler and Jack McLeod present the result of a panel study of young voters during the general election of 1970, with a particular focus on the impact and role of the mass media. The capacity of the mass media to influence the outcome of the election and appropriate campaign policies presents, for a democratic society, crucial research issues.

In the development of political behaviour research, there has been a clear articulation of the point of view that the mass media play an important role both in defining the political situation and in mobilizing limited but politically crucial segments of the population. However, the methodology of survey research tends to produce findings which, if not critically evaluated, lead to a de-emphasis of the impact of the mass media. As a result, in the decade of the 1960s, the view-point of the limited or marginal impact of the mass media in general and, specificially in electoral campaigns, gained ground. The findings of the analysis of Blumler and McLeod are part of a "new look" which reasserts the older orientation. They conclude that the mass media play a discernible role especially for the new voters whose socialisation into the political process was still in progress. In part, we are dealing with the cumulative impact on a new generation of long-term exposure to television. However, the findings are particularly relevant for the issues of the seminar because of the convergence with the problematic concern of "unanticipated consequences." The impact of the mass media was, in actuality, one of reducing the amount of participation. This election campaign resulted, in contrast to previous ones studied by the sample survey, in a decline from the pre-campaign intention to vote to actual turnout. The imagery and the appeals of the campaign led to a calculation (as well as to a sense of indifference) which increased the amount of non-voting.

These findings point to the strain on the electoral system which is the theme of James Spence's paper, "Trends in Political Participation in Britain since 1945". Spence shows through a re-analysis of public opinion poll findings that this strain has in recent years been reflected in the electorate in higher levels of indifference, stronger attachment to the self-conception of being a "political independent" and a marked increase in the shifting of party preference from election to election. He introduces the concept of the political heterogeneity of the electorate to illuminate these developments more than has the traditional idea of voter apathy. These trends can be seen as manifestations of the increased complexity of the social structure and of the inability to build political institutions for effective political participation. Reliance on periodic nation-wide parliamentary elections fails to serve the needs of aggregating and balancing political opinion. Under these conditions, the mass media, paradoxically but understandably, contribute to non-participation.

In general, the work of the seminar on sociological theory and survey research made use of cross-sectional data, or in two cases of panel studies. But again and again, the special role of survey research in trend analysis was emphasized. There can be no doubt that the real power of the survey approach rests in its repeated and long-term reporting of basic trends. This has come in recent years to be renamed the social indicator approach.

There can be no doubt that if the application of sociological theory to survey research is to be developed and extended, it will be in good part by use of trend data and by the linking of the emerging interests in social indicators to traditional and persistent issues of sociological theory and the analysis of social change. Trend data are inherently interesting and indispensable for sociological inquiry. Moreover, trend data are required in order to develop in survey research a concern with the larger societal context; and this is the real burden and contribution of sociological theory to empirical research.

Chapter 2

FAMILY SIZE AND SPACING IN RECENT ENGLISH COHORTS[1]

G. P. Hawthorn

THE PROBLEM

This is a first report of a study of fertility which rests upon two assumptions: that it is important to try to explain recent changes in British fertility and their associated differentials; and that so far success in doing this has been rather limited. The first has been admirably defended in the recent report of the Population Panel set up by the Lord President of the Council in November 1971 (Population Panel 1973) and I shall take it for granted here (but see Hawthorn 1973); the second, however, needs some explanation, since in a narrowly demographic sense we do know something already.

British fertility began to fall in the 1880s. It reached very low levels, lower than any reached either before or since, in the 1930s, rose briefly in the mid-1940s (with a peak in 1947), and then fell again until 1955. Table 1 shows by six conventional measures what has been happening since then. The general fertility rate is obtained by relating the number of births in a given year to the population of women of reproductive age in that year (conventionally taken as 15-44 years). This measure is liable to be affected by the age distribution of women of reproductive age. The gross reproduction rate is freed of the effects of such age distortions and is calculated as a pure measure of fertility. It is the number of daughters a woman would produce, if she survived to the end of her reproductive period, and throughout her life were subject to the age-specific fertility rates of the year for which the gross reproduction rate is calculated.

TABLE 1

NUMBER OF BIRTHS AND BIRTH RATES (GREAT BRITAIN), 1955–1972

Year	Live births (Thousands)	Birth rate per 1,000 population of all ages	General fertility rate per 1,000 women aged 15-44	Reproduction rate		Total period fertility rate
				Gross	*Net*	
1955	760	15.3	74.1	1.09	1.05	2.24
1956	796	16.0	78.2	1.16	1.12	2.38
1957	821	16.4	81.2	1.21	1.16	2.47
1958	840	16.7	83.3	1.24	1.19	2.53
1959	848	16.8	84.0	1.24	1.20	2.56
1960	886	17.4	87.7	1.30	1.26	2.69
1961	912	17.8	89.9	1.35	1.31	2.78
1962	943	18.2	91.3	1.38	1.34	2.84
1963	957	18.3	91.6	1.39	1.35	2.86
1964	980	18.7	93.2	1.41	1.37	2.91
1965	963	18.2	91.7	1.37	1.34	2.83
1966	946	17.8	90.5	1.34	1.30	2.76
1967	928	17.4	89.0	1.29	1.25	2.65
1968	914	17.0	87.7	1.25	1.21	2.57
1969	888	16.4	85.2	1.20	1.17	2.47
1970	872	16.1	83.6	1.16	1.13	2.40
1971	870	16.1	83.8	1.16	1.13	2.39
1972*	(810)	(15.0)	(78)	(1.08)	(1.05)	(2.25)

Source: Office of Population Censuses and Surveys
* Provisional

However, not all women survive to age 45 and the net reproduction rate allows for the effect of mortality. It measures the average number of daughters that would be born to a group of newly-born girls if they were subjected for the first 45 years of their lives to the age-specific fertility and mortality rates of the year for which the rate is calculated. It is therefore a measure of the extent to which a generation of women subject to the fertility and mortality of a particular period would replace themselves by the next generation. A net reproduction rate of unity, if continued indefinitely, would in the long run result in a stationary population and could therefore be taken as "replacement" fertility. At present British rates of mortality the net reproduction rate will be about 2½% lower than the gross reproduction rate, that is, a gross reproduction rate of 1.025 is the equivalent of a net reproduction rate of 1.00.

The total period fertility rate takes account of both male and female births, and is computed in the same way as the gross reproduction rate. As about 106 boys are born for every 100 girls, it will be equal to about 2.06 times the gross reproduction rate. It therefore measures the average number of live-born children per woman which would result if the prevailing age-specific fertility rates were maintained over the whole 30 year reproductive span of women's lives, and if there were no female mortality at all before the end of the reproductive period (Population Panel, 1973: 34-6). All six measures show that fertility, so measured, first rose and then fell over this eighteen year period.

However, as the panel remarked (1973: 36), the measures are based on the experience of single years and so highlight transitory changes. They also take no account of marriage patterns. To overcome the first of these limitations, a cohort analysis may be made, tracing the history of the fertility of women married in successive years. The picture it reveals is shown in Table 2. Two points may be made about it. The first is that the peak period fertility of the last eighteen years, in the early and mid-1960s, can be seen to have been due to exceptionally high age-specific rates at all but the youngest ages. Thus, women married in 1951-55 were tending to have their children rather later than those married in 1956-60, causing a temporary rise in the period rates for the early and mid-1960s. Secondly, however, it is plain that over the years there has been an overall shift of fertility into the younger ages. This reflects two trends: more women were getting married younger, and married women, at least up to the mid-1960s, were having their children sooner after getting married (Table 3). Only in the second half of the 1960s does this tendency seem to have stopped, which no doubt partly explains the very low birth rate for 1972.

We can therefore suggest demographic explanations for the trends in fertility since 1955: a higher proportion married, decreasing ages at marriage, at first a delay, and then an acceleration, and then another delay, in the speed with which married women have had their children (or changes in birth spacing), and lastly an apparent although slight tendency for completed family sizes to rise and then fall again. Demographically we can see the answer, and are only

TABLE 2

AGE-SPECIFIC FERTILITY RATES FOR GIVEN COHORTS OF WOMEN
(GREAT BRITAIN)
(Births per year per thousand women)

Age segment of life in years of age	Period when cohort started childbearing[1]								
	1926 –30	*1931 –35*	*1936 –40*	*1941 –45*	*1946 –50*	*1951 –55*	*1956 –60*	*1961 –65*	*1966 –70*
15–19	(16)	(16)	(16)	16	20*	22	31	41†	49
20–24	(93)	(93)	102	132*	133	158	178†	161	(154)
25–29	(115)	122	151*	139	162	182†	162	(152)	
30–34	92	107*	89	96	105†	89	(79)		
35–39	58*	46	47	50†	41	(34)			
40–44	13	13	13†	10	(8)				
Total period fertility rate (average number of live births per woman)	1.94	1.98	2.09	2.22	2.35	2.44	(2.40)		
Gross reproduction rate of cohort	0.94	0.96	1.01	1.08	1.14	1.18	(1.17)		

SOURCE: Office of Population Censuses and Surveys; General Register Office (Scotland).

[1] Child bearing ages conventionally are taken as 15-44 years (very few births occur outside these ages) but significant numbers of births start at 18 years rather than 15.
* Post-war baby boom 1946-1950.
† Peak period for births 1961-1965.

NOTE: Figures in brackets are those for which partial evidence exists, though not covering the whole of the five year periods concerned. For the earlier cohorts the bracketed figures are those of the year 1938-1939; fertility rates in the 1930s and the second half of the 1920s are thought to have remained fairly stable.

prevented from a full understanding of the data in these terms by the insufficient passage of time between the marriages of the younger cohorts and the present. But how are we to explain the changes in these demographic parameters?

TABLE 3

PROPORTION OF WOMEN HAVING A CHILD WITHIN THE
FIRST TWO YEARS OF MARRIAGE (GREAT BRITAIN), 1951–1970

Year of marriage	% having child within two years
1951	52
1956	56
1961	59
1966	56
1970 (part estimated)	51

SOURCE: Office of Population Censuses and Surveys; General Register Office (Scotland)

THE THEORY

Men have been trying to explain demographic events in general and fertility in particular for a very long time. The history of attempts to do so has been well-documented (United Nations, 1953; Eversley, 1959), and I shall not go into it in any detail here, beyond explaining the thinking behind this study.

It is fair to say that most of the explanations that have been put forward have been of an economic kind. Within such explanations, there has always been if not a contradiction then a definite ambiguity, and it is well illustrated in Malthus himself (Flew, 1970: 7-48). On the one hand, Malthus argued in his *First Essay* that population was a simple linear function of prosperity; the more resources there were, the more it went up, and *vice versa*. On the other hand, in the *Second Essay* and subsequent revisions, he conceded that "prudence" might encourage people at a certain point to "moral restraint", to delay their marriage and to delay or even altogether to restrict their fertility, so that they might retain a standard of living that would otherwise fall if there were more children, or at least more children sooner.

From this ambiguity of Malthus' there arise two quite distinct hypotheses: one, that fertility will rise with income, and the other, that fertility will either cease to be related to income or indeed that it will even fall as income rises. Today, these hypotheses remain somewhat less unresolved (for three reviews, see Hawthorn, 1970; Simon, 1969; 1972). Their resolution is clearly an empirical matter, but it is not a simple one. Consider what each hypothesis implies. In the first, it is assumed that as income rises the taste for other goods or for "higher quality" children does not also increase, or at least, that it does not increase to the extent that no surplus income remains to be disposed of on extra children (Becker, 1960). In the second, however, this assumption is relaxed. There it is assumed that tastes for other goods do indeed rise with income and so offset any tendency for the greater prosperity to lead to higher fertility. In other words, as in the first, the net effect of income on fertility is taken to be positive, but the other consequences of rising income are presumed to cancel it out or even, in the case of those who acquire a disproportionate taste for other goods, to invert it (Duesenberry, 1960).

Given these implications, it is clear that the issue is not going to be decided by the existence or not of simple correlations between income (however measured) and fertility. Witness, as evidence of this, the confusion caused by the fact that in the rich countries the relationship between income and fertility over the past century appears to have been in general negative, by the fact that in the shorter term, over Kuznets cycles and even over business cycles, it appears to be positive, and by the fact that cross-sectional analyses at any one point in time are ambiguous. Simon (1969) has suggested that this confusion may be sorted out by considering more carefully the extent to which the effect of other variables and of income itself may be lagged. He argues that we may safely assume that the effect of income on fertility is indeed positive, but that over the very long term any positive association is destroyed or even inverted by the accumulating effect of factors such as increased education. These factors are themselves initially a function of the rise in income but then take time to work and, when they do, serve to raise the demand for other goods, the opportunity costs to wives of raising children, and the standards required for each child and thus the costs of children. Over the shorter term, these lagged effects have not made themselves felt. And cross-sectional analyses merely show that some groups have reached a point where the other factors have caught up while other groups have not. This suggestion certainly seems to fit most of the facts (Simon, 1972; Heer, 1966).

By doing so, it would at first sight appear also to resolve all the problems. The contradiction, or ambiguity, in the Malthusian and post-Malthusian formulations of the economic theory can be explained, and confident predictions would seem to be in order. However, considerable difficulties remain. First, "income" is not a simple homogeneous variable. At any one point in time, it may be made up of resources other than money earnings, and what may be important about it anyway is not so much what it is at the time that a child is considered as what it will be over a certain period into the future. Potential ("permanent") or expected income may be more important than actual income, and may, like actual income, include many different kinds of resource. Second, the nature and timing of the effects of a change in income are not merely a function of the change in income itself. They will also depend upon the institutional arrangements of the society in question at the time in question. Third, and this remains as the most cogent objection of a set of which the others can be accommodated (Blake, 1968; Namboodiri, 1972), the demand for children may not be wholly elastic. The best associations between fertility and economic indicators have been over the short term of business cycles (for a general review see Simon, 1972: 23-31; for England and Wales, 1955-1970, Busfield and Hawthorn, 1971), and this is almost certainly because what is being affected is the timing of marriages and births and not so much completed family sizes. With regard to the latter, couples may want, say, two children, *whatever* their economic situation, so that variations in this situation affect completed fertility only at the margin. A substantial amount of each couple's fertility will have to be explained in psychological and sociological terms, independent of economic conditions. It is the purpose of this survey and its analysis to explore the relevance of these non-economic variables.

The upshot of these difficulties is that the theoretical ambiguity may have been resolved, but it still cannot give precise predictions (except where it does not apply, as in the case of variations in timing over a business cycle). That is, we may be able to identify the equations appropriate to describe the inter-relationship, but we cannot give determinate values to their terms before the event.

There is, however, a more fundamental difficulty. It revolves around what is implied by the very idea of an economic model of fertility. As Simon (1972: 13-21) says, if one is interested mainly in prediction and control, an aggregative macro-economic approach is adequate in which one merely tests hypotheses about the connections between rates. However, this approach assumes what has to be made explicit if one wishes to understand why couples want and have the number of children that they do at the times that they do, namely that they are rational consumers in the technical, micro-economic sense, gifted with instantaneous and perfect information about "the market" and with the ability to decide upon the optimal course for the maximization of their utilities. There are at least two objections to such an assumption. The first is well explained by Simon himself (1972: 17h):

> The strength of economics, as compared to sociology, has been that the dependent variable in economics is a single agreed-upon goal — maximization of wealth as measured in the agreed-upon yardstick of money. As soon as one admits into the theorizing the possibility of two or more incommensurable goals or yardsticks . . . then the great power of economic analysis is lost. One can no longer make any *a priori* deductions from economic theory and a set of market factors.

It is the classic objection to a utilitarian analysis of anything other than money-wealth maximization (Hampshire, 1972). The second is that the assumption is for empirical reasons patently absurd. People, whether parents or not, are not gifted with perfect and instantaneous information or with the ability (or the inclination, or the time) to decide upon the optimal path for the maximization of what the first objection anyway regards as incommensurable utilities. It is therefore foolhardy seriously to consider such a model.

These are powerful objections, but I do not think that they can be held to be decisive. First, the utilities of, let us say, "family life," time (for a career, or for leisure outside the family) and money are, of course, theoretically incommensurable. We cannot produce a medium of substitution between them that does not vitiate the very premise of their being separate utilities. Nevertheless, it seems to me that people *do* make choices, and that they *do* make choices between such theoretically and technically incommensurable utilities. Accordingly, we are faced with the dilemma of either ignoring this fact and remaining theoretically inviolate or accepting it and so accepting a model that is theoretically impossible to handle. At first sight, it might seem to be resolvable by adopting another theory of choice; but there is no other, or at least, and more precisely, no other that does not in the end force us to translate apparently incommensurable ends or utilities into an identical, commensurable currency.

Second, in objection to the objections, one can also concede that even if we *do* make the kind of choices that theoretically we cannot make we nevertheless make them in a highly imperfect fashion, very uncertain about the appropriateness and the quality of the information that we feed in and in such a way as perhaps, in Herbert Simon's phrase, to satisfy rather than optimise our utilities. Nevertheless, as an ideal type the fiction of economic man (and wife) is a useful one to match against reality. This can be seen by considering its converse.

In his comment on Becker's (1960) original application of the classic utility-maximization model to fertility, Duesenberry (1960) made the simple point that if economics is all about how people make choices, sociology is all about how they don't have any choices to make. Economic man knows only one constraint, that of "income"; sociological man knows no freedom. This is a useful contrast, for it provides an opposing ideal type with which to approach what people actually do. Sociological man's choice is so determined that even when he knows of several courses of action he is so constrained by various social (and psychological) factors that he has no power to choose any other than the one which he does in fact select. Freedman, for instance, writing about fertility, has said (1963):

> One of the fundamental principles of sociology is that when many members of a society face a recurrent common problem with important social consequences they tend to develop a normative solution for it. This solution, a set of rules for behaviour in a particular situation, becomes part of the culture, and the society indoctrinates its members to conform more or less closely to the norms by implicit or explicit rewards and punishments.

One "economic" model derives from a consideration of the importance of economic factors, but is not of course restricted to such factors. Resources need not be ones of money (Becker, 1965, for example, gives an interesting account of "time" as a resource); and choices may be made between wholly non-economic utilities. What has happened is that demographic phenomena have conventionally been assumed to be explicable in terms of economic ones, and for this reason it has contingently come to be the case that the theoretical running in population studies has been made with the choice models of micro-economics. There is no reason to believe that sociological models are inappropriate in population studies, or that economic or "choice" models are not appropriate to other fields of what is usually held to constitute "sociology". The especial interest of two contrary models lies in the extent to which each can explain what the other cannot.

THE HYPOTHESES

Much work has been done in recent years on developing and refining micro-economic theories of fertility; much less on developing and refining sociological ones. There is now, therefore, a considerable number of interesting and testable hypotheses of the first kind. But for the purposes of this paper there is little point in elaborating them all, since I do not yet have the data with which to test them. Accordingly, I shall restrict myself to specifying just three, but three which are nevertheless fundamental to the debate about the determinants of fertility in modern industrial societies.

The first is that, other things being equal, a higher income leads people to have more children (although how many more, and whether the relationship is monotonic, need not here be specified). There is some support already for this hypothesis (D. Freedman, 1963), although, as in other studies, it is difficult to be sure that all other relevant factors have been held constant. If this hypothesis is refuted, of course, doubt is immediately cast upon one of the most basic tenets of the economic theory.

The second is that couples are aware of the financial costs of children, and that this may lead them to restrict their fertility to a level below what in other circumstances they would regard as ideal. I bring data to bear here on only the first of these, although it is clear that if this is refuted then so must the second be. It should be said that against the theoretical expectations of the micro-economists, there is nothing in the literature to suggest that the costs of extra children in industrial societies are a very high proportion of total costs, although definitive work on the costs of children remains to be done.

The third hypothesis provides an interpretation for the refutation of the first two. This is that financial considerations are irrelevant to the determination of completed family size, despite any effect that they may have on the timing of births (or indeed of marriage itself). What is important, rather, is the social pressure existing in the community to have a family of the size considered "proper", a pressure that will be indicated by the perception by couples of their deviance or oddity in not doing so.

These are simple hypotheses. They are, however, relevant to the issue at hand. They can throw some light on the question of whether or not people's financial circumstances in industrial societies affect their fertility. It is less easy to argue that they can throw much light on the question of whether or not "modern" fertility in industrial societies is the outcome of individual, or at least family, choice, as against fertility in "pre-modern", non-industrial societies, which has been held to be the product of general social pressure (Bourgeois-Pichat, 1967: 163; Wrigley, 1969: 192). After all, it might be said that even where couples are avowedly responding to social pressure, they have *chosen* to do so. Nevertheless, the results can reasonably be held to suggest which of the two suppositions corresponds more satisfactorily with the facts.

THE DATA

The Survey

We decided to do a survey for two reasons. First, the kind of information we sought was not available from secondary sources. Second, such surveys on matters other than birth control as had been done had been carried out abroad, so that even if we were to fail in being able to come to the conclusions we envisaged, we would at the very least have been able to produce some useful descriptive material on England.

It was not clear, however, that what had been done in other countries was satisfactory (Hawthorn, 1970). The Princeton Study (Westoff *et al.*, 1961, 1963, 1969), Rainwater's work (1965), and the Growth of American Families study (Freedman *et al.*, 1959; Whelpton *et al.*, 1966), were in their different ways the most useful, but each suffered from an insufficient specification of the theoretical issues at stake. They provided leads rather than conclusions. Nevertheless, there was one respect in which the Princeton and G.A.F. studies were promising, and that was in their longitudinal design. It was clear to us that we either had to follow a cohort of couples over time or to gather retrospective information on the history of a cohort. But we wished to compare cohorts, specifically those building their families in the 1950s and those building theirs in the 1960s, so that by the time (1967) we even thought of doing the study, *some* retrospective work was necessary.

Accordingly, we decided to take a cohort married in the early 1950s and one married in the early 1960s and to ask the couples in each questions about the history and circumstances of their married life and its fertility. The exact cohorts we chose (those married in 1952-57 and 1962-67) were dictated by the fact that the census would provide information on them in 1971 as those married for 15-19 years or 5-9 years. For theoretical as well as practical reasons (Linz, 1969), we decided against a national sample and instead took one from Ipswich. Ipswich had in 1951 been the most representative of towns of over 50,000 in England and Wales (Moser and Scott 1961), and although it had experienced a certain amount of immigration from the Commonwealth since then we did not feel that this overrode the convenience of its being near our own place of work and still felt that although, strictly speaking, we could only generalize from a sample of Ipswich in 1969-70 to Ipswich itself in 1969-70, it nevertheless provided a more secure basis from which to make generalizations to the nation as a whole than any other single area would have done.

Having eliminated those married before 1952, between 1957 and 1962, and after 1967, we proceeded to eliminate couples in which the wife was aged over 44 at the time of interview, wives who were no longer living with their husbands, and women who had been married more than once. This was to avoid the complications arising from such states, and to bring ourselves into line with the O.P.C.S. study which was making the same restrictions (except with regard to cohorts) (Woolf, 1971).

We wished to take a sample of 300 such women, this being what we then considered to be the best compromise between cost and desirability. In a pilot study (Hawthorn and Busfield, 1968) we had used the Ipswich birth register as a sampling frame, but this was unsuitable for the main study: larger families would be over-represented in the sample (and the childless, in whom we were interested, would not appear at all), and it would have been very laborious to extract women of the right date of marriage from it by a random process. So we turned to the electoral register, and estimating that about every twelfth name would produce an address that contained an eligible household, we selected 3600 names from it at random and screened the households at those addresses. Although we used the names to find the addresses, the sample was a sample of households. We were not concerned as to whether the same person as had returned an electoral registration still lived at the address from which he or she had returned it. In the event, we discovered 419 eligible households.

Of these, 129 refused to be interviewed. 31% is a high refusal rate. The O.P.C.S. survey, using the same frame and the same criteria of eligibility (except for the restriction by cohort), was refused by only 11% of the eligible respondents. It failed to contact some 1%, and thus achieved a success rate of 88% as against our 69% (Woolf, 1971:124). Those who agreed to be interviewed and those who did not are compared in Table 4. From this, it is clear that although there was a slight tendency for older and non-manual households to refuse, the differences between the two groups were not large. The

TABLE 4

COMPARISON OF RESPONDENTS AND REFUSALS (%)

	Respondents (N=290)	*Refusals (N=129)*
1. *Cohort*		
3–7 years	57	57
13–17 years	43	43
2. *Wife's age last birthday*		
NA/DK	0	22
15–19	0	0
20–24	19	10
25–29	31	17
30–34	16	16
35–39	25	21
40–44	9	15
3. *Husband's present occupation*		
NA	0	13
Non-manual	28	30
Manual	71	57
4. *Current family size*		
NA	0	15
0	12	8
1	17	19
2	40	35
3	18	9
4	7	8
5	4	2
6	1	2
7+	1	2

one statistically significant difference is that between the percentages of manual households in each group, but if the unknowns in the second are distributed proportionately even this disappears. This is not to say, of course, that there may not be considerable differences between the two groups along dimensions that the screening sheet, from which this information comes, did not tap. For instance, it is perfectly possible that the poor contraceptors refused more than the good ones, and this would bias our data on birth control very considerably.

The Questionnaire

As I have said, we wanted to trace the history and circumstances of the couples' marriages and fertility. We also wished to interview the husband as well as the wife. This had not at that time been done in any study, despite evidence from several that husbands were important in determining actions relevant to fertility it has still only been done in a partial way (in what is otherwise an excellent study, Cartwright, 1970). For practical and ethical reasons, we decided to interview the couple together.

The questionnaire, therefore, had to range over a long period of time (for some, more than seventeen years) and to gather data on two people at once. Not surprisingly, it was long and complex, yet very few showed that the respondents (as distinct from the interviewers) became tired, irritable or careless in answering it. It was arranged as follows:

Section A: screening sheet, administered to original sample of 3600;

Section B: background sheet, requiring information on parents' occupations, respondents' education, income and occupation before marriage, siblings, religion and marriage itself;

Section C: "marriage" sheet, requiring information on housing, occupations, incomes, siblings, marital organisation, networks, ideas about family size, and practice of birth control in period immediately following marriage;

Section P: "pregnancy" sheet, requiring information mentioned above (C) for period preceding each pregnancy (whatever the outcome of that pregnancy);

Section Q: (a) sheet requiring information mentioned above (C) for present period (if not pregnant);

(b) sheet asking general questions about ideals and aspirations and respondents' perceptions of the quality of their lives;

Section R: response sheet, requiring details of the interview (who present, whether whole questionnaire answered, etc.).

All couples were asked to answer the B, C and Q sections, and all those in which the wife had been pregnant to answer as many P sections as there had been pregnancies.

The Questions

The questionnaire was designed and tested in the winter of 1968-1969. It would not be useful here to outline the rationale for each question or set of questions. I shall instead mention two mistakes that we made. The first and less serious relates to income. We used the O.P.C.S. question, which asked for net income from all sources, and, like O.P.C.S. itself, we should have realized that this required respondents to do first a quick sum of gross earnings and then subtract deductions, all in a few moments. In practice, we got mostly reports of gross earnings from employment only, and had to convert these to 1970 prices and then subtract a proportion which represented the average tax deduction for all couples. The result is a highly approximate measure, although relative differences should not have been obscured too much by it. We did, however, ask specifically about other sources of financial help and help in kind, and this should refine the measure a little. Moreover, we asked about income expectations at each time and these replies, together with the income profile over time for each couple, should prove useful. But we have yet to tackle the measurement of potential or, to use the Friedman-Easterlin phrase, "permanent" income.

The second and more serious mistake arises out of not having thought through in 1969 the implications of the theoretical alternative to the economic or "choice" models. As the formulation in the previous section of the relationships implied by this sociological model shows, to test it one needs information on the norms that may exist in the community and the couples' knowledge of them. Of course, it is difficult to find out what the norms *are* in any social situation, and there is no guarantee that even had we deliberately set out to ask about them we would have obtained valid answers. In particular, it is almost impossible in survey research to find out what norms are independent of people's knowledge of them, since the only device open to one is to ask people themselves, such that one is inevitably assessing knowledge at the same time as the very existence of the norms themselves. Nevertheless, questions of the kind: "do

you think that people expect married couples to have children?",
"do you think that they expect married couples to have *at least* a
certain number/*no more than* a certain number?", "have you ever
felt any pressure upon you to have a certain number of children?",
"would you feel odd if you had no children or five or more
children?", etc., might have been relevant. As it is, we shall have to
piece together what indirect indications we can derive from other
parts of our own questionnaire and from other studies. We have
unfortunately missed the opportunity to test directly one of the
most interesting hypotheses about the determination of modern
fertility (Bourgeois-Pichat, *loc.cit.*).

One final point about the questions needs to be considered. A
good part of them is retrospective, in some cases requiring couples to
cast back seventeen years or more. It is clear that the validity of the
answers to some of these questions must be in doubt. A casual
comparison in a sample of questionnaires of the answers to the
questions on marital organization was carried out and this shows that
the similarity between reports of what happened several years ago
and what happens now is often slight. Naturally, this does not
constitute a case for saying that the retrospective replies are valid;
but it does suggest that they may not be wholly invalid.

FINDINGS

The analysis of the data has proceeded in stages. This report is
concerned with the findings of the first stage.

The first point to establish is that the nature and degree of the
differences between the two cohorts in the sample correspond to
those between the two cohorts in England and Wales as a whole. The
comparison in Table 5 is between the fertilities by duration for the
sample and the national population. Two points emerge. First, the
small size of the samples has produced considerable sampling error;
but, second, our figures are all above what one would expect. The
O.P.C.S. study recorded a similar discrepancy between its sample
means and the national ones (Woolf, 1971: 129). It is also possible
that fertility in Ipswich is above the national average. Nevertheless,
the relative differences are similar and I shall assume comparability.

The first finding is the distribution of answers to the question of
whether, if they had had twice as much money during the whole
period of their marriage, the couples would have had any more

TABLE 5

FAMILY SIZE BY DURATION OF MARRIAGE IN 1970

	Ipswich sample	*England and Wales* *
3 years	0.85	0.89
4 years	1.42	1.16
5 years	2.00	1.42
6 years	1.73	1.62
7 years	2.20	1.79
13 years	2.93	2.23
14 years	2.39	2.26
15 years	2.44	2.24
16 years	2.96	2.25
17 years	2.74	2.24

* Registrar General: Statistical Review for England and Wales, 1970, Part II, Table QQ(b).

children (Table 6). This would appear to show that income is not a
constraint for three-quarters of the couples, and moreover, and
perhaps as interestingly, that it does not appear to have been any
more or less of a constraint for couples in the second cohort (who,
on the "business cycle" hypothesis, might have been expected to
have been more aware of such constraints than those in the first).
Of course, answers to such a hypothetical question cannot be taken
as decisive evidence of anything. But if, in Blake's phrase, babies are
to any extent "consumer durables" (Blake, 1968) one would have
expected a different pattern of response. After all, if the question
had been not about fertility but about housing or holidays, then the
replies would almost certainly have been different. At the time of
writing this paper, tabulations of fertility by duration by income in
1969-70 (at the time of the interview) were not available, but they
would not be of much interest anyway; as Easterlin and others have
made clear, the important relationship is likely to be with income at
the time of family formation, not afterwards.

Nevertheless, it cannot be inferred from Table 6 that for most
parents children are not a financial drain. Table 7 indicates that
about two-thirds of all husbands and wives, taken separately, thought
that they were (and as one would expect, the proportion rises with
higher parities). The second part of the same table compares the two
cohorts. Because their children are older and thus presumably more
expensive, one would expect the first cohort of parents to stress the
drain more. But if anything they stress it less (especially the wives),

TABLE 6

CONSTRAINT OF INCOME ON FERTILITY

	(a) All couples (%)			
	No	*Yes*	*DK*	*NA*
Husbands	64	18	2	16
Wives	73	23	1	2
	(b) Those offering an opinion (%)			
	No	*Yes*		
Husbands, Cohort 1	80	20		
Wives, Cohort 1	76	24		
Husbands, Cohort 2	77	23		
Wives, Cohort 2	76	24		

which is not inconsistent with the supposition that the younger cohort may have experienced comparatively greater financial hardship than the older one.

TABLE 7

FINANCIAL DRAIN OF CHILDREN

	(a) All couples with children (%)			
	None	*Little*	*Moderate*	*High*
Husbands	13	23	31	28
Wives	13	21	29	37
	(b) Couples with two children (%)			
	None	*Little*	*Moderate*	*High*
Husbands, Cohort 1	15	23	18	45
Wives, Cohort 1	19	26	21	35
Husbands, Cohort 2	8	30	35	27
Wives, Cohort 2	13	25	30	32

Taken together, Tables 6 and 7 suggest that although most parents feel the cost of children and two-thirds of them consider it to be moderate or heavy, only about a fifth of them concede that they would have had more children if they had had more money. This in turn suggests that if economic considerations are causally important for more than a minority of couples, they must directly affect not completed family size but the spacing of births. This remains to be tested. In terms of the "hypothesis" that the demand for children is a function of the utility of children, income and the cost of children, it would seem from this evidence that it is their utility which is the dominant consideration.

The measurement of utilities is a difficult and ultimately rather arbitrary process, but in order to see whether or not the contrary, sociological hypothesis has any weight it is important to try to distinguish between couples who have children, and a certain number of children, because of the satisfactions they derive from them and couples who have children, and a certain number of children, because it is expected of them (or at least, because they never seriously consider that it is not). As I said earlier, the questionnaire was unfortunately not designed to elucidate this distinction, but something may be said.

We asked couples whether they felt their lives would have been different without children, and if so, in what ways. The results were very clear. Not surprisingly, almost all said that their lives would indeed have been different. At all parities (apart from zero), 45 to 56% of the fathers and 63 to 84% of the mothers said that the most important difference would have been to the emotional quality of their lives. A negligible proportion of each mentioned that they would have been better off financially, and only small minorities (of the order of 10-12%) said that they would have been able to devote themselves more to and perhaps get more out of their employment.

Now for a parent to say that his or her emotional life would have been different without a child or several children (and those with more children indicated that they would have felt more deprived), while no doubt valid and obvious, does not help us to decide whether the deprivation would have been strictly personal, regardless of what others expected of them, or whether it would have been because in not having children, or in not having a certain number, they would have felt uneasy or even upset at violating the expectations of others. Expectations of this kind very probably do exist. Rainwater, for example, describing couples in three American cities, considered that there was a clear norm to have children, embodied in the proposition that "one shouldn't have more children

than one can support, but one should have as many as one can afford."
And a recent pilot study in England, not yet published, finds that
some respondents do refer to what is described as an "acceptable,"
"respectable" number.[2]

My own opinion, however, would be that although such
expectations do exist, and may even be widespread enough for a
majority to know about them, they are not causally very important.
That is, there very probably does exist an assumption that one
should marry, and having married, should have children, and it is
possible that the sanctions are sufficiently unpleasant to make most
people conform to it; but I doubt whether, even if it does exist, the
assumption that in having children one should have a certain number
is accompanied by similar sanctions. Bourgeois-Pichat, or at least
Wrigley, may be right: decisions about family size may have become
much more a matter for individual discretion. (It would be possible
to test for the difference between the two. If Wrigley were right,
that "social" sanctions have been replaced by "family" sanctions,
then there should be an association between the fertility of siblings;
if, on the other hand, Bourgeois-Pichat is right, there should be no
such association. Unfortunately, we do not have the data to do this
for our sample, which would anyway be difficult because of the
problem of married siblings being at different durations of marriage.
None of the other post-war studies contains the necessary
information either.)

So, whether couples value children in themselves for themselves
or whether their valuation is an expression of the satisfactions of
fulfilling social expectations remains unclear. *A priori*, the
economists would incline to the first, the sociologists to the second.
I do not yet have the evidence to decide.

CONCLUSIONS

Because much of the relevant material from the survey has yet to
be analysed, I have only been able to present a fragment of the
evidence necessary to explain the problem outlined at the beginning
of this paper and to test the "hypotheses" also outlined above.
Moreover, with regard to the latter, I have pointed out that we have
in this survey unfortunately not asked all the most relevant questions.
Nevertheless the findings so far suggest the conclusion that economic
considerations are not predominant in parents' minds when they

decide not to have any more children (although they may be when they consider their *timing*).

NOTES

1. The study described here is being done in conjunction with Joan Busfield, Michael Paddon and Diana Barker, for whose advice and help l am grateful; none of them, however, is responsible for the interpretations offered here, which remain my responsibility alone.

2. It should also be said that this study reports three-quarters of its respondents as giving "economic" reasons for their family size.

REFERENCES

BECKER, G.S. (1960). An Economic Analysis of Fertility. UNIVERSITIES-NATIONAL BUREAU COMMITTEE FOR ECONOMIC RESEARCH. *Demographic and Economic Change in Developed Countries*. Princeton: Princeton University Press. 209-31.

———— (1965). A Theory of the Allocation of Time. *Economic Journal* 75. 493-517.

BLAKE, J. (1968). Are Babies Consumer Durables? *Population Studies* 22. 5-25.

BOURGEOIS-PICHAT, J. (1967). Social and Biological Determinants of Human Fertility in Non-Industrial Societies. *Proceedings of the American Philosophical Society* 3. 160-63.

BUSFIELD, N.J., HAWTHORN, G.P. (1971). Some Social Determinants of Recent Trends in British Fertility. *Journal of Biosocial Science Supplement* 3. 65-77.

CARTWRIGHT, A. (1970). *Parents and Family Planning Services*. London: Routledge.

DUESENBERRY, J.S. (1960). Comment. UNIVERSITIES-NATIONAL BUREAU COMMITTEE FOR ECONOMIC RESEARCH. *op.cit.* 231-234.

EASTERLIN, R.A. (1972). The Economics and Sociology of Fertility: a Synthesis. Mimeo.

EVERSLEY, D.E.C. (1959). *Social Theories of Fertility and the Malthusian Debate*. London: Oxford University Press.

FLEW, A. (ed.) (1970). *Malthus: An Essay on the Principle of Population*. London: Perguin.

FREEDMAN, D. (1963). The Relation of Economic Status to Fertility. *American Economic Review*. 53. 414-427.

FREEDMAN, R. (1963). Norms for Family Size in Underdeveloped Areas. *Proceedings of the Royal Society,* Seires B. 159. Part 974. 220-245.
FREEDMAN, R., WHELPTON, P.K., CAMPBELL, A.A. (1959). *Family Planning, Sterility and Population Growth.* New York: McGraw-Hill.
HAMPSHIRE, S. (1972). *Morality and Pessimism.* The Leslie Stephen Lecture. Cambridge: Cambridge University Press.
HAWTHORN, G.P. (1970). *The Sociology of Fertility.* London: Collier-Macmillan.
———— (1973). *Population Policy.* London: Fabian Society.
————, BUSFIELD, N.J. (1968). Some Social Determinants of Family Size: Report of a Pilot Study. Mimeo.
HEER, D.M. (1966). Economic Development and Fertility. *Demography* 3. 423-444.
LEIBENSTEIN, H. 1973. *The Economic Theory of Fertility Decline.* Discussion Paper No. 292. Institute of Economic Research. Cambridge, Mass.: Harvard University.
LINZ, J.J. (1969). Ecological Analysis and Survey Research. DOGAN, M., ROKKAN, S. (eds.). *Quantitative Ecological Analysis in the Social Sciences.* Cambridge, Mass., M.I.T. Press 91-132.
MOSER, C.A., SCOTT, W. (1961). *British Towns.* Edinburgh, Oliver and Boyd.
NAMBOODIRI, N.K. (1972). Some Observations on the Economic Framework for Fertility Analysis. *Population Studies* 26. 185-206.
POPULATION PANEL (1973). *Report.* London: H.M.S.O.
RAINWATER, L. (1965). *Family Design.* Chicago: Aldine.
SIMON, J.L. (1969). The Effect of Income on Fertility. *Population Studies* 23. 327-341.
———— (1972). The Effect of Economic Conditions upon Fertility: Review, Analysis, Prediction. Mimeo.
UNITED NATIONS. DEPARTMENT OF ECONOMIC AND SOCIAL AFFAIRS (1953). *The Determinants and Consequences of Population Trends.* ST/SOA/ Series A/17. 53. XIII. 3. New York: United Nations.
WESTOFF, C.F. *et al.* (1961). *Family Growth in Metropolitan America.* Princeton: Princeton University Press.
———— (1963). *The Third Child.* Princeton: Princeton University Press.
———— (1969). *The Late Years of Childbearing.* Princeton: Princeton University Press.
WHELPTON, P.K., CAMPBELL, A.A., PATTERSON, J.E. (1966). *Fertility and Family Planning in the United States.* Princeton: Princeton University Press.
WOOLF, M. (1971). *Family Intentions.* London: H.M.S.O.
WRIGLEY, E.A. (1969). *Population and History.* London, Weidenfeld and Nicholson.

Chapter 3

POSITIVE DISCRIMINATION IN EDUCATION:
INDIVIDUALS, GROUPS AND INSTITUTIONS

J.H. Barnes and H. Lucas*

THE POLICY OF POSITIVE DISCRIMINATION

A dominant theme of policy research in education has been the documentation of how far schools reflect, rather than affect, their social context. Educational institutions seem to produce an academic ranking of each generation which follows closely the socio-economic ranking of their parents.[1] This observed performance is seen to be in painful contradiction with the moral implications of a democratic ideology — that educational opportunities should be equal, and educational experiences should be universal and open. And reformers are devoting enormous efforts to change it and to make equality of opportunity a more cogent reality.[2]

But the tensions for educational policy and for research have neither been resolved nor receded with time. If anything they have become more severe as the disparity between the performance of schools and the developing demands on them has grown. The old search for equality of opportunity, seen in terms of individuals fulfilling some notion of their potential and gaining access to the more selective levels of education, has moved on. Some see the issues now to be concerned more with equality of *results* between groups than with opportunities for *access* open to individuals. It is argued that education should not reflect the divisions current in society, simply providing opportunities for some to ascend the ladder of privilege; it should, in fact, be judged by the extent to which it transcends those divisions, and provides convergent experiences for its subjects.[3] Thus in its performance, education seems to persist as a means whereby society perpetually renews the conditions of its own existence, reflecting the extant and dominant distribution of adult roles. Yet many believe that it ought to be an agency of social reform, redistributing access to and transforming the nature of adult roles.

In this paper we report our attempts to clarify the nature and identify the possible outcomes of one series of policies which have been designed to promote greater equality in British primary education: "positive discrimination in the allocation of educational resources . . . in favour of areas and schools where children are most severely handicapped by home conditions."[4]

The policy was first proposed by the Plowden Council in its report, in 1967, on "primary education in all its aspects."[5] Their formulations were designed to encompass an extremely complex series of interactions, many of which they implied rather than specified. Children in educational priority areas were seen to be surrounded by a "seamless web of circumstance,"[6] where everything was causing everything else. Individuals and institutions were interacting together in a downward spiral of deprivation, making identification of cause or consequence redundant — perhaps impossible. The basic dynamic appears to have been as follows: various non-educational characteristics of groups of children — the colour of their skin, the occupation of their father, the financial circumstances of their family — are determinants of their educational performance. The effect of combinations of these attributes on a child's capacity to perform successfully at school is cumulative. The Council identified this as "cumulative deprivation", a situation which, they said, occurred when one deprivation "reinforced" another. Children subject to these cumulative deprivations are not scattered at random across the population. They are concentrated in certain (primarily urban) areas and schools where their interaction together, and with an environment "ingrained with the grime of generations," increased the cumulative effect of disadvantage. Situations in the schools are thus a consequence, and then become a further cause of disadvantage for the children attending them. The concentration of disadvantaged families in poor neighbourhoods has consequences for their community institutions, which lack coherent organization and suffer from poor leadership. And to complete the circle, disorganization at the community and family level contributes further to the educational effects of initially non-educational circumstances: race, social class, income, etc.

In some respects the policy proposed by the Council to deal with this situation was clear and unambiguous. It was to be an educational policy; and one which had relatively moderate resource implications. Marginal increments to the total volume of resources available to education were to be diverted to educational priority areas and their children and schools. The main weapon in the attack on multiple deprivation was to be more effective schools.[7] Secondly "objective criteria for the selection of educational priority schools and areas" were provided.[8] The policy would be focused on the poor; but it would not require poor people to identify, and to risk stigmatizing, themselves in order to receive help. The target for the policy was to be disadvantaged areas and the schools in them.

In other respects the Council's recommendations are less easy to understand. In particular, although their concern for disadvantaged schools and areas is unequivocal, it occasionally becomes muddled with a further concern: for disadvantaged groups and individuals and their families. Certainly the Report moves very easily from one to the other without recognizing the consequences of their change of focus. And further, it is not clear what the effects of positive discrimination on its recipients are intended to be. The Council advised, for instance, that "the first step must be to raise the schools with low standards to the national average. The second quite deliberately to make them better."[9] The target for the policy here is schools; but it is not clear whether "better" refers specifically and only to the volume of resources going to the schools, to the opportunities available to, or to the actual performance of the children in them. Initial priority should, they urged, be given "to the schools which by our criteria contain the ten per cent of most deprived children;"[10] but for a longer term programme they envisaged an extension of positive discrimination beyond "an arbitrary figure of ten per cent of the population."[11] (Notice that the target for the policy has moved from schools to people). Both in the long and the short term, a national policy of positive discrimination should "favour *schools* in *neighbourhoods* where *children* are most severely handicapped by *home* conditions"[12] (authors' italics).

Our analysis has been directed towards a clarification of these two issues: of who can be helped, and of what can be achieved by a policy of positive discrimination in favour of educational priority area schools. In the first section of text below we examine the concept of educational disadvantage itself. We attempt to identify the disadvantaged children in one inner city population. We ask whether the notion of disadvantage is a meaningful way to characterize their social and educational situation. And we attempt to place the phenomenon in the context of its social geography by exploring how far disadvantaged or poor children are concentrated in disadvantaged or poor areas. From this we are able to estimate possible upper limits to the scope of the policy expressed in terms of who can be helped. In the second section of text we examine what effect a discriminatory policy can have. This necessarily involves an attempt to identify an effect from the social and educational context of schools which exists independently of the circumstances of individual children. Presuming that a discriminatory policy will operate in some way to counteract this contextual effect, we once again estimate the upper limits to the scope of the policy. The data we use were largely gathered at the individual level; and we would contend that such a heterogeneous concept as educational disadvantage can only be studied in this way. But at the same time our concern is largely with the policy consequences for groups of children and for schools. We would contend in this respect that, while educational policies might be designed to help particular groups of individuals (and these groups might be very small and homogeneous), policies can hardly be expected to accommodate the unique life situations of particular individuals. Teachers do this while teaching children; we are unsure what a policy for it would look like other than in some very general and perhaps rhetorical sense.

SOURCES OF DATA

The data used were all derived from work undertaken by the Research and Statistics Group of the Inner London Education Authority (the ILEA) during the period 1968-1971. It should be remembered that the original data were collected in order to provide the Authority with descriptive material on its primary schools and their children. Certainly the child data are in a number of ways unreliable and inadequate for our purposes.[13] And our findings can only be applied with confidence to inner London. We were aware of these limitations throughout the analysis, and have taken account of them when presenting our conclusions.

Information on the Schools: From the Index of Relative Institutional Deprivation

During 1967-1968 the Research and Statistics Group of the ILEA developed an Index to identify primary schools which answered to the Plowden Council's definition of educational priority area schools.[14] The criteria included in the Index were either those recommended by the Plowden Council or conveniently near equivalents. The measures of each of the criteria were either school-based or collected for a notional catchment area for all primary schools in the ILEA.[15] School scores on each of the measures were scaled to conform to a distribution between 0 and 100; and these scaled scores were summed to derive an equally weighted, composite, institutional score. Schools were then ranked, according to their composite score, to create an Index of Relative School Deprivation.

A basic premise of our analysis is that the logic of this Index is an adequate and acceptable way to identify educational priority area schools. We offer no defence of the Index, except to say that there was substantial agreement between the schools' rank positions on it and practitioner assessments of their relative positions. It was, and still is, used by the ILEA as one basis for allocating extra resources to schools thought to need help; and in spite of its limitations which are discussed in the account of its construction, it appears to have few rivals as an attempt to identify disadvantaged schools or areas as targets for positive discrimination.

Information on the Children: From the ILEA Literacy Survey

At the same time as the construction of its Index of EPA Primary Schools, the ILEA conducted the first stage of a survey of reading performance in one age cohort of children in its junior schools. All junior schools in the Authority were asked to test all children who were in their second junior school year (the 8+ group) on a reading test (the Sentence Reading Test A).[16] In addition, class and head teachers were asked to complete a questionnaire giving a range of background information on each child.[17] Towards the end of the school year 1970-1971 all junior schools in the Authority were again asked to test all children in the same cohort on a parallel form of the original reading test. The cohort was then in its last year in primary school (the 11+ group).

Table 1 (below) shows the absolute size of that cohort of ILEA children from their birth year in 1960 to their year of transfer to secondary school in 1971. The table shows, firstly, that the cohort was growing smaller at a net rate of 2.7% per annum for each year it was in ILEA primary schools and, secondly, that a reading test score was achieved for a very high proportion of the universe of children. We nevertheless need to be extremely careful when speaking about the performance of the whole cohort.[18],[19]

TABLE 1

CHANGES IN THE SIZE OF THE AGE COHORT OVER TIME

Year		Size	Change	% Change
1960:	Birth Cohort	56,642	−18,499	−32.7
1965:	Cohort 5+ years old	38,143	− 864	− 2.3
1966:	" 6+ " "	37,279	− 1,001	− 2.7
1967:	" 7+ " "	36,278	− 1,152	− 3.2
*1968:	" 8+ " "	35,126	− 977	− 2.8
1969:	" 9+ " "	34,149	− 980	− 2.9
1970:	" 10+ " "	33,169	− 803	− 2.4
*1971:	" 11+ " "	32,366		
Mean Net Percentage Change 1965-1971				− 2.7

* Time of initial reading survey: 31,308 Children Tested
* Time of second reading survey: 31,731 Children Tested
Derived from ILEA Statistics

A file was created containing both school and child-based data. We set out the main items placed on this file in Table 2. But briefly, all infant schools were excluded together with any junior schools on whom there were no data from the schools' Index of Deprivation. As we had measures from the child data on only eight variable Index of Schools was constructed for the file. To the new file, already containing both the school scores and their rank position on this new Index, were added equivalent variables for each individual child together, where these were available, with the reading test scores. We then added three other pieces of data to characterize schools: the proportion of semi-skilled and unskilled workers' children in each school, the proportion of immigrant children in each school and the score and rank position of each school on the original ILEA Schools' Index of Relative Deprivation.

TABLE 2

MAIN DATA ITEMS USED IN THE ANALYSIS

1.	*Data on the Schools*	*Data Used*
A.	*Source: ILEA Schools Index*	
i.	School's scaled score on the EPA Index	
ii.	School's rank position on the EPA Index	To identify the EPA Schools and to arrange schools into Quartiles. (See Tables 4, 4.1, and 6)
iii.	School's scaled score on the EPA Index amended by removing factors of overcrowding of houses and housing stress	To characterise schools for the regression analysis. (See Tables 9, 11 and 12)
iv.	School's rank position on the amended Index	

B.	*Data from the Literacy Survey averaged over all the children in the same school*	
i.	Percentage of children whose parent or guardian was a semi-skilled or unskilled manual worker	To characterise schools for the regression analysis. (See Table 8)
ii.	Percentage of children who were immigrant. (that is, stated country of origin was not the United Kingdom or the Republic of Ireland)	To characterise schools for the regression analysis. (See Table 8)

2.   Data on the Children

		For the Index of Disadvantage (See Note 21) Tables 3, 4, 4.1, 6, 7 and 7.1	For the regression analysis. Only if the following data were available. Tables 5, 8, 9, 10, 11 and 12
C.	*Source 1968 Literacy Survey*		
i.	Country of Origin of the child	X	X
ii.	Number of schools attended by the child	X	
iii.	Number of teachers who had taught the child	X	
iv.	Number of absences during one term	X	
v.	Family size	X	X
vi.	Whether the child received free school meals	X	X

TABLE 2 CONTINUED

MAIN DATA ITEMS USED IN THE ANALYSIS

---

2.   *Data on the Children cont.*

		For the Index of Disadvantage (See Note 21) Tables 3, 4, 4.1, 6, 7 and 7.1	*For the regression analysis. Only if the following data were available. Tables 5, 8, 9, 10, 11 and 12*
C.	*Source 1968 Literacy Survey cont.*		
vii.	Occupation of parent or guardian (a proxy measure for social class)	X	X
viii.	Child's standardised score on the SRA Reading Test		(X)
C.	*Source 1971 Literacy Survey*		
i.	Child's standardised score on the SRB Reading Test		
ii.	Child's rank position on a Verbal Reasoning Test completed prior to transfer to secondary school	X (N.B.).	

N.B.   Children whose position was unknown were dropped for the analysis presented in Table 6.

DISADVANTAGED CHILDREN: THE ECOLOGICAL FALLACY[20]

It is our conclusion that, in as far as they were concerned to help poor children or children in disadvantaged or deprived circumstances, the analysis of the Plowden Council which led it to advocate an educational priority area or school programme was based on a methodological fallacy. The fallacy occurs when ecological methods of analysis are used: when aggregated or averaged data are used to characterize areas or institutions. It is caused by a concentration on the principal or dominant pattern, and a failure to recognize the variation or heterogeneity. The fallacy in this particular case does not take account of the diversity within any group of educational priority schools, of the wide distribution of circumstances to which children outside any such group of schools are subject, nor does it recognize the logical jump between a counting of separate problems and the identification of a condition of cumulative disadvantage or deprivation. In advocating a priority area or school programme to meet the needs of poor children, the Council went beyond conclusions which could have been born out by analysis of its data.

The policy consequences are that, as a device for helping poor children, positive discrimination through schools can only be disappointing. Most poor families do not live in poor areas; they are widely scattered throughout the population. A policy which discriminated in favour of the most disadvantaged 10 per cent of schools, could only help a relatively small proportion of the total number of poor or disadvantaged children. And trying to bring help to more of them by expanding the number of schools would run into diminishing returns: as more schools were added in to the programme, so the rate at which relatively privileged children were included would increase faster than the rate for disadvantaged children. In effect, positive discrimination in favour of the most dis-advantaged schools establishes for itself criteria which limit the number of disadvantaged people that can be reached.

Children at Risk

We came to this conclusion once we had found the numbers and the various proportions of children, inside and outside priority area schools, who were at risk on criteria equivalent to those which had been used to identify the schools. Tables 3, 4 and 4.1 summarise our findings. For each of the school criteria on which we had individualised data, children were assigned an at-risk or not at-risk score; and these scores were added together to create a cumulative index.[21] For analysis using the individual items, we said simply that children were either at-risk or not at-risk. For the analysis using the cumulative index, we said that children with high scores (five or more out of a maximum of eight) were at risk of being disadvantaged. For the sake of clear exposition we call these the disadvantaged children, but we think there should be more investigation of a "condition of disadvantage" before a positive diagnosis is made. We said children with low scores on the index (zero or one) were not at risk. We call these the non-disadvantaged children. They cannot be called a privileged group because their "objective" circumstances have been defined by a series of negatives: they were not immigrants, not unskilled or semi-skilled workers' children, they were not from large families, etc. Schools are grouped in two ways for Tables 3 and 4 and 4.1. The "Least Privileged Group" are those junior schools

TABLE 3

PROPORTION OF CHILDREN AT-RISK AND NOT AT-RISK ON THE SINGLE ITEMS OF RISK

	Immigrant Children %	High Pupil Mobility %	High Teacher Mobility %	High Absenteeism %	Large Families %	Free Meals %	Low Verbal Reasoning Scores %	Low Social Class %
LEAST PRIVILEGED GROUP OF SCHOOLS (E.P.A. Schools) N = 4,158								
Not at risk	67.75	81.48	70.66	73.71	57.96	68.22	49.86	37.45
At-risk	30.57 32.25	14.14 18.52	23.74 29.34	17.27 26.29	34.53 42.03	29.56 31.76	30.47 50.14	50.07 62.55
Don't Know	1.68	4.38	5.60	9.02	7.5	2.2	19.67	12.48
ALL OTHER SCHOOLS N = 26,338								
Not at-risk	83.55	84.20	81.65	75.67	67.46	82.79	64.09	52.11
At-risk	16.45 16.45	13.03 15.80	15.15 18.34	17.59 24.33	27.59 32.53	16.57 17.21	17.80 35.91	38.40 47.89
Don't know	—	2.77	3.19	6.74	4.94	0.64	18.11	9.49
TOTAL N = 30,496								
Not at-risk	81.56	83.99	79.97	75.48	65.90	80.73	62.19	49.98
At-risk	18.22 18.44	13.05 16.00	16.53 20.03	17.52 24.52	28.55 34.10	18.42 19.27	19.52 37.81	39.96 50.20
Don't know	0.22	2.95	3.50	7.00	5.55	0.85	18.29	10.06
Number of cases of risk in the least Privileged Schools: Number of cases of risk in all other schools	1:3.2	1:5.4	1:4.0	1:5.9	1:4.9	1:3.4	1:4.5	1:4.9

which were included in the 150 primary schools having the highest scores on the ILEA Index of Schools. We call these the EPA Schools in the text below, because they are the group which conform most strongly to the Plowden Council's definition of educational priority area schools.[22] The second way in which schools are grouped (for Table 4.1) is into approximate quartiles on the ILEA Index of Schools; this enables us to illustrate the effect, in terms of the individual children who would be encompassed, of extending the range of schools in any educational priority area programme.

The proportions of the total population at-risk on the individual items in the analysis varies from 16 per cent, in the case of high pupil mobility, to 50 per cent in the case of low social class (see Table 3 above). The overall pattern is that, in each case, between one in five and one in three of the cohort are at risk on these items, although the proportions are higher for social class and low verbal reasoning.

As could be expected, the proportions of children at risk in the EPA Schools are higher than in the total population; but they only go above fifty per cent on those two items whose incidence in the population is also significantly high. On two items, pupil mobility and high absenteeism, the incidence in the EPA Schools is similar to that which could be expected in any other group of schools in this population.

Although children with these individual at-risk characteristics are a higher proportion of the population of EPA Schools than they are of the population generally, their total number is far greater outside the EPA Schools. For instance, we might wish to say that immigrant children are concentrated in under-privileged EPA Schools; but from our evidence, for every immigrant child that is in an EPA School three are not. There are five times as many children at-risk because they come from large families outside the EPA Schools than there are inside them. There are five times as many unskilled and semi-skilled workers' children, three and a half times as many children receiving free school meals and four and a half times as many children with low verbal reasoning scores outside the EPA Schools than there are in them.[23]

It might be argued that, although the incidence of individual situations of need is widely spread throughout the population, cumulative disadvantage is a phenomenon more common to the EPA Schools. Tables 4 and 4.1 show our findings on this matter. (See Note 21 for the way in which the index of disadvantage was constructed). In the total cohort eleven thousand four hundred children, or one in three, had scores of zero or one. We can say that these children are not disadvantaged. However, two and a half thousand children, or one in every twelve, were multiply disadvantaged on our measures and according to our definition.

TABLE 4

INDIVIDUALS AT-RISK ON THE CUMULATIVE CHILD AT-RISK INDEX OF DISADVANTAGE IN THE LEAST PRIVILEGED GROUP OF SCHOOLS

(a) By school group by level of risk
(b) By level or risk by school group

(a) *Least Privileged Group of Schools: The EPA Schools*

Level of Risk	Least Privileged Schools	All Other Schools	Total
	%	%	%
0	6.0	14.5	13.3
1	15.4	25.5	24.1
2	22.1	24.7	24.3
3	21.8	18.0	18.5
4	17.9	10.6	11.6
5+	16.8	6.7	8.1
Base (=100%)	4,158	26,338	30,496

(b) *By Level of Risk*

Level of Risk		Least Privileged Schools	All Other Schools	Total
0	%	6.1	93.9	100
1	%	8.7	91.3	100
2	%	12.4	87.6	100
3	%	16.1	83.9	100
4	%	21.0	79.0	100
5+	%	28.2	71.8	100
Total	%	13.6	86.4	100

TABLE 4.1

INDIVIDUALS AT-RISK ON THE CUMULATIVE CHILD AT-RISK INDEX OF
DISADVANTAGE IN THE SCHOOLS GROUPED INTO
APPROXIMATE EPA QUARTILES

(a) By school group by level at-risk
(b) By level of risk by school group

(a)   Schools Grouped into Quartiles

Level of Risk	Least Privileged Quartile	Second Quartile	Third Quartile	Most Privileged Quartile
	%	%	%	%
0	6.7	11.4	14.0	22.2
1	17.5	22.3	26.9	30.4
2	23.0	24.5	25.4	24.0
3	21.6	20.3	18.0	13.5
4	16.8	12.4	10.1	6.6
5+	14.3	9.0	5.5	3.3
Base (=100%)	7,029	9,122	7,670	6,675

(b)   Level of Risk

Level of Risk		Least Privileged Quartile	Second Quartile	Third Quartile	Most Privileged Quartile
0	%	11.6	25.6	26.4	36.4
1	%	16.8	27.6	28.0	27.6
2	%	21.9	30.2	26.3	21.6
3	%	26.8	32.8	24.5	15.9
4	%	33.6	32.0	21.9	12.6
5+	%	40.5	33.3	17.1	9.0
Total	%	23.0	29.9	25.2	21.9

As with the single at-risk items, these children comprise a
significantly higher proportion of the EPA Schools than of the total
population: 16.8 per cent as opposed to 8.1 per cent (Table 4). Even
so, even in the EPA Schools, the disadvantaged group are
outnumbered by children who are not disadvantaged: for every three
children in these schools who are at risk of being disadvantaged, four
are not.

Perhaps most significantly, less than one third of the multiply disadvantaged children are in the EPA Schools. In other words, resources going to these schools reach 13.6 per cent of all the children in the cohort, but only 28.2 per cent (two out of every seven) of the disadvantaged children in it. It would clearly be unrealistic to expect all the disadvantaged children to be in the disadvantaged EPA Schools. And it is an open question what proportion of them it would be regarded as satisfactory for any schools programme to pick up. Indeed, given limited resources, a school or area policy acts as an effective rationing device.

But what seems to us important is that the logic of discriminatory school or area policies constrains the upper limit to their effectiveness seen in this way. The policy can only be discriminatory if some schools are excluded; but excluding some schools excludes some disadvantaged children. Table 4.1b illustrates the point. By encompassing half the schools in this analysis, a school programme of positive discrimination could bring benefit to 74 per cent of the disadvantaged children; but 40 per cent of the children who were not disadvantaged would also be included. By expanding to three quarters of all schools (78 per cent of all children), 90 per cent of high risk children could be reached but so also would nearly two thirds of the non-disadvantaged group. Nine per cent of disadvantaged children are in the most privileged quartile of schools, where they comprise 3 per cent of the population. To help this group, a school programme would need to include all schools and all children; it could hardly then be discriminatory according to the conventional definitions.

We believe that the results of this part of our analysis confront the policy of discrimination in favour of EPA Schools with a paradox. It seems likely that the majority of disadvantaged children are not in disadvantaged areas, and the majority of children in disadvantaged areas are not disadvantaged. At the least this means that policies to assist disadvantaged schools or areas should not be seen as alternatives to policies which are focused on groups of children, whether these groups are to be identified in terms of single or combined indicators of need.

Further, we might wish to develop the policy by saying that any help for disadvantaged children which was channelled through a positively biased schools' programme should be differentially weighted according to the proportion of disadvantaged children in each school. But if such a programme were to be sensitively adjusted to the needs of different groups of children, it would need to take account of their relative positions within a school as well as the presence of their disadvantage measured on "objective" indicators of need. In other words, once the policy moves from one which simply discriminates between schools to one which accommodates intra school differences, it must recognize other parameters. We illustrate something of what we mean by this in the text below, when we move from analysis of the children's circumstances to say something about their behaviour.

Reading Performance and Objective and Relative Disadvantage

We used performance on the reading test, given at the beginning of the children's second year in the junior school, to compare their objective and their relative situations seen in behavioural terms. We used this because, effectively, there was no other available measure of the children's behaviour.[24] Clearly it provides a narrow view of a child's relative position in a school and other measures might have given different results. But every primary school tries to teach this skill, and its acquisition is seen to be particularly important for children of this age.[25] Given this, it seems to us that reading performance is a powerful indicator of the degree to which a child is being assimilated into the main academic culture of the school.

Tables 5 and 6 provide basic descriptive statistics on the reading performance of the children in this analysis. For Table 5 groups of children have been categorized according to four objective need indicators (see Note 27). In table 6 children are ranked according to their level of risk of being disadvantaged and by the previous school groupings.[26] It is important to be clear what can be inferred from these tables. They represent the extant reading performance of groups of children: performances which are a consequence of the interaction of all kinds of factors. In the second section of the paper we attribute variations in reading performance to possible effects: but for the moment we wish to illustrate the actual situation, at one point in time, regardless of the apparent reason for it.

Not surprisingly our broad findings are that, as children's objective circumstances become more disadvantaged, so their reading performance tends to be lower. But the actual size of the differences found between privileged and underprivileged children do seem to be disturbingly large. The performance of disadvantaged children in the

TABLE 5

MEAN READING SCORES FOR GROUPS OF CHILDREN

(a)   *according to Social Class*
(b)   *for West Indian Immigrant and groups born in the United Kingdom*
(c)   *according to Family Size*
(d)   *according to Receipt of Free School Meals*

		N	Mean Score	S.D.
Total		22,614	95.5	15.28
(a) Social Class				
	Social Class I	1,872	107.4	14.59
	Social Class II	3,539	100.4	14.43
	Social Class III	7,662	96.0	14.29
	Social Class IV	5,073	92.5	13.72
	Social Class V	4,468	89.1	13.95
(b) Non-Immigrant and West Indian Immigrant Groups				
Non-Immigrant	Social Class I	1,845	107.5	14.64
	Social Class II	3,425	100.7	14.45
	Social Class III	7,113	96.6	14.35
	Social Class IV	4,432	93.3	13.81
	Social Class V	3,793	90.2	14.19
West Indian Immigrant	Social Class I	27	–	–
	Social Class II	114	91.8	13.78
	Social Class III	549	88.9	13.47
	Social Class IV	641	87.2	13.04
	Social Class V	675	83.1	12.55
(c) Family Size Small Families				
Non-Immigrant	Social Class I	1,512	107.9	14.74
	Social Class II	2,765	101.4	14.49
	Social Class III	5,381	97.4	14.40
	Social Class IV	3,117	94.1	13.94
	Social Class V	2,430	91.5	14.53
West Indian Immigrant	Social Class I	17	–	–
	Social Class II	71	93.5	14.12
	Social Class III	295	89.1	13.46
	Social Class IV	290	87.5	13.60
	Social Class V	294	83.8	12.81

TABLE 5 CONTINUED

		N	*Mean Score*	*S.D.*
(c) Family Size cont.				
Large Families				
Non-Immigrant	Social Class I	333	105.7	14.18
	Social Class II	660	97.7	14.28
	Social Class III	1,732	93.9	14.20
	Social Class IV	1,315	91.3	13.48
	Social Class V	1,363	87.9	13.55
West Indian Immigrant	Social Class I	10	–	–
	Social Class II	43	88.8	13.22
	Social Class III	254	88.6	13.49
	Social Class IV	351	86.8	12.56
	Social Class V	381	82.6	12.35
(d) Receipt of Free Meals				
No Free Meals Small Families				
Non-Immigrant	Social Class I	1,469	108.1	14.70
	Social Class II	2,647	101.7	14.52
	Social Class III	5,187	97.6	14.40
	Social Class IV	2,910	94.5	13.92
	Social Class V	2,099	92.1	14.60
West Indian Immigrant	Social Class I	15	–	–
	Social Class II	59	93.0	14.04
	Social Class III	252	89.7	13.61
	Social Class IV	247	88.0	13.72
	Social Class V	215	84.4	12.88
No Free Meals Large Families				
Non-Immigrant	Social Class I	282	106.0	13.92
	Social Class II	505	99.0	14.06
	Social Class III	1,220	94.7	14.35
	Social Class IV	836	92.4	13.66
	Social Class V	693	89.5	13.70
West Indian Immigrant	Social Class I	5	–	–
	Social Class II	25	–	–
	Social Class III	164	89.0	13.70
	Social Class IV	206	87.1	13.08
	Social Class V	193	82.4	12.80

TABLE 5 CONTINUED

		N	Mean Score	S.D.
(d) Receipt of Free Meals cont.				
Free Meals Small Families				
Non-Immigrant	Social Class I	43	99.0	15.84
	Social Class II	118	95.4	13.64
	Social Class III	194	92.2	14.26
	Social Class IV	207	89.6	14.23
	Social Class V	331	87.4	14.13
West Indian Immigrant	Social Class I	2	—	—
	Social Class II	12	—	—
	Social Class III	43	86.2	12.52
	Social Class IV	43	84.7	12.93
	Social Class V	79	82.0	12.59
Free Meals Large Families				
Non-Immigrant	Social Class I	51	103.9	15.53
	Social Class II	155	93.3	14.99
	Social Class III	512	91.8	13.85
	Social Class IV	479	89.4	13.18
	Social Class V	670	86.2	13.40
West Indian Immigrant	Social Class I	5	—	—
	Social Class II	18	—	—
	Social Class III	90	87.9	13.12
	Social Class IV	145	86.3	11.79
	Social Class V	188	82.7	11.87

EPA Schools is slightly below that of similar children in the privileged schools. But at the same time, there are senses in which the relative position of disadvantaged children in privileged schools is actually worse than it is in EPA Schools. In absolute terms disadvantaged children appear to be poor readers whatever sort of school they are in. In privileged schools, where average reading performances are high, low performing disadvantaged children are therefore relatively worse off.

Table 5 shows the average reading scores for groups of children with various home background factors or characteristics of family circumstance controlled.[27] The average reading score for the whole group of children, for instance, is 95.5. When the occupation of the children's father (our proxy for social class) is controlled, the averages range from 107.4, for the children of professional and managerial workers, to 89.1, for unskilled workers' children. The range of average scores, when all four of the factors have been controlled, is twenty six points of reading score (more than two years of reading age): between the average score of professional and managerial workers' children, who were born in the United Kingdom, who do not receive free school meals and who come from small families and the children of West Indian Immigrant unskilled workers, whether or not they receive free school meals and irrespective of their family size.

A simple comparison of mean scores does not recognize that, in every case, there is nearly as much variation in score within one of these groups as there is within the whole population. In order to illustrate the size of the differences between groups, therefore, we prefer to use a measure of the extent to which the various distributions of score overlap each other.[28]

The reading performance of 50 per cent of the whole population represented in Table 5 falls below 95.5. The performance of 86 per cent of West Indian Immigrant unskilled workers' children falls below this point. In other words, 86 per cent of this group of West Indian Immigrant children score below the average for the population. Seventy five per cent of all West Indian Immigrant children score below the average for the non-immigrant children in the analysis. Seventy seven per cent of non-immigrant professional workers' children score above the average for all non-immigrant children. Ninety seven per cent of West Indian Immigrant unskilled workers' children score below the average for non-immigrant professional workers' children; and 71 per cent of West Indian Immigrant unskilled workers' children score below the average for non-immigrant unskilled workers' children. For whatever reason, differences in reading performance between privileged and disadvantaged children appear to be very large indeed.

A similar calculation from the mean and standard deviation of scores in Table 6 simply confirms this. The differences in mean score between zero risk children and children with a score of five or more on the index of disadvantage is of the order of twenty-two points (nearly two years of reading age); and 96 per cent of the high risk children score below the average for the zero risk group.

The average reading performance of high risk children in EPA Schools is only one point of score below their average performance in all other schools, while high risk children in the most privileged

TABLE 6

INDIVIDUALS AT-RISK ON THE CUMULATIVE CHILD INDEX OF
DISADVANTAGE: MEAN READING SCORE AND STANDARD DEVIATION

(a) By the least privileged group of schools by level of risk
(b) By the schools grouped into "quartiles" by level of risk

(a) Least Privileged Group of Schools

Level of Risk	Least Privileged Group of Schools (N = 3284)		All Other Schools in the Index of Privilege (N = 21360)		Total (N = 25952)	
	Mean	S.D.	Mean	S.D.	Mean	S.D.
0	98.8	12.7	104.1	13.3	103.8	13.3
1	94.4	13.2	99.6	13.6	99.1	13.7
2	90.6	13.3	94.9	14.4	94.4	14.3
3	85.7	12.2	90.3	13.9	89.6	13.7
4	82.5	13.3	85.7	13.7	85.0	13.7
5+	80.7	12.1	81.9	12.5	81.5	12.4
Total	88.0	14.0	95.5	15.2	94.6	15.2

(b) Schools Grouped into "Quartiles"

Level of Risk	Least Privileged Quartile (N = 5581)		Second Quartile (N = 7292)		Third Quartile (N = 6291)		Most Privileged Quartile (N = 5480)	
	Mean	S.D.	Mean	S.D.	Mean	S.D.	Mean	S.D.
0	99.6	13.3	101.8	12.9	103.9	13.3	106.5	13.1
1	95.6	13.1	98.1	13.1	99.2	13.6	102.2	14.0
2	91.2	13.5	93.1	13.9	95.3	14.1	98.2	15.0
3	86.6	13.0	88.6	13.3	91.3	13.7	94.1	14.6
4	83.1	13.3	84.8	13.7	85.9	13.5	89.6	14.1
5+	80.6	12.1	81.4	12.2	83.2	12.7	84.2	13.3
Total	89.2	14.4	93.0	14.7	95.9	14.8	100.4	15.1

quartile of schools do slightly better in an absolute sense: the difference of mean scores between disadvantaged children in EPA and in the most privileged quartile of schools is therefore of the order of three and a half points. In other words, 53 per cent of high risk children in EPA Schools score below the average for high risk children in all other schools, but 61 per cent fall below the average for high risk children in the privileged schools. On the other hand, looking at intra school differences, high risk children in privileged schools are worse off relative to their classmates. Again the point can be illustrated with reference to distributions of score. Eighty per cent of high risk children score below the average for the total population; 70 per cent score below the average for EPA Schools; and 86 per cent score below the average for the most privileged group of schools.

Clearly disadvantaged children in privileged schools have potentially more access to privileged children. But from this piece of analysis we do not know whether either of the groups take advantage of whatever opportunities this offers or whether, if they did, either would benefit from it. We do know that high risk children in privileged schools do slightly better than similarly defined groups of children in EPA Schools. But it should be remembered that, in every case, the reading performance of groups of disadvantaged children is extremely low, that the difference between their scores in different sorts of school is relatively small, and that the performance of high risk children is more deviant for privileged schools and closer to the average in EPA Schools.

We have previously demonstrated that there is only a loose correlation between the objectively measured and accepted distribution of disadvantaged schools and the spread of similarly identified groups of children. The geographical distribution of children at risk of being disadvantaged is not confined to a particular sample of schools; and school programmes of positive discrimination cannot be alternatives to other programmes of help for children in need. We can now also say with some confidence that educationally disadvantaged circumstances are themselves diverse.[29] The behaviour, measured in terms of reading performance, of groups of disadvantaged children is different from that of privileged groups, and from groups that are not disadvantaged. But we have also illustrated that groups of children whose circumstances are identical on objective indicators (that is, they are all at risk of being disadvantaged) can be in quite different social and educational situations. It may be that it is more pleasant in some way for disadvantaged children to be in privileged schools; it is certain that their group performance is low wherever they are. Once again we can ask what follows. At the very least programmes of positive discrimination must face the low performance of groups of disadvantaged children wherever they are: with concentrations of low performance in EPA Schools and extreme diversities in performance between groups of children in privileged schools.

The Nature of Child Disadvantage

We had established that child disadvantage can only be adequately studied with data gathered at the individual and not the aggregate level. Our empirical evidence at least raised the possibility that, in addition to its objective dimensions, there were relative and possibly therefore subjective aspects to disadvantage. We tried lastly, to investigate the content of disadvantage as it was identified by the objective indicators. We wanted to discover whether a series of relationships could be established between the objective measures in the child index which approximated to a latent variable (of deprivation or disadvantage).

When people talk of seeing disadvantaged or deprived children they mean that they can *see* poor or black or badly clothed or dirty children. We think they *mean* something more, however. They mean that some children are subject to a particular substantive condition. This may need to be observed or measured through observable criteria; but it is thought to exist in the same way that, say, productivity in factories, or bravery in soldiers, or aggression in a species, or even intelligence in human beings is thought to exist. Our findings indicate that, in as far as this phenomenon of disadvantage is to be identified through the at-risk criteria we had constructed, people who believe this are probably wrong. The at-risk index is a definition of need rather than an approximation to a latent variable of multiple deprivation.

Table 7 shows the relationships between any two at-risk indicators for the total population.[30] By far the strongest relationship exists, unsurprisingly perhaps, between the large families and the free school meals indicators (r = 0.333). A second level of relationship exists between the social class, large families, free meals, low verbal reasoning and immigrant items: the correlation coefficients in this case range between 0.107 and 0.225. Given the numbers involved the other relationships are extremely weak; and we decided to concentrate the later stages of our analysis on only those variables that were strongly related together.[31]

Table 7.1 summarizes the results of principal components analysis to test directly for the existence of the latent variable of multiple

TABLE 7

CORRELATIONS BETWEEN INDIVIDUAL AT-RISK ITEMS
IN THE TOTAL POPULATION

Immigrants	1.0							
High Number of Schools Attended	0.078	1.0			N = 25949			
High Number of Different Teachers	0.059	0.074	1.0					
High Absentee Rate	−0.053	0.086	0.113	1.0				
Large Family	0.133	0.066	0.022	−0.005	1.0			
Free Meals	0.107	0.096	0.041	0.022	0.333	1.0		
Low Social Class	0.108	0.047	0.032	0.046	0.143	0.225	1.0	
Low Verbal Reasoning Score	0.109	0.043	0.022	0.036	0.110	0.146	0.168	1.0

deprivation.[32] The largest factor has, as could be predicted, a high weighting for free school meals, family size, low verbal reasoning, low social class and immigrants. It accounts for only 21 per cent of the variance, however; and in such an analysis, on any eight variables, at least 12.5 per cent must be explained by the first component.

There appears thus to be a large degree of heterogeneity in the population. Any linear construct of "multiple deprivation" using these variables would strictly involve adding together measures of *separate* conditions of need. It could hardly be said that they were estimating a series of underlying factors of deprivation.

From this evidence, although we would concede that the terms "disadvantage" and "deprivation" provide a convenient shorthand for the many different social situations that they are used to cover, it should be clear that the shorthand devices cannot replace more precise and if necessary more elaborate understandings of those situations.

SCHOOL CONTEXT AND FAMILY CIRCUMSTANCE

The first stage of our analysis was focused on the concept of child disadvantage, and was concerned to establish upper limits to what school- and area-based programmes can achieve as devices for rationing and allocating resources. But there is a second proposition implied by the policy of positive discrimination in favour of schools: that disadvantaged schools themselves somehow affect performance

TABLE 7.1

PRINCIPAL COMPONENTS ANALYSIS ON INDIVIDUAL AT-RISK ITEMS ON THE TOTAL POPULATION

Component		1	2	3	4	5	6	7	8
Component Variance		1.7044345	1.1416622	0.9910582	0.9593481	0.9159591	0.8226776	0.8126737	0.6521867
Percentage Added to Total Variance	%	21.31	14.27	12.38	12.00	11.45	10.28	10.16	8.15
Accumulated Value of Total Variance	%	21.31	35.58	47.96	59.96	71.41	81.69	91.85	100
Immigrants		0.324301	0.114425	0.597226	0.433012	0.039429	0.066769	0.564314	0.114427
High Number of Schools Attended		0.233239	−0.385418	0.408864	0.325134	0.664119	0.041089	−0.274751	0.077072
High Number of Different Teachers		0.013665	−0.580760	0.284987	0.215164	−0.612530	−0.028984	−0.372091	0.045182
High Absentee Rate		0.090471	−0.066531	−0.433303	−0.692644	0.067294	−0.062081	0.588555	0.043019
Large Family		0.474388	0.197956	0.024917	−0.431875	−0.256472	−0.025709	0.166910	−0.619840
Free Meals		0.526151	0.125984	−0.202766	−0.344021	−0.168198	−0.023548	−0.090910	0.073585
Low Social Class		0.425316	0.038550	−0.324700	0.240905	0.058862	0.762065	−0.142564	−0.222762
Low Verbal Reasoning Score		0.361657	0.043547	−0.301289	0.541104	0.274653	−0.584608	−0.254490	−0.421115

irrespective of the home circumstances of children. Certainly there was some evidence for this from the first stage of our analysis; the average reading performance of disadvantaged children in privileged schools was slightly higher than their performance in EPA Schools (See Table 6). In the text below we report our conclusions from an attempt to investigate this more directly. We first of all attempted to identify an effect of school context on reading performance, which was independent of the family circumstances of children; and we secondly converted our findings into statistics which establish upper limits to the effectiveness of discriminatory policies to overcome this effect.

Schools in the United States

The question of how far differences between different school situations have independent effects on the distribution of educational performance is a matter of debate in the United States. The main source of data for the debate is the 1965 "Survey of Equality of Educational Opportunity" conducted and initially analysed by Coleman and associates.[33] Many of the major findings of the initial Coleman Report have been confirmed by later reanalysis: the differences seem to have arisen over their interpretation and significance.[34] Our findings, although similar to those on the American school system, are different in a number of important respects. A brief outline of the main evidence on inequalities of conditions and performance in American elementary schools may be helpful, therefore, to set our results in context.

It seems clear that the 1965 Coleman Survey was conducted in order to document the fact that there were dramatic inequalities in school facilities in the United States, particularly for minority groups, and further, that these inequalities in resources were directly related to school performance. Analysis of the data revealed that there were inequalities in resources between regions and states; but that, within regions, school resources were more similar than had been supposed. Since those regions which had relatively poor resources tended to be those with higher concentrations of minority group children, there were overall differences between the volume of educational resources available to minority group and to white children. But the larger part of the difference was accounted for by a regional effect. In any case it was found that differences in traditional resource levels bore little or no relationship to differences in school performance levels.

The average school performance of minority group or poor children was found to be lower at every stage of schooling than that of the average white pupil. Family circumstances were found to have the strongest explanatory power over performance levels.[35] But the "human resources" available to schools were found to have a significant impact on levels of performance, even when the family characteristics of individual children and levels of expenditure had been controlled. Subsequent reanalysis of the data has found that family background factors are, if anything, more strongly related to achievement levels than Coleman and associates originally asserted.[36] But the reanalysis has not destroyed the main Coleman findings on the effect of schools: that it is the resources contributed to a school by the other people in it that most affect levels of performance. Further, the effect of schools on performance is strongest for those groups of children whose family circumstances are likely to be the most disadvantaged. Coleman has succinctly restated the case:

". . . the strongest inference that can be drawn from the results is that the resources most important for a child's achievement in school are the cognitive skills in his social environment in school, including his fellow students as well as his teachers, and that these effects are strongest for the children with least educational resources outside school . . . Other resources, on which school systems spend much money, appear unimportant; and lower class students do better in absolute terms rather than worse (as one might have predicted) in schools where their *relative* achievement is low due to the presence of higher-performing middle-class students."[37]

The major American findings of interest to us for this analysis, therefore, are above all that we should be moderate in our expectations of what schools can do to overcome adverse extra-school circumstances. Secondly, we should expect evidence that variation in the human resources available to schools, in particular in the mixture of pupils in the school, affect performance levels more than variations in more traditional expenditures or resources; and thirdly we should expect schools to have more effect on the performance of children from poor homes than they have on privileged children.

The Effect of Environmental Disadvantage

Our concern was to identify the effect of poor environmental conditions on the school performance of groups of children. We used three measures of school environment for this, the first two of which depicted characteristics of the pupils in each school (the proportion of immigrants and the proportion of unskilled and semi-skilled workers' children). The third was a composite measure of the relative circumstances of each school according to the logic of the original ILEA Schools' Index (see pages 47 and 48 and Table 2); we call this the measure of school context.

In order to avoid possible misunderstandings, it is important to be clear what our analysis cannot show about the behaviour of schools. We had no measure of the relative volume of resources going to different schools; and we can say nothing about an effect on the performance of children from variations in traditional school resources. In only one sense (namely teacher mobility)[38] did we have data on the characteristics of the teaching force; and we do not identify the characteristics or the behaviour of teachers as a separate variable. We had no data on the attitudes or affective behaviour of teachers, children or their parents; and we can say nothing about how these might mediate between family circumstance, reading performance and schools as we characterized them. We can say nothing from this analysis about intra school processes or the possible effect of different curricula or teaching methods.

We wished to find answers to five related but conceptually distinct questions: all of which can be answered at the macro-level and all of which relate to the justification for a priority area or schools strategy.

(1) Can an independent contextual effect (of relative institutional disadvantage) on reading performance be identified and its strength measured?

(2) If there is such a contextual effect, are different groups of children differently affected by it?

(3) Irrespective of any contextual effect across all schools, is there a significantly strong effect on the performance of groups of children in the most disadvantaged schools?

(4) In addition to any contextual effect which might be identified among groups of children in their second year in junior school, is there an effect on the changes in reading performance taking place between the beginning of the second and the end of the fourth year in junior school?[39]

(5) How strong is the independent effect of schools compared to the effects of various measured characteristics of the circumstances of families?

Children were included in the analysis to establish the school contextual effect only if four pieces of information were available on their family circumstance: the occupation of their father, whether they were children born in the United Kingdom or were immigrants from the West Indies, whether or not they came from large families and whether or not they received free school meals.[40]

The method of analysis used was to compute how far the measured variation in reading performance for groups of children could be "explained" by the measured characteristics of schools. We wished to avoid assuming that the effect of schools on different groups of children was the same or homogeneous. Indeed, given the American findings that schools have most effect on disadvantaged children and the argument of the Plowden Council that the effect of environmental disadvantage was most strongly felt by the most deprived children, this assumption was one we wanted to investigate. Therefore, the explained variation was computed separately for each group of children defined by social class, immigrant and family status, etc.[41] The regression coefficient given in the tables below is a line of best fit between the measured school characteristic and the reading score of each child, calculated separately within each group. In virtually all cases it has a negative value, indicating that as the school context becomes less advantaged so reading performance tends to deteriorate, even when various family characteristics have been controlled. The explained variance (the R^2 value) is a measure of the improvement that can be made in the prediction of a child's actual reading score by using the characteristic of the schools, rather than the average score of the group of children in that particular regression equation. It is therefore a measure of the strength of the independent effect of school context on the reading performance of children, when the various characteristics of family circumstance have been controlled for (see Note 41).

The proportion of the total variation in reading scores explained by any of the factors included in the analysis never reaches above 20 per cent and most of the time it is below 10 per cent. In other words we always fail to explain more than 80 per cent of the total variation in scores. We do not consider this to be surprising. The regression analyses were attempts to discover how far the derived, standardised distribution of scores was biased, or could be attributed to various family, or group, or institutional factors which educational policies might hope to affect. Included in the unexplained variances are errors in the measurement of reading scores, of child background characteristics and of school context. The unexplained variation would, in addition, be due to possibly random factors like the alertness and motivation of particular children on the day of the test, and also to variables which were not measured – the most significant of which would probably be the intelligence of individual and groups of children. More of the variation in reading performance could in principle be explained by the inclusion of more data in the analysis.[42] But to repeat, we were interested in that part of the variation which can be explained or controlled; and which therefore, if they are to increase equality of opportunity or of performance, educational policies must do something about.

A School Effect due to the Social Class and Immigrant Status Characteristics of a Child's Peers

We found no significant pattern of independent effects on variations in reading performance from the social or immigrant mix of pupils in the school.

A proportion of the overall variation in reading performance could be explained by the concentration of unskilled and semi-skilled workers' children in schools. But this was reduced to between 1 and 2 per cent when occupation of father had been controlled (see table 8). We doubt the educational significance of apparent effects of this size.

There was virtually no independent effect on overall variations in reading performance from the concentrations of immigrant children. This is hardly a surprising finding when most schools have very few immigrant children in them. Sixty-five per cent of the non-immigrant children in the analysis are in schools where less than 10 per cent of the children are immigrant; 44 per cent of them are in schools where less than 5 per cent of the children are immigrant; and only 3.4 per cent are in schools which contain more than 40 per cent immigrant children. (Appendix Table A 3).

Using the same body of data but a different method of analysis, Little and Mabey found that for children born in the United Kingdom . . . "there is a marked fall in attainment of children in schools with more than 60 per cent immigrants; (and) . . . there is very little difference . . . in the mean scores of children in schools between 10 and 50 per cent immigrant concentration." They also found that "immigrant children were only marginally affected by the immigrant concentration in the school."[43]

TABLE 8

READING SCORE AND SOCIAL AND IMMIGRANT MIX
REGRESSION SERIES

Reading score regressed against:
1. *Concentration of low social class children in the school.*
2. *Concentration of immigrant children in the school.*

For groups of children controlling:
  (a) *By Social Class (I and V only are displayed).*
  (b) *By West Indian Immigrant and groups born in the United Kingdom*
  (c) *By Family Size*
  (d) *By Receipt of Free School Meals*

		1. Class Concentration		2. Immigrant Concentration	
		Regression Coefficient	R^2	*Regression Coefficient*	R^2
Total		−.18	.0429	−.17	.0229
(a) Social Class					
	Social Class I	−.12	.0203	−.11	.0062
	Social Class V	−.10	.0133	−.15	.0227
(b) Non-Immigrant and West Indian Immigrant Groups					
Non-Immigrant	Social Class I	−.12	.0195	−.09	.0038
	Social Class V	−.10	.0134	−.11	.0085
West Indian Immigrant	Social Class I	−	−	−	−
	Social Class V	−.07	.0052	−.00	.0000
(c) Family Size Small Families					
Non-Immigrant	Social Class I	−.13	.0216	−.08	.0032
	Social Class V	−.11	.0150	−.09	.0057
West Indian Immigrant	Social Class I	−	−	−	−
	Social Class V	−.11	.0219	−.02	.0037
Large Families					
Non-Immigrant	Social Class I	−.09	.0104	−.18	.0117
	Social Class V	−.08	.0094	−.15	.0171
West Indian Immigrant	Social Class I	−	−	−	−
	Social Class V	−.04	.0017	+.01	.0002

TABLE 8 CONTINUED

		Regression Coefficient	R^2	Regression Coefficient	R^2
(d) Receipt of Free Meals					
No Free Meals Small Families					
Non-Immigrant	Social Class I	−.13	.0214	−.08	.0032
	Social Class V	−.11	.0150	−.09	.0054
West Indian	Social Class I	−	−.	−	−
Immigrant	Social Class V	−.14	.0226	−.07	.0071
No Free Meals Large Families					
Non-Immigrant	Social Class I	−.08	.0078	−.14	.0069
	Social Class V	−.08	.0082	−.14	.0133
West Indian	Social Class I	−	−	−	−
Immigrant	Social Class V	.00	.0000	−.02	.0005
Free Meals Small Families					
Non-Immigrant	Social Class I	−	−	−	−
	Social Class V	−.11	.0185	−.06	.0031
West Indian	Social Class I	−	−	−	−
Immigrant	Social Class V	−	−	−	−
Free Meals Large Families					
Non-Immigrant	Social Class I	−	−	−	−
	Social Class V	−.08	.0091	−.16	.0203
West Indian	Social Class I	−	−	−	−
Immigrant	Social Class V	−.08	.0089	+.04	.0030

Our analysis obscured identification of the presence of any such "tip-off" concentrations of immigrant children. We would point out, however, that the Little and Mabey method of comparing mean scores, without regard for variation of score around the mean, tends to dramatise the strength of relatively small differences. Further, even if the differences in score which they found are seen to be educationally significant, relatively small numbers of children are involved. For instance, 0.1 per cent of the non-immigrant population which remain in the cohort for our analysis are in schools with more than 60 per cent immigrant children — the point at which a strong deterioration in the reading score of non-immigrant children was found; and two out of three non-immigrant children are in schools

with less than 10 per cent immigrant children — the point at which
some deterioration in the attainment of non-immigrant children
began. With the overall net size of the cohort of children falling at
the rate of 2 per cent per annum, class sizes will tend to become
smaller as the cohort becomes older. In this situation, relatively small
movements of children could obviate any possible impact of
certainly the heaviest concentrations of immigrant children on the
reading performance of non-immigrant children.

A School Effect due to the Environmental Context

We found that there was an effect on reading performance from
the total school context. Reading performance was significantly
lower the more disadvantaged the school — at least for groups of
children from the United Kingdom.

It makes a difference to the reading performance of groups of
non-immigrant children whether they go to schools which are
privileged or disadvantaged on the measure we used. The differences
exist irrespective of the family circumstances of the children. They
tend to become unstable when groups are homogeneous with respect
to the four characteristics of family circumstance, but the overall
pattern remains and the instability leads to high as well as to low
proportions of explained variation. This independent contextual
effect is slightly stronger for United Kingdom children from
non-manual workers' homes than for children from manual workers'
homes: respectively 6 per cent and 4 per cent of the variation in
reading performance is explained by it (see table 9).

There is no significant school contextual effect on the variation in
reading scores for groups of West Indian Immigrant children. We had
found that the average reading performance of West Indian Immigrant
children in this cohort was low irrespective of the occupation of their
father (see table 5). From this subsequent finding we must say,
further, that whether they are in privileged or disadvantaged schools
makes far less difference to the reading performance of West Indian
Immigrant children than it does to non-immigrant children.

With this evidence we can answer the first two of our questions
concerning the justification for programmes to combat the effect of
relatively disadvantaged school environments. There *is* an effect of
relative institutional deprivation on the school performance of
children. It *does* affect different groups of children in different ways:

TABLE 9

READING SCORE AND SCHOOL PRIVILEGE REGRESSION SERIES

Reading score regressed against relative privilege
score of school for groups of children controlling:

(a)   by Social Class
(b)   by West Indian Immigrant and groups born in the United Kingdom
(c)   by Family Size
(d)   by Receipt of Free School Meals

		Regression Coefficient	R^2
Total		−.34	.0674
(a) Social Class			
	Social Class I	−.26	.0378
	Social Class II	−.29	.0485
	Social Class III	−.26	.0418
	Social Class IV	−.18	.0218
	Social Class V	−.27	.0478
(b) Non-Immigrant and West Indian Immigrant Groups			
All Non-Immigrant Children		−.31	.0579
Non-Immigrant	Social Class I	−.26	.0367
	Social Class II	−.26	.0408
	Social Class III	−.24	.0352
	Social Class IV	−.16	.0163
	Social Class V	−.25	.0409
All West Indian Immigrant Children		−.16	.0140
West Indian Immigrant	Social Class I	—	—
	Social Class II	−.02	.0009
	Social Class III	−.19	.0194
	Social Class IV	−.14	.0118
	Social Class V	−.16	.0148
Non-Immigrant	Non Manual	−.30	.0581
	Manual	−.24	.0366
West Indian Immigrant	Non Manual	−.14	.0098
	Manual	−.15	.0135

TABLE 9 CONTINUED

		Regression Coefficient	R^2
(c) Family Size			
Small Families			
Non-Immigrant	Social Class I	−.24	.0333
	Social Class II	−.24	.0368
	Social Class III	−.23	.0324
	Social Class IV	−.15	.0143
	Social Class V	−.24	.0378
West Indian Immigrant	Social Class I	−	−
	Social Class II	−	−
	Social Class III	−.15	.0129
	Social Class IV	−.10	.0053
	Social Class V	−.23	.0271
Large Families			
Non-Immigrant	Social Class I	−.31	.0556
	Social Class II	−.29	.0550
	Social Class III	−.25	.0396
	Social Class IV	−.16	.0189
	Social Class V	−.24	.0456
West Indian Immigrant	Social Class I	−	−
	Social Class II	−	−
	Social Class III	−.24	.0308
	Social Class IV	.08	.0037
	Social Class V	−.12	.0096
(d) Receipt of Free Meals			
No Free Meals Small Families			
Non-Immigrant	Social Class I	−.24	.0326
	Social Class II	−.24	.0351
	Social Class III	−.22	.0302
	Social Class IV	−.15	.0141
	Social Class V	−.24	.0359
West Indian Immigrant	Social Class I	−	−
	Social Class II	−	−
	Social Class III	−.15	.0129
	Social Class IV	−.12	.0075
	Social Class V	−.27	.0365

TABLE 9 CONTINUED

		Regression Coefficient	R^2
(d) Receipt of Free Meals cont.			
No Free Meals Large Families			
Non-Immigrant	Social Class I	−.31	.0533
	Social Class II	−.25	.0418
	Social Class III	−.23	.0308
	Social Class IV	−.12	.0104
	Social Class V	−.25	.0475
West Indian Immigrant	Social Class I	—	—
	Social Class II	—	—
	Social Class III	−.37	.0626
	Social Class IV	−.06	.0020
	Social Class V	−.05	.0018
Free Meals Small Families			
Non-Immigrant	Social Class I	—	—
	Social Class II	−.11	.0085
	Social Class III	−.28	.0514
	Social Class IV	−.08	.0035
	Social Class V	−.21	.0292
West Indian Immigrant	Social Class I	—	—
	Social Class II	—	—
	Social Class III	—	—
	Social Class IV	—	—
	Social Class V	—	—
Free Meals Large Families			
Non-Immigrant	Social Class I	—	—
	Social Class II	−.37	.0893
	Social Class III	−.28	.0563
	Social Class IV	−.19	.0288
	Social Class V	−.21	.0346
West Indian Immigrant	Social Class I	—	—
	Social Class II	—	—
	Social Class III	—	—
	Social Class IV	−.08	.0057
	Social Class V	−.20	.0280

NOTE: See Table 5 for mean scores for these groups of children.

but in ways contrary to the forecast of the Plowden Council and expectations from the American data analysis. Across the whole population, the more privileged the home circumstances of groups of children, the more their performance is depressed by the apparent effect; and the less advantaged their home circumstances, the less children are affected by school context.

We can illustrate these points by establishing what, in principle, would be the upper limits to the impact of a programme of positive discrimination through schools. We can ask, first of all, what would be the impact on the distribution of individual scores of a policy which overcame the effects of the school context. Clearly the distribution of scores would be reduced by the amount now attributable to it.[44] But the effect, in this case, would be to reduce the spread of individual scores in the population by a maximum of only 3.4 per cent. And so we must say that policies of positive discrimination which successfully overcame the total effect of school context would do little to reduce the spread of performance among individual children.

But the target for the Plowden Council's programme of positive discrimination was to be more specific than this. The programme was to bring help to the most disadvantaged 10 per cent of the population, initially raising them to the national average and subsequently improving their position even more (see page 45. We might ask therefore, what would be the effect of a policy which did this for groups of children in the bottom 10 per cent of schools, bearing in mind that the measured effect of school context is different for different groups of children.[45]

We are speculating here about a possible future situation from evidence on the present; we do not identify what could be done to bring about that situation. We are providing theoretical upper limits to the impact of discriminatory policies and not positive forecasts or practical recommendations. To do even this we must assume that any transformation in scores brought about by a successful policy would be linear: that to make the most disadvantaged group of schools as good as the average would, in principle, be to make their effects on reading performance the same as those currently produced by the average schools. The validity of the assumption may be questioned; but it is necessary to ask what would be the consequences of not accepting it. All that could be said, if it were unacceptable, would be that improving schools will cause them to have as yet unknown effects on the performance of the children in them. Clearly in all policy there is an element of what we hope will happen in addition to what might reasonably be predicted. These transformations establish the reasonable predictions from evidence on schools as they operate at present; the creation of new futures is beyond their scope.

If, therefore, we say that the purpose of a programme of positive discrimination through schools is to overcome the disadvantages they currently impose on the children in them, then we can assess the maximum reduction in the spread of scores that would result from a successful policy. In this case we would need to say that the differences in score between groups of children in the most disadvantaged 10 per cent of schools and groups, with the same home situation, but in the average school would be reduced by:

$$(z) \times (r) \times (s)$$

where z is equal to the number of standard deviations between the overall group mean and the mean of the bottom 10 per cent of children in that group (1.9): r^2 is equal to the amount that the total variation in scores would be reduced if the effect now attributable to school context for the group of children in question were removed: and s is equal to the standard deviation of scores for the group in question (See Note 45).

Thus, policies of discrimination which overcame the effect of school context in the most disadvantaged 10 per cent of schools would narrow the gap in performance between groups of children in those schools, and similarly defined groups in the average school, by the following amounts:

For the children of Non-Immigrant Non-Manual Workers:	by 6.90 points of score or months of reading age.
For the children of Non-Immigrant Manual Workers:	by 5.28 points.
For children of West Indian Immigrant Non-Manual Workers:	by 2.70 points.
For the children of West Indian Immigrant Manual Workers:	by 2.93 points.

The effect of such policies, far from tempering differences between groups which resulted from factors outside the school situation, would be to reinforce them. Positive discrimination which made the most disadvantaged schools as good as the average schools would increase the differences in performance between groups of children defined in terms of their family circumstances.

A School Effect due to
Different Magnitudes of Contextual Disadvantage

We investigated whether the most disadvantaged schools had effects on the performance of groups of children in them which were different to the effects of the least disadvantaged schools: whether there were different apparent contextual effects at different concentrations of institutional disadvantage.

For this analysis schools were grouped into thirds acccording to their score on the eight variable school index, and the variations in reading performance for the groups of children were regressed against variations in school contextual score for the three groups of schools.

The small numbers of West Indian Immigrant children in each regression equation makes confident interpretation of the results for these groups impossible, and we focused on the pattern of results for children born in the United Kingdom grouped by the occupation of their father. From Table 10 it can be seen that the variations within the three groups of schools are dramatically smaller than for the total population of schools. Further, the variations remain roughly similar for heavily disadvantaged and for privileged schools. In other words, there are no significant differences between the effects from the most disadvantaged and the least disadvantaged group of schools on the reading performance of the children in them.

In one sense this is not a surprising result. For this analysis the groups of schools were in each case relatively homogeneous with respect to variations in measured levels of contextual disadvantage; and so their independent effects became correspondingly smaller. But it could have been otherwise. The logic of the Plowden principle of "cumulative disadvantage" means that as schools become more disadvantaged so the consequences for children attending them become progressively more detrimental. To repeat: we did not find this. There is an effect of school context operating across the whole population of schools in this analysis; but it is not confined to, and it is not especially powerful in, a particular group of heavily disadvantaged schools.

Although for this piece of analysis the explained variances were in every case below 2 per cent and were below 1 per cent for most cases, there is the semblance of a pattern to the situations where the variance is between 1 and 2 per cent. Children born in the United Kingdom, whose fathers are semi-skilled and unskilled workers and

TABLE 10

READING SCORE AND SCHOOL PRIVILEGE
GROUP REGRESSION SERIES

Reading score is regressed against relative privilege score of school with schools grouped into the most, *mid- and least privileged third of scores* for groups of children controlling:

(a)   By Social Class
(b)   By West Indian Immigrant and groups born in the United Kingdom

Most Privileged Third of Scores— The Lowest Scores for Disadvantage on the Schools Index		*N*	*Mean*	*Regression Coefficient*	R^2
Total		3,452	102.4	−.44	.0144
(a) Social Class					
	Social Class I	664	110.3	−.35	.0103
	Social Class II	797	104.9	−.45	.0194
	Social Class III	1,096	100.6	−.36	.0106
	Social Class IV	519	97.0	−.10	.0010
	Social Class V	376	95.4	−.16	.0014
(b) Non-Immigrant and West Indian Immigrant Groups					
Non Immigrant	Social Class I	663	110.3	−.34	.0101
	Social Class II	790	105.0	−.45	.0192
	Social Class III	1,077	100.8	−.32	.0086
	Social Class IV	498	97.1	−.12	.0013
	Social Class V	362	95.6	−.16	.0014
West Indian	Social Class I	—	—	—	—
Immigrant	Social Class II	—	—	—	—
	Social Class III	—	—	—	—
	Social Class IV	—	—	—	—
	Social Class V	—	—	—	—
Mid-Privileged Third of Scores					
Total		16,084	95.2	−.30	.0180
(a) Social Class					
	Social Class I	1,105	106.2	−.27	.0130
	Social Class II	2,449	99.7	−.20	.0085
	Social Class III	5,592	96.0	−.21	.0100
	Social Class IV	3,738	92.6	−.12	.0033
	Social Class V	3,200	89.7	−.32	.0227

TABLE 10 CONTINUED

Mid-Privileged Third of Scores cont.

		N	*Mean*	*Regression Coefficient*	*R²*
(b) Non-Immigrant and West Indian Immigrant Groups					
Non-Immigrant	Social Class I	1,083	106.4	−.26	.0115
	Social Class II	2,377	100.0	−.19	.0075
	Social Class III	5,214	96.5	−.17	.0068
	Social Class IV	3,296	93.3	−.10	.0025
	Social Class V	2,733	90.7	−.26	.0148
West Indian	Social Class I	—	—	—	—
Immigrant	Social Class II	72	92.1	—	—
	Social Class III	378	89.5	−.30	.0195
	Social Class IV	442	87.5	+.11	.0030
	Social Class V	467	83.6	−.24	.0119

Least Privileged Third of Scores —
the highest scores for disadvantage on the Schools Index.

		N	*Mean*	*Regression Coefficient*	*R²*
Total		3,208	89.3	−.24	.0059
(a) Social Class					
	Social Class I	113	101.8	−.16	.0016
	Social Class II	312	94.3	−.08	.0006
	Social Class III	1,006	90.6	−.02	.0000
	Social Class IV	840	89.3	−.16	.0028
	Social Class V	937	84.9	−.24	.0080
(b) Non-Immigrant and West Indian Immigrant Groups					
Non-Immigrant	Social Class I	109	101.6	−.12	.0010
	Social Class II	277	94.8	−.07	.0004
	Social Class III	847	91.3	−.03	.0001
	Social Class IV	661	90.4	−.24	.0062
	Social Class V	736	85.8	−.22	.0071
West Indian	Social Class I	—	—	—	—
Immigrant	Social Class II	35	90.4	—	—
	Social Class III	159	86.9	+.01	.0011
	Social Class IV	179	85.3	+.06	.0004
	Social Class V	201	81.7	−.35	.0162

who are in the most disadvantaged schools, and United Kingdom children whose fathers are non-manual and skilled manual workers but who are not in the most disadvantaged schools, are the groups for whom the proportions of explained variation in reading score are largest. This by itself proves nothing; but it opens up an interesting speculation. For instance, we might say that although privileged groups of children are affected by their school context in most schools, they are not further affected by the most disadvantaged schools: in other words, once privileged children are in heavily disadvantaged schools it does not matter how much more disadvantaged the schools become. Similarly we could speculate that, although disadvantaged non-immigrant children appear to be affected by the degree of institutional disadvantage in the most disadvantaged schools, it matters less to them once they are in relatively more privileged schools.

Effects of Family Circumstance

In order to provide a further framework within which the relative size of the overall independent school effects might be seen, we calculated the variation in reading performance which could be attributed to the measured characteristics of home circumstances. Table 11 presents our findings.[46]

TABLE 11

VARIATIONS IN READING SCORES INDEPENDENTLY EXPLAINED
BY HOME BACKGROUND CHARACTERISTICS OF GROUPS OF CHILDREN

	Explained variation %
Occupation of Father	9.35
Whether the child was of United Kingdom or West Indian Immigrant origin	3.01
Contribution of all four family background characteristics: Father's occupation, immigrant status, size of family, receipt of free school meals.	14.30
Cumulative child at risk index	19.06

With school effects explaining between 4 and 6 per cent of the variations in reading score for groups of United Kingdom children and 1 per cent for West Indian Immigrants, it is clear from Table 11 that the circumstances of families explains more of the variation in reading performance than do the circumstances of schools.

These again are perhaps not surprising findings but their implications for educational policy remain highly significant. To begin with, the measure of the socio-economic status of the children's father dominates the other measures — both of school context and of other family characteristics. Secondly there is an effect of the immigrant status of groups of children which is independent of social class. The distinction in this cohort between West Indian Immigrants and children born in the United Kingdom explains a 3 per cent variation in reading performance which cannot be attributed to the father's occupation. Thirdly, once these two factors, social class and immigrant status, are taken into account, the remaining variance explained by the characteristics of home circumstances, family size and free school meals, appears far less important.

Making the same assumptions as were made over the calculation of the maximum impact of discriminatory policies operating against the apparent effect of schools on groups of children, we used the variances explained by family circumstance to estimate upper limits to the impact of policies on these effects. Thus in principle, the impact of policies which removed the effect of socio-economic status on the reading performance of groups of children would narrow the gap in performance between children in the bottom 10 per cent on that dimension of inequality and the average child in the population by *8.7 points* of reading score: an amount equivalent to the same number of months of reading age. Similarly, the removal of differences attributable to a distinction between West Indian Immigrant children and children born in the United Kingdom would mean that differences in reading performance between the bottom 10 per cent of children and the average child on that dimension would become smaller by *4.9 points*. Policies operating against the effects of all four family circumstance characteristics could have an effect of *10.8 points* on the gap between the bottom 10 per cent and the average child; and the upper limit to a totally effective policy against cumulative disadvantage (as measured on the at-risk index) would narrow the gap in performance between the most disadvantaged 10 per cent of children and the average child by *12.5 points* of score, or over a year of reading age.

Changes in Score

We attempted, lastly, to examine the changes in score taking place in the cohort over time, and to relate these to measured characteristics of family circumstance and school context.

Analysis of the "Equality of Opportunity" cross-sectional data in the United States had shown that the differences between the average verbal ability levels of groups was greater in the higher than in the lower school grades.[47] Cohort studies in this country had similarly shown that both vocabulary and reading performance of groups of low working class children deteriorated with reference to national norms between the ages of eight and eleven.[48] These findings were highly significant for us because they implied that schools provide divergent experiences for children and that, in consequence, the longer children attend school the more the average performances of privileged and underprivileged groups are likely to differ.

Comparison of the average scores of the total age groups in ILEA schools at the time of the first and second reading surveys showed them to be remarkably similar.[49] We isolated the children who were present at both test times and on whom there was adequate family circumstance data, and calculated individual change scores over the period.[50]

Our first finding was that average change scores are very small no matter how we define each group of children. The children of United Kingdom professional and managerial workers improved by an average of one and a half standard points; and the children of West Indian Immigrant unskilled workers, who came from large families and received free school meals, lost ground by an average of one and a quarter standard points over the period (see Table 12). The second finding makes it necessary to be extremely circumspect about conclusions to be drawn from even these small changes in score. The variations about the average scores are considerable for each group and they nullify any straight comparison of average scores.

It is necessary to be clear what kind of results an analysis of the kind we performed could, in principle, give. We examined differences between two standardized scores.[51] Essentially, therefore, consideration could only be given to those changes which would

TABLE 12

CHANGES IN READING SCORE AND SCHOOL PRIVILEGE

Changes in reading score were regressed against relative privilege score of original school for groups of children controlling:

- *(a)*   *by Social Class*
- *(b)*   *by West Indian Immigrant and groups born in the United Kingdom*
- *(c)*   *by Family Size*
- *(d)*   *by Receipt of Free School Meals*

		N	Mean	S.D.	Regression Coefficient	R^2
Total		18,596	+0.25	10.6	−.01	.00
(a) *Social Class*						
	Social Class I	1,438	+1.48	10.8	+.01	.00
	Social Class II	2,853	+0.54	10.3	.00	.00
	Social Class III	6,354	+0.10	10.6	−.02	.00
	Social Class IV	4,224	+0.14	10.6	+.01	.00
	Social Class V	3,727	−0.07	10.9	+.01	.00
(b) *Non-Immigrant and West Indian Immigrant Groups*						
All Non-Immigrant Children		16,907	+0.28	10.6	−.01	.00
Non-Immigrant	Social Class I	1,421	+1.48	10.9	+.01	.00
	Social Class II	2,757	+0.55	10.3	−.01	.00
	Social Class III	5,871	+0.13	10.6	−.02	.00
	Social Class IV	3,686	+0.18	10.6	−.01	.00
	Social Class V	3,172	−0.08	10.9	.00	.00
All West Indian Immigrant Children		1,689	−0.09	10.7	+.07	.00
West Indian	Social Class I	–	–	–	–	–
Immigrant	Social Class II	96	+0.08	11.4	–	–
	Social Class III	483	−0.27	10.5	+.04	.00
	Social Class IV	538	−0.12	10.4	+.12	.02
	Social Class V	555	−0.01	11.0	+.04	.00
(c) *Family Size*						
Small Families						
Non-Immigrant	Social Class I	1,154	+1.65	11.1	+.02	.00
	Social Class II	2,222	+0.57	12.1	−.01	.00
	Social Class III	3,948	+0.32	11.2	+.13	.00
	Social Class IV	2,582	+0.39	10.7	.00	.00
	Social Class V	2,042	+0.21	10.9	+.01	.00

TABLE 12 CONTINUED

		N	Mean	S.D.	Regression Coefficient	R^2
(c) Family Size cont.						
West Indian	Social Class I	—	—	—	—	—
Immigrant	Social Class II	59	−0.98	10.7	—	—
	Social Class III	248	−0.59	10.4	−.06	.00
	Social Class IV	233	+0.60	9.4	−.03	.00
	Social Class V	232	+0.85	10.5	+.02	.00
Large Families						
Non-Immigrant	Social Class I	267	+0.73	10.0	−.01	.00
	Social Class II	535	+0.49	10.4	.00	.00
	Social Class III	1,428	−0.35	10.7	−.02	.00
	Social Class IV	1,104	−0.31	10.4	−.01	.00
	Social Class V	1,130	−0.59	10.8	−.01	.00
West Indian	Social Class I	—	—	—	—	—
Immigrant	Social Class II	34	+1.78	12.5	—	—
	Social Class III	235	+0.07	10.7	+.11	.03
	Social Class IV	305	−0.06	11.1	+.04	.00
	Social Class V	323	−0.62	11.3	+.05	.00
(d) Receipt of Free Meals						
No Free Meals Small Families						
Non-Immigrant	Social Class I	1,120	+1.66	11.03	+.02	.00
	Social Class II	2,130	+0.68	10.22	.00	.00
	Social Class III	4,269	+0.29	10.59	−.02	.00
	Social Class IV	2,416	+0.38	10.74	.00	.00
	Social Class V	1,769	+0.28	10.89	.00	.00
West Indian	Social Class I	—	—	—	—	—
Immigrant	Social Class II	48	+0.27	10.59	—	—
	Social Class III	212	−0.73	10.36	−.07	.01
	Social Class IV	197	+0.80	9.48	−.03	.00
	Social Class V	168	+0.60	10.66	+.02	.00
No Free Meals Large Families						
Non-Immigrant	Social Class I	226	+0.98	10.14	−.04	.00
	Social Class II	409	−0.61	10.58	−.01	.00
	Social Class III	1,021	−0.18	10.76	−.02	.00
	Social Class IV	699	−0.25	10.56	.00	.00
	Social Class V	583	−0.27	10.87	−.02	.00

TABLE 12 CONTINUED

		N	Mean	S.D.	Regression Coefficient	R^2
(d) Receipt of Free Meals cont.						
No Free Meals Large Families cont.						
West Indian	Social Class I	—	—	—	—	—
Immigrant	Social Class II	—	—	—	—	—
	Social Class III	145	−0.74	10.49	+.20	.07
	Social Class IV	180	+0.31	12.14	+.04	.00
	Social Class V	171	−0.06	12.08	+.06	.01
Free Meals Small Families						
Non-Immigrant	Social Class I	34	+1.26	11.83	—	—
	Social Class II	92	−1.19	10.03	—	—
	Social Class III	174	+0.10	10.22	+.05	.00
	Social Class IV	166	+0.58	10.52	−.01	.00
	Social Class V	273	−0.28	10.67	+.06	.01
West Indian	Social Class I	—	—	—	—	—
Immigrant	Social Class II	—	—	—	—	—
	Social Class III	36	+0.25	10.46	—	—
	Social Class IV	36	−0.47	8.41	—	—
	Social Class V	64	+1.52	9.93	—	—
Free Meals Large Families						
Non-Immigrant	Social Class I	41	−0.66	8.93	—	—
	Social Class II	126	+0.07	9.95	+.04	.00
	Social Class III	407	−0.75	10.53	−.03	.00
	Social Class IV	405	−0.41	10.25	−.04	.00
	Social Class V	547	−0.93	10.78	.00	.00
West Indian	Social Class I	—	—	—	—	—
Immigrant	Social Class II	—	—	—	—	—
	Social Class III	90	+1.39	10.83	—	—
	Social Class IV	125	−2.06	9.31	+.07	.00
	Social Class V	152	−1.25	10.39	+.05	.00

result in a reordering of the children's relative performance between the two test times. A change in rank position relative to peers could be estimated; absolute changes in reading performance had already been accommodated by the standardization process.

On this basis we were able to find no contributions of importance from either school context or family circumstance to changes in hildren's relative positions over time (school contextual contribution xplained none of the variance whatsoever and the home background ariables explained 0.5 per cent of the variation). Thus we must onclude that, while on average the more privileged groups appear to mprove their position and the less privileged groups appear to lose round, any pattern is swamped by random variations which are ssociated with neither school context nor family circumstance.

CONCLUSIONS

In this paper we have reported our attempts to analyze data on ne cohort of junior school children in inner London in order to say ome thing more about educational disadvantage and about policies f positive discrimination through schools in order to meet it. In articular we have tried to establish upper limits to those policies oth in terms of their potential coverage and their possible effects. rom the data available to us we have come to fourteen specific najor conclusions:

1. Using single item indicators: between one in four and one in six of the children in need are in the EPA Schools.
2. Using an indicator of cumulative disadvantage: for everv two disadvantaged children who are in EPA Schools, five are outside then.. And in the EPA Schools themselves, disadvantaged children are outnumbered by children who are not disadvantaged.
3. Irrespective of the schools they attend, there is about two years difference in the average reading age of disadvantaged and non-disadvantaged children when those children are between eight and nine years old.
4. The average reading performance of disadvantaged children in the EPA Schools is approximately three months behind that of disadvantaged children in the most privileged schools. The two groups are respectively nineteen months and sixteen months behind a national norm, and eight months and sixteen months behind the average for their group of schools.
5. We could find no evidence of a substantive content to a condition which people call disadvantage. It seems to refer to many different situations of need.
6. Once the occupation of father has been controlled, there is no effect on variation in reading performance of either the low social class composition or the concentration of immigrant children in a school.
7. There is a pattern of independent effects on variations in reading performance from the overall context of a school. This pattern holds up even when groups of children are homogeneous with respect to the occupation of their father, their immigrant status, the size of their family and whether or not they receive free school meals.

8. This is not a school contextual effect which is concentrated in a particular group of EPA Schools. It operates across the whole population.

9. Policies of discrimination which overcame this effect would do little to equalize performance between *individual* children.

10. Policies which overcame it would substantially reduce the gap in performance between identically defined groups of children in different sorts of school. The strongest impact of such a policy would be felt by the children of professional and managerial workers who were born in the United Kingdom. For that group, the gap between their performance in the most disadvantaged 10 per cent of schools and in the average school would be closed by 7 points of score or months of reading age.

11. The group of children least affected by discriminatory policies which overcame the effects of school context would be West Indian Immigrants. This group is significantly less affected by its school context than are non-immigrant children.

12. The effect of school context on variations in reading performance is considerably less than the effect of characteristics of family circumstance.

13. In addition to having average reading performances which were below their non-immigrant contemporaries when they were aged between eight and nine, in addition to being less affected by school context than their contemporaries at that stage, the average change in score of the West Indian Immigrant group remained virtually constant between the two test times, while the score of the non-immigrant group improved slightly.

14. There were no changes in the relative ordering of reading scores taking place in the cohort between the second year and the last year in the junior school which could be attributed to the effect of school context or to family circumstance.

The validity and general applicability of these findings can be criticized in a series of ways and it is instructive to list some of the main ones here. The data were for only one age-group of children from inner London, mainly for one point of time, five years ago. The information is in some senses faulty. It is also inadequate (See notes 13 and 18). In particular we must be careful about what can be inferred from measured performance in one reading test. There is no information on intra school processes, or on teacher skills, or on schools which have effects on their children which are quite different from the measured dominant pattern. Quite possibly policies which improved schools would change their impact on the performance of the children. For determined critics the list can go on. We think that these points should be considered carefully and we have tried to qualify our findings in the text without littering it with apologies.

At the same time two issues seem to us of overriding importance. The first comes from the logic of the data rather than from its precise quantification. Educational disadvantage is a very heterogeneous concept. School and area policies to tackle it set for themselves limits which prevent complete coverage. In order to bring discriminatory help to disadvantaged or needy children such policies will need to become substantially more complex, accommodating both intra school and area processes and other dimensions of the phenomenon. If school and area policies are to retain their original simplicity, they must be complemented with other, perhaps new and different policies which help the disadvantaged children who will inevitably be left out.

The other issue does rely on accurate measurement and correct analysis. But we think here that the questions we raise should be taken seriously even by those who may wish to question our findings. Consider the conclusions we derive from the analysis. Policies which successfully overcame the effect of school context and improved the performance of schools, would equalize performance between schools. But they would do little to equalize performances between individuals — perhaps nobody would expect them to. But also, equalizing the performance of schools could do little to equalize opportunities between individuals. In addition, because the effect of school context is stronger for privileged groups than for less privileged ones, equalizing the performance of schools would increase inequalities in performance between groups.

At the very least this raises questions about what it is appropriate and realistic to expect from schools. If what is desired is to maximize the opportunities available to all children irrespective of which school they go to, then, on this evidence, inequalities in performance between groups will increase. If what is desired is to reduce inequalities in performance between all children, then, again on this evidence, more powerful policies than school reform will be needed. If what is desired is to reduce inequalities in performance between groups, then, on this evidence, reforms will be needed which transform the relationships between schools and their social context. Further, a community of interest could not be assumed between all the families whose children attend the most disadvantaged schools; whether the policy is to improve or to transform those schools, again on this evidence, different groups will have different amounts to gain (and to lose) by it. It seems reasonable to ask the question both of schools as they operate now and of a policy of positive discrimination to change them. Who is expected to benefit?

APPENDIX

Distribution of United Kingdom and West Indian Immigrant Children by Social Class in Schools:

- — by low social class concentration in the school
- — by immigrant concentration in the school
- — by relative privilege score of the school
- — by schools grouped into thirds on their relative privilege scores.

APPENDIX 1

PUPILS IN SCHOOLS WITH VARYING PERCENTAGES OF LOW SOCIAL CLASS CHILDREN

United Kingdom children　　(a) by school by social class,　　(b) by social class by school.

(a) By School

	Percentage of low social class children in the school										
	0-10 %	10-20 %	20-30 %	30-40 %	40-50 %	50-60 %	60-70 %	70-80 %	80-90 %	90-100 %	Total %
Social Class											
1	49.4	25.4	16.3	10.7	6.6	5.4	3.2	1.9	1.6	—	8.5
2	30.0	29.8	23.4	17.1	16.3	14.4	13.3	9.9	8.1	4.1	16.5
3	16.5	31.7	39.1	44.2	40.6	34.0	28.0	21.7	11.9	2.0	34.7
4	3.4	7.8	13.6	16.2	20.6	26.0	28.1	31.7	35.0	32.7	21.7
5	0.8	5.3	7.7	11.9	15.9	20.2	27.4	34.7	43.3	61.2	18.7
Base (=100%)	237	1,126	2,464	2,852	5,367	3,912	2,776	1,780	621	98	21,233

(b) By Social Class

	0-10 %	10-20 %	20-30 %	30-40 %	40-50 %	50-60 %	60-70 %	70-80 %	80-90 %	90-100 %	Base (=100%)
% 1	6.5	15.8	22.2	16.8	19.5	12.0	4.9	1.8	0.6		1,805
% 2	2.0	9.6	16.4	13.9	25.0	16.0	10.5	5.0	1.4		3,509
% 3	0.5	4.8	13.1	17.1	29.6	18.0	10.5	5.3	1.0		7,370
% 4	0.2	1.9	7.3	10.0	24.0	22.1	16.9	12.3	4.7	0.7	4,607
% 5	0.1	1.5	4.8	8.6	21.6	20.0	19.3	15.7	6.8	1.5	3,942
Total	1.1	5.3	11.6	13.4	25.3	18.4	13.1	8.4	2.9	0.5	21,233

[93]

APPENDIX 2

PUPILS IN SCHOOLS WITH VARYING PERCENTAGES OF LOW SOCIAL CLASS CHILDREN

West Indian Immigrant children   (a) by school by social class,   (b) by social class by school

(a) By School

| | Percentage of low social class children in the school | | | | | | | | | | |
	0-10 %	10-20 %	20-30 %	30-40 %	40-50 %	50-60 %	60-70 %	70-80 %	80-90 %	90-100 %	Total %
Social Class											
1			3.2	2.4	1.9	1.2	0.5	—			1.4
2			8.1	9.7	4.0	4.7	7.9	3.6			5.7
3			41.9	39.4	34.5	26.9	19.3	19.1			27.5
4			30.6	23.0	32.8	31.5	34.8	29.4			31.8
5			16.1	25.5	26.7	35.7	37.6	47.9			33.6
Base (=100%)	1	10	124	165	475	591	420	194	73	17	2,070

(b) By Social Class

	0-10 %	10-20 %	20-30 %	30-40 %	40-50 %	50-60 %	60-70 %	70-80 %	80-90 %	90-100 %	Base (=100%)
% 1		3.6	14.3	14.3	32.1	25.0	7.1	—	3.6		28
% 2		0.9	8.5	13.6	16.1	23.7	28.0	5.9	2.5	0.9	118
% 3		1.1	9.1	11.4	28.8	27.9	14.2	6.5	0.7	0.4	570
% 4	0.2	0.3	5.7	5.8	23.7	28.1	22.2	8.7	4.3	1.1	659
% 5			2.9	6.1	18.3	30.4	22.7	13.4	5.3	1.0	695
Total	0.1	0.5	6.0	8.0	23.0	28.6	20.3	9.4	3.5	0.8	2,070

APPENDIX 3

PUPILS IN SCHOOLS WITH VARYING PERCENTAGES OF IMMIGRANT CHILDREN

(a) by school by social class,   (b) by social class by school

Percentages of Immigrant Children in the school

(a) By School

Social Class	0-10 % United Kingdom children	10-20 %	20-30 %	30-40 %	40-50 %	50-60 %	60-70 %	70-80 %	80-90 %	90-100 %	Total %
1	10.5	6.9	6.2	4.0	6.2	3.6	—	—			8.5
2	16.7	15.7	14.5	18.8	19.6	16.9	—	—			16.5
3	33.7	36.2	36.0	36.3	37.1	35.6	—	—			34.7
4	21.0	21.9	24.0	23.3	19.8	28.4	—	—			21.7
5	18.1	19.3	19.3	17.5	17.3	15.6	—	—			18.7
Base (=100%)	14,019	3,887	1,789	1,003	469	225	28	4			21,424

(b) By Social Class

	0-10 %	10-20 %	20-30 %	30-40 %	40-50 %	50-60 %	60-70 %	70-80 %	80-90 %	90-100 %	Base (=100%)
% 1	76.2	14.0	5.8	2.1	1.5	0.4	—	—			1,924
% 2	66.3	17.2	7.3	5.3	2.6	1.1	0.1	—			3,534
% 3	63.8	19.0	8.7	4.9	2.4	1.1	0.1	—			7,402
% 4	63.6	18.5	9.3	5.1	2.0	1.4	0.2				4,623
% 5	64.6	19.0	8.8	4.5	2.1	0.9	0.2				3,941
Total	65.4	18.1	8.4	4.7	2.2	1.1	0.1	—			21,424

APPENDIX 4

PUPILS IN SCHOOLS WITH VARYING PERCENTAGES OF IMMIGRANT CHILDREN

West Indian Immigrant children   (a) by school by social class,   (b) by social class by school

Percentage of Immigrant Children in the school

	0-10 %	10-20 %	20-30 %	30-40 %	40-50 %	50-60 %	60-70 %	70-80 %	80-90 %	90-100 %	Total %
(a) By school											
Social Class											
1	1.3	1.6	1.2	1.1	1.6	1.6	—	—			1.4
2	6.6	5.8	6.2	7.9	4.5	6.9	—	—			5.7
3	23.8	30.6	25.5	23.4	28.9	30.9	—	—			27.5
4	34.4	31.1	32.1	31.3	31.8	32.4	—	—			31.8
5	33.9	30.8	35.0	36.4	32.2	28.2	—	—			33.6
Base (=100%)	227	428	420	368	374	188	51	24			2,080
(b) By Social Class											*Base (=100%)*
% 1	—	—	—	—	—	—	—				28
% 2	11.7	19.5	20.3	22.7	13.3	10.2	2.3				128
% 3	9.5	23.0	18.8	15.1	18.9	10.2	2.8	1.8			570
% 4	11.8	20.2	20.5	17.5	18.1	9.3	1.2	1.5			659
% 5	11.1	19.0	21.2	19.3	17.8	7.6	3.5	0.6			695
Total	10.9	20.6	20.2	17.7	18.0	9.0	2.5	1.2			2,080

PUPILS IN SCHOOLS WITH VARYING SCORES ON THE RELATIVE PRIVILEGE: UNDER PRIVILEGE SCALE.

United Kingdom children   (a) by school by social class,   (b) by social class by school.

(a) By School

Social Class	Privileged %	%	%	%	%	%	%	%	%	%	%	%	%	Under privileged %	Total %
1	18.1	18.3	24.3	17.5	11.4	9.4	5.8	5.0	3.0	4.9	4.4	2.2	2.1	—	9.0
2	26.7	31.6	22.2	21.2	18.6	14.9	17.5	14.6	13.7	11.9	9.4	9.2	9.9	—	16.6
3	37.1	29.8	29.1	33.4	34.3	36.6	36.3	35.4	34.2	34.3	35.9	21.5	21.8	—	34.4
4	15.5	14.1	15.2	14.6	19.2	20.5	22.6	24.5	28.4	25.4	25.7	24.5	22.5	—	21.5
5	2.6	6.2	9.2	13.3	16.5	18.6	17.8	20.4	20.8	23.5	24.6	42.6	43.7	—	18.5
Base (=100%)	116	531	950	1,793	3,509	2,982	3,293	3,271	1,648	1,210	855	404	142	19	20,723

(b) By Social Class

	Privileged %	%	%	%	%	%	%	%	%	%	%	%	%	Under privileged %	Base (=100%)
% 1	1.1	5.2	12.5	16.9	21.5	15.1	10.2	8.9	2.6	3.2	2.0	0.5	0.2	0.2	1,855
% 2	0.9	4.9	6.1	11.0	19.0	12.9	16.7	13.9	6.5	4.2	2.3	1.1	0.4	0.1	3,444
% 3	0.6	2.2	3.9	8.4	16.9	15.3	16.8	16.2	7.9	5.8	4.3	1.2	0.4	0.1	7,138
% 4	0.4	1.7	3.2	5.9	15.1	13.7	16.7	18.0	10.5	6.9	4.9	2.2	0.7	0.1	4,455
% 5	0.1	0.9	2.3	6.2	15.1	14.5	15.3	17.4	9.0	7.4	5.5	4.5	1.6	0.2	3,831
Total	0.6	2.6	4.6	8.7	16.9	14.4	15.9	15.8	8.0	5.8	4.1	2.0	0.7	0.1	20,723

APPENDIX 6

PUPILS IN SCHOOLS WITH VARYING SCORES ON THE RELATIVE PRIVILEGE: UNDERPRIVILEGE SCALE

West Indian immigrant children   (a) by school by social class,   (b) by social class by school

(a) By school

Social Class	Privileged %	%	%	%	Under privileged %	%	%	%	%	%	%	%	%	%	Total %
1	—	—	—	—	3.6	3.8	1.9	1.4	—	0.7	1.1	—	—	—	1.3
2	—	—	—	—	4.3	6.2	3.8	6.1	5.3	6.9	5.7	4.8	—	—	5.5
3	—	—	—	—	30.2	28.5	29.3	24.4	27.7	27.5	32.2	21.9	—	—	27.6
4	—	—	—	—	37.4	28.5	30.3	30.5	34.4	35.5	30.5	15.2	—	—	31.8
5	—	—	—	—	24.5	33.1	34.7	37.6	32.5	29.3	30.5	58.1	—	—	33.8
Base (=100%)	—	4	15	40	139	130	314	423	375	276	174	105	25	—	2,020

(b) By Social Class

	Privileged %	%	%	%	Under privileged %	%	%	%	%	%	%	%	%	%	Base (=100%)
% 1	—	—	—	—	—	—	—	—	—	—	—	—	—	—	27
% 2	—	—	0.9	2.7	5.4	7.2	10.8	23.4	18.0	17.1	9.0	4.5	0.9	—	111
% 3	—	—	0.5	2.5	7.5	6.6	16.5	18.5	18.7	13.6	10.1	4.1	0.9	—	557
% 4	—	0.4	1.1	1.9	8.1	5.8	14.8	20.1	20.1	15.2	8.2	2.5	2.0	—	643
% 5	—	0.3	0.6	1.5	5.0	6.3	16.0	23.3	17.9	11.9	7.8	8.9	0.9	—	682
Total	—	0.2	0.7	2.0	6.9	6.4	15.5	20.9	18.6	13.7	8.6	5.2	1.2	—	2,020

APPENDIX 7

PUPILS IN SCHOOLS GROUPED INTO THE MOST PRIVILEGED AND LEAST PRIVILEGED THIRDS OF SCORE

	United Kingdom children — (a) by school group by social class; (b) by social class by school group				West Indian Immigrant children — (a) by school group by social class; (b) by social class by school group			
	Most Privileged %		Least Privileged %	Total %	Most Privileged %		Least Privileged %	Total %
(a) By School Group								
Social Class 1	19.6		4.1	9.0	–	1.6	0.7	1.3
2	23.3		10.5	16.6	–	5.2	6.0	5.5
3	31.7		32.2	34.2	–	27.3	27.6	27.6
4	14.7		25.1	21.5	–	32.0	31.0	31.8
5	10.7		28.0	18.5	–	33.8	34.7	33.8
Base (=100%)	3,390	14,703	2,630	20,723	59	1,381	580	2,020
(b) By Social Class				Base (=100%)				Base (=100%)
% 1	35.7	58.4	5.9	1,855	–	–	–	27
% 2	22.9	69.0	8.0	3,444	3.6	64.9	31.5	111
% 3	15.1	73.0	11.9	7,138	3.4	67.9	28.7	557
% 4	11.2	74.0	14.8	4,455	3.3	68.7	28.0	643
% 5	9.4	71.3	19.2	3,831	2.1	68.5	29.5	682
Total	16.4	71.0	12.7	20,723	2.9	68.4	28.7	2,020

NOTES

* This work was begun when both of its authors were members of the Research and Statistics Group of the ILEA and was continued and completed by them after they had left. The paper represents the view of its authors and not those of the ILEA.

1. Those institutions which appear to have strong redistributive functions are those which are privileged in terms of selective restrictions on access to them. For instance, the *Robbins Committee* on higher education in Great Britain found that once they were in higher education, working class children did at least as well as those from middle class homes — whether this was measured in terms of the type of degree achieved or in terms of wastage rates. On the other hand, there were large variations in rates of access to higher education: 41 per cent of children from non-manual families who were born in 1940-1941 and had measured IQs of 130+ entered full-time higher education, whereas 30 per cent of such children from manual workers' families did so. Seventeen per cent of non-manual workers' children with IQs below 114 went into full-time higher education, whereas 6 per cent of manual workers' children with similar measured intelligence did so. *Westergaard and Little's* (1964) collation of data on class differences in access to education showed the grammar schools effectively to be selecting for access to higher education: "one in four (of the cohort they studied) was at a secondary grammar school at 13; one in ten was still at school at 17; while one in twenty-five went on to university. . . . At 11-13 a professional or managerial family's child had nine times as high a chance of entering a grammar school or independent school as an unskilled worker's child. Some years later, at 17, he had nearly thirty times as high a chance as the others of still being at school . . . One in every four of the non-manual, middle class children who entered a grammar school type course at 11+ eventually went to a university; but only one in fifteen to one in twenty of the grammar school entrants from unskilled working class homes did so."

2. See Passow (1971) and Smith and Little (1971) for surveys of the United States programmes. See Halsey (1972) for an account of the educational priority area programmes in British primary schools, and Benn and Simon (1972) and Rubinstein and Simon (1973) for accounts of the reform of British secondary education.

3. See Evetts (1970) for a discussion of the development of the concept of equality of opportunity in Britain. See Coleman (1969) for an analysis leading to advocacy of equality of performance between groups. See Jencks (1972) for a conceptual and empirical analysis of the opportunities for equality between individuals. Halsey (1972) advocates a further development of the concept. He sees the need for diversity of educational contents between schools and areas. Education should, he argues, be one of the means which would enable local communities to transform their own local situation. This further development assumes an actual or potential community of interest in particular schools and areas; we comment in the conclusions to this paper on how far our analysis would lend support to such an assumption.

4. See *Plowden* (1967), Chapter 5, passim.

5. The terms of reference of the *Plowden Council* were "to consider primary education in all its aspects, and the transition to secondary education." Although this reference was enormously wide, in a strictly formal sense the Council was not allowed to investigate all aspects of child socialisation and child poverty. Its recommendations for positive discrimination through the agency of schools should perhaps be seen in this light.

6. *Plowden* (1967). paragraph 131.

7. The research commissioned by the Council found that a relatively small amount of the variation in children's education performance could be attributed to "the state of the school" (a variable composed largely of the characteristics of the teachers in the school). The regression analysis of this material found respectively 28%, 20% and 17% of the between school variance explained by "Parental Attitudes," "Home Circumstances" and "School Variables." See Plowden (1967), Volume II, Appendix 4, Table 3. In other chapters in the Report, the Council stressed the importance of parental attitudes to children's performance at school. Yet only one of the thirteen specific and precise recommendations for an educational priority area policy is related to parental attitudes; at least nine of them, on the other hand, are recommendations for extra resources to be channelled to schools in priority areas.

8. The objective critera were:
(a) Occupation
(b) Size of Families
(c) Supplements in Cash or Kind from the State
(d) Overcrowding and Sharing of Houses
(e) Poor Attendance and Truancy
(f) Proportions of Retarded, Disturbed or Handicapped Pupils
(g) Incomplete Families
(h) Child unable to speak English
Plowden (1967), Paragraph 153.

9. Ibid. Paragraph 151.

10. Ibid. Paragraph 169.

11. Ibid. Paragraph 171.

12. Ibid. Paragraph 174.

13. Undoubtedly the main problem of using the ILEA Literacy Survey as a research source was the understandable reliance on uncorroborated teacher information and opinion. One difficulty was the probable lack of uniformity between teachers and schools in their interpretation of the questions. This, we suggest, arose not only for questions involving child relationships at school and the degree of home stimulation (only a tiny proportion of immigrant homes were though to be "stimulating"), but also for supposedly factual items such as country of origin and parental occupation (the proportion of semi-skilled manual occupations in many schools was so low as to give rise to the speculation that some teachers misplaced this category). Secondly, it was precisely those groups in which we were most interested, those with high at-risk scores, for which information was often not available (for West Indian Immigrant children there was no information on the guardian's occupation in some 20 per cent of cases). See Goodacre (1969). for a discussion of teacher perceptions of the home background of the children they teach.

Secondly, the data were inadequate for our purposes. For instance, it would have been most interesting to have had some measure of the children's IQ's. However, the only available measure – the child's rank position on a verbal reasoning test – although designed to measure something akin to IQ was also, in part, a measure of child vocabulary. We could see no way of using this variable without considerably confusing any interpretation of our analysis. Further, the measure was not taken directly from an individual's test performance. Tests administered to all children were marked anonymously; schools were subsequently told the number of children which they could place in particular categories and individual children were then assigned a rank score for purposes of secondary school selection. The "goodness of fit" between a child's actual performance on the initial test and subsequent assignment to a rank position was not known. Lastly the data were available for children two and a half years after the initial reading test. We used this information for the at-risk index, but excluded it from the regression analysis (See below notes 18, 21, 26 and 27).

14. A full account of the construction of the index of schools is given by Little and Mabey in Shonfield and Shaw (1973).

15. Of the 10 variables in the ILEA Index, four were area based and collected from Census material (unskilled employed males, overcrowding of houses, housing stress and family size). The remaining six (proportion of immigrants, incidence of receipt of free school meals, high pupil absenteeism, high teacher mobility, high pupil turnover, low verbal reasoning scores) were all school based. A notional catchment area of the schools was calculated, for county schools, as an area within one quarter of a mile radius from the school. When the Index was constructed the density of population in inner London was 40.6 people per acre. Broadly then, the population in the notional catchment area of a London primary school at the time was slightly more than 5,000 people.

16. This test, and its parallel version, was constructed for use in the National Foundation for Educational Research's study of streaming in primary schools. See Barker Lunn (1970). The Sentence Reading Test A is standardized on a national sample of English children to have a mean of 100, a standard deviation of 15, a range from 70 to 140 points and a standard error of measurement of approximately 3.5 points.

17. It has not proved possible to print the questionnaire. Copies may be obtained from the authors at the Centre for Studies in Social Policy, London.

18. The overall response rate was very high, but the amount of missing data caused serious problems (See note 13). We needed to adopt different methods to deal with this at different stages of the analysis. For the regression analysis, we only dealt with cases on which there were complete data (see note 27). For the calculation of the at-risk scores, we counted a case with unknown data on a specific item as at-risk (see note 21). This caused problems when we wished to calculate the reading performance of at-risk groups, particularly with regard to the verbal reasoning scores. Not only were these indirect measures, but a substantial proportion of the children who were present in ILEA schools in 1968 (when the initial reading performance was measured) had left by 1971 (when the verbal reasoning rank assignments were allocated (see Table 3)). We therefore

discounted children whose verbal reasoning position was unknown for the calculation of mean reading scores (Table 6).
reasoning position was unknown for the calculation of mean reading scores (Table 6).

19. There was an additional problem: the SRA reading test was standardized by NFER on a sample from the whole of England. When used for the ILEA children it was found that many more of them than expected scored the minimum possible standardized score of 70. To have included these children, and used the 70 score for them, would have considerably biased the mean score for disadvantaged groups as these had a high proportion of 70 scorers. To have eliminated such children from the analysis would have had a similar effect. Our resolution to this problem was as follows:

i. We assumed that scores between 71 and 139 (the true range of the SRA test) were from a truncated normal distribution.

ii. We estimated the mean of this normal distribution using the scores between 71 and 139.

iii. We used this to estimate a mean score for children scoring below 71.

iv. The children scoring 70 were included in the analysis but were given the mean score derived in (iii).

20. We are grateful to Keith Hope at Nuffield College, Oxford, whose comments on an earlier draft of this section of the paper helped us clear our ideas on the general form of this fallacy. See Keith Hope (1969). For an extended discussion of the analysis of ecological data see Dogan and Rokkan (1969).

21. The table below shows how the child index was created. The source of the measures was in every case but one the data collected in the Literacy Survey. The verbal reasoning scores were added to the children's file at the time of their assessment for transfer to secondary school, two and a half years after the first stage of the survey (see Notes 13 and 18). Data not known were taken as at-risk.

Criteria	*Child counted as at-risk if:*
1. Occupation of Father:	Father was a semi-skilled or unskilled manual worker, he was unemployed or his occupation was not known.
2. Family Size:	By adding together the number of parents and the number of siblings of school age and living at home, the family was six or more.
3. Cash Supplements to the Family: Receipt of Free School Meals:	The child received free school meals.
4. Handicapped Pupils: Low Verbal Reasoning:	Child was in group 6 or 7 on the secondary school transfer profile (the lowest scoring 25 per cent). Children whose profile score was not known were included in the analysis presented in Tables 3 and 4 and 4.1 but excluded for Table 6 (See note 18).

Criteria	*Child counted as at-risk if:*
5. Immigrant Pupils:	The stated country of origin was other than the United Kingdom or the Republic of Ireland.
6. Teacher Turnover:	He had been taught by more than one class teacher over the previous year.
7. Pupil Turnover:	He had attended more than two schools to date.
8. Poor Attendance:	Child was absent for more than one third of possible occasions.
CUMULATIVE INDEX OF RISK	Items on which a child was found to be "at-risk" were summed together. The higher the score achieved, the greater the chance of being disadvantaged.

22. Teachers in this group of schools all received extra increments to their salary as part of the national piogramme of positive discrimination which followed the publication of the *Plowden Report*. See Chapter 3 of Halsey (1972) for an account of the sequel to the publication of the Report. Schools receiving the salary allowances were seen to have been "nationally recognized as EPA." In addition, the ILEA allowed these schools the maximum of extra resources available in its own attempts to help EPA Schools.

23. The Tables in the Appendix provide further data on the distribution of children. They show the numbers and proportions of English and West Indian Immigrant children (by social class) in schools characterized by the proportion of immigrant and of unskilled and semi-skilled workers' children in them.

24. We considered the possibility of constructing an index of "socialization" based on questions concerning the teacher's perceptions of a child's attitudes and relationships at school. For the reasons outlined in 13 above we abandoned this idea. We considered that any answers to such questions were probably too closely related to reading performance to be useful in forming an independent criterion measure.

25. See the forthcoming Schools Council Study, *Aims of Primary Education*.

26. Children whose verbal reasoning rank position was unknown were dropped for this analysis. (See Note 18).

27. Children were only included in the calculation of these mean scores — as for the regression analysis presented in Tables 8 to 12 — if all four items of family characteristic were known: the occupational group of their family, their immigrant status, the family size and receipt of free school meals. The West Indian Immigrant group was isolated because it was the only sufficient large, relatively homogeneous immigrant group; all other immigrant children were dropped from this analysis.

28. Throughout the analysis we assume that the scores for any group are normally distributed. Given this assumption, it is simple to calculate what percentage of children in a group fall below any given score. See Blalock (1972).

29. The Plowden Council considered recommending that measures of parental attitudes be used in addition to their "objective criteria". They rejected this on the grounds of difficulty and unreliability. It should be noted that the

heterogeneity of disadvantaged circumstances we have identified is not revealed by adding more variables into the analysis, although clearly this is possible in principle.

30. If we have two measurements Xi and Yi for each of n individuals we may define a linear correlation between the two sets of measurements

$$r_{xy} = \frac{\Sigma(X_i - \overline{X})(Y_i - \overline{Y})}{(\text{Standard Deviation X})(\text{Standard Deviation Y})}$$

which varies between +1 and −1 and has the following properties

   i. If X is large when Y is large and vice versa rxy will be close to +1.

  ii. If X is small when Y is large and vice versa rxy will be close to −1.

 iii. If X and Y vary independently of each other rxy will be close to zero.

(See Blalock (1972)).

The question arises, how are we to interpret a correlation which is close neither to zero nor ±1? Unfortunately this is largely a matter of personal decision based on experience. Certainly there is no reason to say, for example, that a correlation of 0.5 indicates a relationship which is twice as strong as that indicated by a correlation of 0.25.

31. But the verbal reasoning was dropped for the reasons outlined above (See notes 13 and 18).

32. Whenever we have a battery of measurements on a group of subjects it is natural to attempt to construct a simplified model, in which variation among the subjects over the battery variables can reasonably be explained by their position on one or two, preferably independent, underlying "dimensions": in the present case dimensions of deprivation. A Principal Components Analysis (see for example Hope (1969)) seeks systematically to construct such dimensions in order of their explanatory importance, that is, the percentage of the original variation which can be attributed to each, by considering linear combinations of the original battery variables.

33. See Coleman et al (1966).

34. See Mosteller and Moynihan (1973).

35. See Coleman et al (1966), Chapter 3 passim. Two types of argument are presented to support this. The first shows that there are differences between black and white groups on entry into school, which persist over time spent in school. The second results from estimates of various school and family input factors derived from individual student-level correlation and regression analysis.

36. See Marshall Smith in Mosteller and Moynihan (1973) for an extended critique of the findings in Chapter 3 of the Coleman Report.

37. See Coleman (1970).

38. Teacher mobility was one of the variables used in the index to identify the ILEA's disadvantaged Schools. See Little and Mabey in Shonfield and Shaw (1973).

39. In effect, between the time of the first (SRA) and second (SRB) test times.

40. See note 27. Only cell sizes greater than 100 were said to be reliable.

41. For the purposes of regression analysis we assume a simple linear relationship between one variable (the reading ability of a child) and another (the deprivation score of his school) that is:

Y (child score) = a + b x X (school deprivation score)

where a and b are two constants, which we select such that the equation is a "best fit" to the data: that is, it explains as much as possible of the total variation in scores. From this equation we can see that a change of 1 unit in X produces a change of b units in Y. Similarly if X varies by 1 standard deviation, Y varies by:

b x (standard deviation of X).

From correlation and regression theory it is easy to show that

b x (standard deviation of X) = r_{xy} x (standard deviation of Y)

and it is this quantity which we use in our subsequent calculations.

42. See Jencks (1972) for analysis which includes a far greater range of data on American schools and children than were available to us. It should be remembered that Jencks is concerned with the individual as his prime unit of analysis. We illustrate our findings in terms of their consequences for schools, groups and for individuals.

43. See Little and Mabey in Donnison and Eversley (1973).

44. In order to estimate the maximum school effect on variations in reading score among individuals we established the maximum reduction in standard deviation that could be brought about by equalizing the school effect. Thus

Standard Deviation	$(\sqrt{1 - R^2_{xy}})$ x	(Standard Deviation)
(after adjusting		(before adjusting for
for the school effect)		the school effect)

where R_{xy} is the correlation between school disadvantage score and child reading score.

45. In order to estimate the maximum school effect on the mean score for groups we considered the outcome of decreasing the school disadvantage score from its average value in the most disadvantaged 10 per cent of schools to its value in the average school. Suppose this involves a change of N standard deviations in school disadvantage score, that is, of X (see note 41), then for the change in group average reading score (Y) we have:

Change in Y = N x b_{yx} x Standard Deviation of X for the group.
where b_{yx} is the regression coefficient of Y on X.
or
Change in Y = N x r_{xy} x Standard Deviation of Y for the group.

46. Although there are considerable difficulties in using regression techniques with classification level variables, we considered it very important to have comparable measures using the family background variables. We therefore produced estimates of R^2_{xy}, the proportion of variance in reading score explained by these variables, and used these in the same way that we used the R_{xy} between school disadvantage score and reading score.

47. See Coleman et al. (1966).

48. See Douglas et al. (1968).

49. See ILEA (1972).

50. We took all children who had reading scores on both the 1968 and the 1971 test and calculated the change in score for each child. Unfortunately we were unable to say whether children had changed schools within the ILEA over this period.

51. Unfortunately the 1968 reading test had been standardized by the teachers before the results were returned to the ILEA. Although raw scores were available for the 1971 survey, this meant we could not standardize scores for those children who were in both surveys.

REFERENCES

BENN, C. and SIMON, B. (1972) *Half Way There: A Report on the British Comprehensive School Reform*, Second edition. Harmondsworth: Penguin Education.

BLALOCK, H.M. (1972) *Social Statistics*, Second edition. New York: McGraw Hill.

COLEMAN, J.S. *et al.* (1966). *Equality of Educational Opportunity*. Washington, DC: U.S. Government Printing Office.

COLEMAN, J.S. *et al.* (1969). *Equal Educational Opportunity.* (an expansion of the Winter 1968 Special Issue of Harvard Educational Review). Cambridge Mass: Harvard University Press.

COLEMAN, J.S. (1970). "Reply to Cain and Watts", *American Sociological Review*, vol. 35, no.2, pp. 242-252.

DOGAN, M. and ROKKAN, S. (1969). *Quantitative Ecological Analysis in the Social Sciences.* Cambridge, Mass.: MIT Press.

DONNISON, D. and EVERSLEY, D. (eds.) (1973). *London: Urban Patterns, Problems and Policies.* London: Heinemann.

DOUGLAS, J.W.B. *et al.* (1968). *All Our Future: A Longitudinal Study of Secondary Education*. London: Peter Davies.

EVETTS, J. (1970). "Equality of Education Opportunity: The Recent History of a Concept". *British Journal of Sociology*, vol. 21, pp.425-430.

GOODACRE, E.J. (1969). *Teachers and Their Pupils' Home Backgrounds: An Investigation into Teachers' Attitudes and Expectations in Relation to Their Estimates and Records of Pupils' Abilities, Attributes and Attainment.* Slough: National Foundation for Educational Research in England and Wales.

HALSEY, A.H. (1972). *Educational Priority: Vol. 1, EPA Problems and Policies.* London: HMSO.

HOPE, K. (1969). *Methods of Multivariate Analysis.* London: University of London Press.

HOPE, K. (1972). "Social Research, the Fifth Estate". Unpublished lecture given to the Sociology Section of the British Association meeting at Leicester.

Inner London Education Authority. (1972). *Literacy Survey, 1971 Follow-up: Preliminary Report.* Report to the Education Committee, ILEA 203, December 1972.

JENCKS, Christopher *et al.* (1972). *Inequality: A Reassessment of the Effect of Family and Schooling in America.* New York: Basic Books.

LUNN, J. Barker. (1970). *Streaming in the Primary School: A Longitudinal Study of Children in Streamed and Non-streamed Junior Schools.* Slough: National Foundation for Educational Research in England and Wales.

MOSTELLER, F. and MOYNIHAN, D.P. (eds.). (1972). *On Equality of Educational Opportunity.* Papers deriving from the Harvard University Faculty Seminar on the Coleman Report. New York: Random House.

PASSOW, A.H. (1971). *Urban Education in the 1970s: Reflections and A Look Ahead.* New York: Teachers College Press.

PLOWDEN, Lady (Chairman). (1967). *Children and Their Primary Schools.* A Report of the Central Advisory Council for Education (England). London: HMSO.

ROBBINS, Lord (Chairman). (1963). *Report of the Committee on Higher Education.* London: HMSO. (Cmnd 2154).

RUBINSTEIN, David and SIMON, B. (1973). *The Evolution of the Comprehensive School, 1926-1972.* London: Routledge and Kegan Paul.

Schools Council. *Aims of Primary Education.* Forthcoming.

SHONFIELD, A. and SHAW, S. (eds.) (1973). *Social Indicators and Social Policy.* London: Heinemann Educational Books.

SMITH, George and LITTLE, A.N. (1971). *Strategies for Compensation: A Review of Educational Projects for the Disadvantaged in the United States.* Paris: OECD.

WESTERGAARD, J. and LITTLE, A.N. (1964). "The Trend of Class Differentials in Educational Opportunity in England and Wales." *British Journal of Sociology,* Vol. 15, No.4, pp. 301-316.

Chapter 4

THE ATTITUDES TO WORK, EXPECTATIONS AND SOCIAL PERSPECTIVES OF SHIPBUILDING APPRENTICES

Richard Brown

THEORETICAL ORIENTATION

This chapter is concerned with the relationship between men's immediate social context and their perceptions of society and their own place in it. The basic assumption is that social consciousness reflects primary social experiences, rather than position in a socio-economic (or any other sort of) category; that there is a relationship between men's expectations and social perspectives and their location in the various milieux in which they live.

There is a considerable body of work related to this general theme. In studies of class and of conceptions of the class structure, in particular, a number of writers have suggested that subjective perceptions of class, or more general "images of society", are to be explained in similar terms. One of the most influential of these studies is Lockwood's account of the "Sources of Variation in Working Class Images of Society" which draws on a large number of research reports to construct three ideal types of manual worker. (Lockwood 1966). The basic assumption of this paper, and its opening sentence, is that "for the most part men visualise the class structure of their society from the vantage point of their own milieux, and their perceptions of the larger society will vary according to their experiences of social inequality in the smaller societies in which they live out their daily lives." A considerable body of recent research has been devoted to the examination, more or less directly, of Lockwood's argument and of the utility of his "types"; for the most part, even if Lockwood's discussion is criticized, these investigators have continued to assume that there is a relationship between milieux and social consciousness (see Bulmer 1972).

A rather different but related body of work has been concerned with the sources of men's expectations of and orientations to, in particular, the world of work. The most notable example of this is the investigation of the affluent manual worker by Goldthorpe and his colleagues, in which a crucial part of the argument is the assertion that "the values and motivations that lead workers to the view of work they have adopted must be traced back,so far as this is possible, to typical life situations and experiences" (Goldthorpe *et al.* 1968: p.185). A good deal of recent research has investigated "orientations to work" among other groups of employees and the approach outlined by Goldthorpe and colleagues has been criticized in a number of important respects (see Brown 1973). Of particular relevance to this paper is the criticism that "orientations to work" are typically much more strongly influenced by the experience of work than is allowed for in the case of the "affluent workers". As in the case of studies of social imagery, however, the critics for the most part also accept the basic assumption that orientations and expectations are to be explained in terms of men's social experience whether it be in the family, in the community and/or at work.

The research to be described focused on a particular problem within this general area of interest., It was concerned with two cohorts of shipbuilding apprentices who were studied over a period of two and a half years as part of a more general research project on shipbuilding workers. As we shall see this situation had both advantages and disadvantages so far as the general problem area is concerned. It provided an opportunity, however, to try to discover how far the orientations to work and the general social perspectives of the apprentices were affected by the experience of work and of being trained for their eventual roles as adult shipbuilding craftsmen. In general terms the assumptions underlying the research were that the apprentices' attitudes, expectations and "world views" would change over the training period, particularly insofar as this training involved contact with adult shipbuilding workers in the context of normal shipyard work; that these changes would tend to be towards a situation where apprentices shared the same attitudes and social perspectives as adult shipbuilding workers; and that differences among the apprentices would be related to differences in their immediate social experience. The data available are insufficient to explore these assumptions completely satisfactorily, but the analysis will be directed towards this end.

BACKGROUND OF THE ORIGINAL SURVEY

The Shipbuilding Research Project

Between 1967 and 1970 the author was engaged with three colleagues in a relatively intensive study of and in a Tyneside shipyard.[1] The investigation, supported by the SSRC, was entitled "The Orientations to Work and Industrial Behaviour of Shipbuilding Workers on Tyneside" and was designed to achieve two main objectives: to provide a sociological description of this particular occupational category for comparison with other occupations (miners, lorry drivers, fishermen, etc.) who have been similarly studied; and to assess the importance, in explaining attitudes and behaviour, on the one hand of the technology of the industry (shipbuilding can be described as a "craft" industry) and on the other of the orientations to work of the workers (who were supposedly "traditional proletarians").

The main project involved extended periods of observation in the yard, and interviews with managers, foremen, shop stewards and a sample of workers. In terms of the interest in "orientations to work", however, it was important also to investigate those currently entering the industry, and the main channel for skilled workers (who comprise two thirds or more of shipbuilding's manual labour force) is via apprenticeship. The discussion of orientations to work by Goldthorpe and his colleagues had stressed that they should be seen as "an important independent variable relative to the in-plant situation" (1968: p.183); shared definitions of the situation were seen as resulting from a process of self-selection in the context of near full employment, so that workers sought out jobs which, so far as possible, met their expectations. An alternative explanation would be that orientations to work and shared definitions of the situation resulted from socialization within the work context, which would mean that the technology and other aspects of the in-plant situation might well be of much greater importance than Goldthorpe and his colleagues appeared to allow.

Thus we were concerned with trying to establish the attitudes, priorities, expectations and social perspectives of school leavers recruited to shipbuilding as apprentices; with trying to assess what changes took place over the period of apprenticeship; and with comparing the attitudes etc. of apprentices with those of adult shipbuilding workers, especially those who were the next older generation. Did the apprentices' background in and knowledge of the shipbuilding "communities" from which they mostly came mean that they entered the industry already sharing the expectations and attitudes of adult shipbuilding workers?[2] Did the experience of working in the industry lead to significant changes in attitudes and social perspectives away from those derived from the more "middle class" world of the school? These questions were of importance in the context of the main study, and are of relevance to the general problem area already described. The data collected to attempt to answer them, however, can be analyzed in more detail so as to consider differences and relationships within the cohorts as well as changes over time.

Apprenticeship

Craftsmen have dominated the labour force in shipbuilding since the earliest days of the modern shipbuilding industry in the second half of the nineteenth century. In a period when in many industries production work was increasingly carried out by relatively unskilled workers, and craftsmen were reduced to a maintenance role, if they remained at all, the Trade Unions of skilled shipbuilding workers have been able to preserve the main production tasks for their members. They have done this in the context of a massive overall decline in employment in the industry in the post-1945 period, and of very high rates of unemployment for much of the period between the wars. This has been possible partly because of the absence of technical changes in the industry comparable to the introduction of mass production and assembly line working; and partly perhaps because it served the employers' purposes to have a skilled labour force available, so that despite the costs of some loss of control over the labour market and of demarcation disputes they lacked the incentive to challenge it. For whatever reasons, however, the union controls over recruitment have meant that with few exceptions (men who gained a skilled worker's card by some other means) all skilled shipbuilding workers have served their time as apprentices, though not necessarily in the shipbuilding industry. All except four of the 208 skilled shipbuilding workers we interviewed had completed an apprenticeship, and four-fifths had done so in shipbuilding or the related industries of ship-repair and marine engineering.

In the past serving one's time as an apprentice meant learning the skills of one's trade by working alongside other craftsmen, and perhaps in some cases continuing formal education on craft courses at nightschool or by means of day release. More recently some employers, including the firm we were concerned with, introduced more highly organized training schemes, including off-the-job training in a Training School or centre. With the passing of the Industrial Training Act and the establishment of the Shipbuilding Industry Training Board in 1964, such more highly formalized and supervized schemes of training became essential if firms were to receive grants.

In the case we studied apprentices for all trades (except painters) spent their first year in training off the job in the firm's training centre; after a short induction course the first three months of this period were spent on common basic training, gaining knowledge of and an insight into the work of all trades as well as receiving theoretical and practical instruction in ship construction more generally; the remaining nine months were devoted to training for the specific trade or group of trades in which the apprentice was to specialize (or was going to be allowed to, as the apprentice's own preferences were not always granted). Training consisted of classroom instruction and, for the major part of the time, practical work in workshops, together with day release to attend a local Technical College. Some production work might be done in the workshops under supervision, but only a very limited amount of time was spent in the yard on visits of observation, to see a launch, and so on.

In their second year the great majority of apprentices spent their time working in the yard on production work, though this work was planned to provide a variety of experience and the apprentices' progress was supervised by members of the training staff. A few apprentices remained in the centre for some or all of their second year, but in all cases the remaining three years of apprenticeship were spent in the yard on production work. Indeed as apprentices became older and more knowledgeable they could be found on occasions working independently or in the company of other apprentices rather than adult craftsmen.

The Training Centre was deliberately not called a training school so as to emphasize the change from school to the world of work. However, it seems likely that, because of the nature of the activities there, including classroom instruction and the teacher-pupil type relationship between instructors and apprentices, a school-like ethos continued to some extent. Indeed the author's colleague, who sat in on part of one induction programme, commented, "in the initial part of the course the point was made several times to the boys that they were not now at school. At the same time, the first morning of the course seemed to be devoted in large part to 'dos and don'ts' on safety, punctuality, manners, etc. Sanctions were also mentioned several times; that is, expulsion from the school." Increasingly, of course, they would be likely to become aware of and familiar with the situation in the shipyard itself, which they entered fully in the second year of their training.

THE EMPIRICAL STUDY

We began our apprentice study in the summer of 1967. At that time one cohort of apprentices, who had entered the industry in 1966 were just about to leave the Training Centre, and a cohort of new entrants just about to enter it. These two groups, or sub-samples of them, provided the material on which this chapter is based.

Members of each of the two former groups of apprentices (the 1966 entrants and the 1967 entrants) were questioned on three occasions: in the summer of 1967, in the summer of 1968, and in the early spring of 1970. Whilst the apprentices were in the centre it was possible to obtain completed questionnaires from almost the whole population, though there were some non-respondents on every occasion due to absence and wastage. When the boys left the centre, however, they went to work in any one of a number of shipyards on Tyneside and we were only able to follow up those who went to the yard in which the centre itself was situated. This meant that the numbers completing questionnaires in the second or later years of training were only a sub-sample, not selected at random, of the cohort of entrants. This was unfortunate but unavoidable; it is possible, though, to compare the sub-sample with the original cohort. The numbers involved and their distribution can be set out as follows:

	1966 Entrants	*1967 Entrants*
Questioned on entry to Training School	–	204 (in 1967)
Questioned on completion of one year off-the-job training	126 (in 1967)	145 (in 1968)
Questioned after 1-1½ years on-the-job-training	47 (in 1968)	56 (in 1970)
Questioned after c.2½ years on-the-job training	38 (in 1970)	–
Completed questionnaires on all three occasions	37	52

The main sources of information were questionnaires which were completed by the apprentices themselves. We were also able to talk with various members of the Training Centre staff and to observe something of the apprentices' activities in the centre and in the yard. The use of self-completion questionnaires was dictated by the lack of resources for interviewing and by the fact that it would have been very difficult if not impossible to obtain time and facilities to interview at work. In 1967 and 1968 the questionnaires were completed in the Training Centre under the supervision of a member of the research team, who explained the purpose of the research and was available to answer questions. In 1970 the majority of respondents had to be contacted by post, as they were at those stages in their apprenticeship working in a great number of different locations in the yards; this caused a further decline in the number of completed questionnaires. The questionnaires had the same basic content in all cases, though some changes in detail were made in the light of experience, and it was only necessary to ask certain questions (for example, about school) on one occasion. They were designed to secure information about the following main areas:

Social origins: father's occupation; contacts with shipbuilding through kin and/or friends; place of residence; secondary schooling.

Social networks: occupations entered by friends at school and respondent's evaluation of them; occupations of current friends.

Priorities in choosing a job; assessment of apprenticeship.

Attitudes to work, and assessment of present job in comparison with other trades in shipbuilding, and with jobs outside the industry.

Aspirations with regard to promotion and jobs in the future.

Attitudes towards the firm and management; Trade Unions; and certain industrial relations questions.

General social perspectives, in particular in relation to the class structure.

The majority of questions were closed-ended (and answers to open-ended questions were necessarily brief), so that there was some danger (not too serious, it is hoped) of imposing the investigator's definitions of the situation on respondents. A number of the questions were included in the interview schedule for adult shipbuilding workers.

In addition to the problems which arise due to the use of highly structured questions in questionnaires, the data obtained have certain limitations for the purpose of this analysis. The numbers in the matched sub-samples are small, and the relationship between sub-samples and the original cohort may be biased in certain ways. In terms of their social characteristics, origins and education the apprentices are a very homogeneous population, and this limits the extent to which differences between them can be related to "face-sheet" variables; they are all male, in the same age group, from a small number of very similar localities, having received an education for the same number of years in the same sort of school; they work in the same industry, under one employer and are engaged in a limited range of occupations of more or less the same status. On the other hand it was possible to question these two cohorts of apprentices over a relatively long period (2½ years) and to do so within the context of a more general investigation in shipbuilding which means that the findings can be placed in context, and that some comparison can be made between apprentices and adult shipbuilding workers. The relative homogeneity of the population also means that the influence of such internal differences as do exist can perhaps be seen more clearly.

HYPOTHESES TESTED IN THE ANALYSIS

In the light of the discussion so far it is possible to formulate certain expected findings from the data obtained from the apprentices.

(1) Entering apprenticeship in shipbuilding is to move from an environment of school and family/community to one of work and family/community. The school is likely to transmit certain broadly speaking 'middle class' values which will differ from the 'working class' values of adult shipbuilding workers: for example, the desirability of promotion and a career; the possibility of getting ahead by one's own efforts; the legitimacy of existing distributions of

authority; and the underlying harmony of interests of management and workers. To say the least, such perspectives are not unambiguously endorsed in working class communities, and are challenged by the experience of working in an industry like shipbuilding.

Although the family community situations of most apprentices remained constant over the sort of period we have investigated, to move from school to work can be expected to produce changes in attitudes and social perspectives towards a more 'working class' position.

(2) In terms of the above argument the most marked change can be expected to occur in the second and subsequent years of apprenticeship; the Training Centre continues a school-like influence for a time. **Hence, although there may be changes in attitudes and expectations with the move from school (and family/community) to a Training Centre (and family/community), there can be expected to be greater changes with the move from Training Centre to shipyard.**

(3) Outside work the social relations and social situation of the apprentice may remain relatively unchanged, though his status in the family, for example, is likely to change once he starts working and earning. **Although the experience of being employed and at work is likely to affect any boy's perceptions of a wide range of issues and situations, it can be expected that this influence will be greater with reference to work-related issues than to more general social perspectives.**

(4) As we shall see the majority of apprentices have contacts with and knowledge of the shipbuilding industry before starting work. They differ, however, in the extent of these contacts. It can be expected that those with more prior contacts will have greater knowledge of the industry and will tend to have absorbed, to a greater extent, the expectations and perspectives held by adult shipbuilding workers. **Hence, apprentices with least prior contact with the industry may be expected to differ most in their outlook from adult shipbuilding workers and subsequently to experience the more marked change in attitudes and expectations.**

(5) The apprentices are each part of a network of friends, but these networks differ in the extent to which they are composed of others also working in the shipbuilding industry. **Hence, the greater the extent to which an apprentice's network is composed entirely of shipbuilding workers, the greater the degree to which his attitudes and perspectives will resemble those of adult shipbuilding workers.**

BASIC DESCRIPTIVE FINDINGS

A preliminary examination of some of the "hypotheses" can be made on the basis of straightforward tabulations of the apprentices' responses over the three years. These have been grouped under the following headings:

1. Attitudes to work
2. Apprenticeship
3. Aspirations
4. Attitudes to the firm and to management
5. Attitudes to Trades Unions
6. Social perspectives

These headings are not mutually exclusive but will allow us to consider the areas of interest in the probable order of their decreasing salience to the apprentices themselves. Where possible the replies of adult shipbuilding workers, aged 21-30, have been tabulated alongside the apprentices' replies for comparative purposes.

1. Attitudes to Work

The questions about job priorities revealed similar, though not identical patterns of replies. The relative importance of financial rewards differs slightly at any one time and in changes over time, but it is the most important criterion in general for apprentices as it is for adult shipbuilding workers. Indeed, taking Table 1c into account as well, earnings appear to be regarded as of increasing importance as apprenticeship continues. Security of employment is of decreasing importance and this is surprising given its ranking by adult shipbuilding workers. On the other hand the declining importance attributed to promotion prospects is what was expected and is in line with the responses of adult shipbuilding workers (though the second set of statements in Table 1c is out of line with this). As we shall see below, aspirations do change during the period of apprenticeship.

Turning from these extrinsic rewards to intrinsic rewards (interesting work, good conditions, etc.) they are at all stages accorded lesser importance as the basis for evaluating jobs by both apprentices and adult shipbuilding workers, except in the case of the 1966 entrants after 3½ years at work in answer to the question tabulated in Table 1a.[3] There is evidence however to suggest that they are seen as increasingly important as apprenticeship proceeds, though a good deal depends on the context of the question; the changing frequency of mention of financial rewards in Table 1a may be compared with the steadily increasing emphasis on the amount of money earned as the most important thing about a job in Table 1c.

TABLE 1*

ATTITUDES TO WORK IN GENERAL

(a)   What kind of things do you look for in a good job?

Years of Apprenticeship		Frequency of Mention (per cent) 0	1	2/2½	3½
Financial Rewards	1966		(78)78	84	70
	1967	(82)79	83	77	
Interesting and	1966		(33)46	46	62
Varied Work, etc.	1967	(48)37	50	67	
Security	1966		(35)41	43	32
	1967	(40)44	40	25	
Future Prospects	1966		(39)35	41	8
	1967	(53)44	44	19	
Conditions of	1966		(33)19	27	38
Work	1967	(33)35	31	33	
Friendly	1966		(13)14	8	22
Workmates	1967	(8) 8	16	8	

*   In these tables, and in Tables 2, 3, 8, 9 and 10, the format is as follows:

		Apprentices				Adult Shipbuilding workers aged 21-30
Year of Apprenticeship		0	1	2/2½	3½	(Completed 5-15 years in employment)
Year of Question:	1966 Entry		1967	1968	1970	1969
	1967 Entry	1967	1968	1970		
Number of	1966 Entry	–	(126)37	37	37	
Respondents	1967 Entry	(204)52	52	52	–	71†

Figures in brackets are the numbers of those who completed the questionnaire in the first year, from which the two sub-samples were drawn.

†   Includes 7 respondents who were not skilled (i.e. apprenticed) shipbuilding workers.

TABLE 1 CONTINUED

(b)   Which three of the following do you think are the most important

Year of Apprenticeship		Frequency of Mention (per cent)				
		0	1	2/2½	3½	5-15
Good Wages	1966		(62)65	78	81	85
	1967	(61)65	81	83		
Safe and Steady Job	1966		(40)49	46	27	47
	1967	(57)66	38	25		
Having Good Workmates	1966		(38)35	49	57	21
	1967	(31)38	42	44		
Good chances of Promotion	1966		(37)41	19	19	23
	1967	(43)37	42	35		
Good Conditions	1966		(24)22	19	27	27
	1967	(31)33	31	17		
Interesting Work	1966		(42)43	32	38	38
	1967	(36)37	31	52		
Being Near Home	1966		(14)11	16	22	27
	1967	(13)14	13	15		
Having responsibility for one's own work	1966		(15)16	27	19	20
	1967	(15)10	18	13		
Good bosses	1966		(9)11	5	3	11
	1967	(11)10	8	10		

One characteristic of the replies in Table 1b is interesting though not statistically significant. This can be seen if data from Table 1b are represented as follows (see also Table 1a):

		1967	1968	1969	1970
		(Per cent)			
Good Wages	Adult			85	
	1966 Entry	(62)65	78		81
	1967 Entry	(61)65	81		83
Safe and Steady Job	Adult			47	
	1966 Entry	(40)48	46		27
	1967 Entry	(57)67	38		25

(c) Statements about Work.
Which statement do you agree with most?

Year of Apprenticeship	Frequency of Mention (per cent)				
	0	*1*	*2/2½*	*3½*	*5-15*
Having an interesting job and good workmates are the most important things about work					
1966	•	—	57	43	
1967	(45)42	35	37		20
The amount of money you earn is the most important thing about a job					
1966		—	27	51	
1967	(12)13	27	37		49
Good bosses and a satisfactory job are the most important things about work					
1966		—	14	5	
1967	(29)35	38	30		(28*)
A man's working life is like a ladder which he climbs up from rung to rung until he reaches the top					
1966		(55)70	49	51	
1967	(51)48	52	63		38
If a man has a steady job and a good wage, he should be content					
1966		(44)30	49	43	
	(36)38	46	31		56

* Not comparable because statement asked about bosses and *security*.

The frequency of mention of "good wages" and "a safe and steady job" appears to be related closely to the year in which the question was put rather than to the stage of apprenticeship. This "finding" gives an added dimension to any formulation of what is meant by "social situation", that of the particular (micro-) historical period. The years 1968-1969 were a period in which all wage agreements in the yard were radically renegotiated and in which a two-year guarantee of security of employment was offered by management as part of these productivity agreements. As wages were so much under discussion it is not surprising that they were so frequently mentioned; and the marked decline in interest in job security in 1970 may reflect the existence of relative job security for all employees at this time. The adult shipbuilding workers may emphasize security more because of their greater domestic responsibilities; 74 per cent of them were married, and 62 per cent had children.

2. Apprenticeship

The general pattern of replies to a question designed to find out what the apprentices considered the advantages of training for a skilled job was similar to that relating to questions about jobs in general (Table 2). Good pay was consistently the most frequently

TABLE 2

APPRENTICESHIP

Which three of the following do you think are the most important advantages of having a trade?

Year of Apprenticeship		Frequency of Mention (per cent)			
		0	1	2/2½	3½
Good Pay	1966		(62)71	68	74
	1967	(72)71	83	81	
Secure Employment	1966		(55)61	70	39
	1967	(62)71	67	38	
Varied and interesting work	1966		(45)47	52	65
	1967	(45)38	63	54	
Good chance of getting on	1966		(43)49	17	25
	1967	(49)50	38	40	
Being able to make your own decisions	1966		(19)25	22	38
	1967	(14)12	18	27	
Scope to use your skills	1966		(22)11	32	22
	1967	(24)29	12	29	
Competence in use of tools and techniques	1966		(2) –	11	21
	1967	(8)14	6	21	
Important work	1966		(11)11	13	3
	1967	(15)12	6	6	
Good Social Position	1966		(16) 6	8	8
	1967	(8) 4	8	4	

chosen factor. In this case too security of employment was less stressed in 1970, and the intrinsic characteristics of a skilled man's work (its interest and variety, responsibility, etc.) were increasingly stressed over the apprenticeship period; and the possible opportunities for advancement were less often mentioned.

3. Aspirations

The apprentices were asked both what sort of job they expected to have in ten years' time, and what sort of job they would like to have in ten years' time if they could have any job. The answers to these questions were very varied in terms of which occupations were specified, but very similar over the two and a half years and as between the two questions in that the great majority of all responses to both questions on all occasions was either the sort of jobs for which the apprentices were training (that is, skilled manual work), or closely related jobs of a similar or only slightly higher status (for example, foreman, draughtsman). Very few aspired to attain, or had realistic expectations of attaining, unambiguously middle class or managerial positions.

Schools (and to a lesser extent the Training Centre) might be expected to inculcate a belief in the opportunity and desirability of upward mobility at work, especially among their more able pupils. As we have already seen, opportunities for promotion appeared to be decreasingly important as a job characteristic as the boys gained experience of the world of work. This declining emphasis on the desirability, and even more sharply on the possibility, of promotion is reflected in the answers to questions about promotion to foreman (Table 3a and b). It appears as if the Training Centre is relatively successful in sustaining a belief in the possibility and desirability of becoming a foreman, but after the first year of apprenticeship there is evidence of a decline in positive answers to both questions. The questions about promotion to managerial position produced a different pattern (Tables 3c and d). At all stages it is seen as more desirable; very few apprentices or adult shipbuilding workers see it as likely; and there is no consistent pattern of change over time.

Finally, in one respect at least the process of apprenticeship appears to be unsuccessful in that it produces a decline in the proportion of boys who expect to stay in the industry (Table 3e).

It is possible to try to highlight these changes in orientations to

TABLE 3

ASPIRATIONS

Year of Apprenticeship	Frequency of Mention (per cent)				
	0	1	2/2½	3½	5-15
(a) Would you like to become a foreman?					
Very much or* 1966		(50)54	38	27	41
quite a lot 1967	(61)63	79	56		
(b) What chance do you think you have of becoming a foreman?					
Very good chance† 1966		(50)52	33	17	41‡
or good chance 1967	(38)39	54	44		
(c) What about the idea of becoming a member of management, e.g. Department Manager? Would you like this?					
Very much or* 1966		(59)60	41	54	48
quite a lot 1967	(60)56	63	75		
(d) What chance do you think you have of becoming a manager?					
Very good chance† 1966		(10) 5	11	5	16‡
or good chance 1967	(13)10	14	18		
(e) Do you think you will stay in shipbuilding?					
Yes 1966		(51)38	19	27	
1967	(50)60	31	33		

* Alternatives: 'not much' and 'not at all'
† Alternatives: 'not much chance' and 'no chance at all'
‡ 'Good or Moderate' (alternatives 'Not very good' and 'hopeless')

work by selecting for closer examination those items on which some changes in emphasis have occurred. Four such items have been chosen:

(i) the choice or mention of "good wages", "financial rewards", etc. in answer to any or all of the following three questions:
  Which three of the following do you think are the most important advantages of having a trade? (9 items listed).
  What kind of things do you look for in a good job? (open-ended).
  Which three of the following do you think are most important in a job? (9 items listed).
  The number of mentions in any case could range from none to three.
(ii) the mention of "interesting and varied work", etc. in answer to the open-ended question "what kind of things do you look for in a good job?".
(iii) the mention of "future prospects", "the chance to get ahead", etc. in answer to the same question.

(iv)   the choice of "safe and steady job" in answer to the question "which three of the following are most important in a job?".

TABLE 4

FINANCIAL REWARDS

(a) 1966 Entry	*Number of Mentions after 3½ years training*			
Number of Mentions after one year	*(per cent)* *0,1, or 2*	*3*	*Total*	*N*
0, 1 or 2	22	38	60	22
3	14	27	41	15
Total	35	65	100	37
N	13	24	37	
(b) 1967 Entry	*Number of Mentions after 2½ years training*			
Number of Mentions at start of training	*(per cent)* *0,1, or 2*	*3*	*Total*	*N*
0, 1 or 2	25	29	54	28
3	13	33	46	24
Total	38	62	100	52
N	20	32	52	

As can be seen in Table 4, in both cohorts there was a distinct, and very similar, increase in the number of apprentices who mentioned financial rewards in answer to all three of the questions. All the changes were not however in one direction; when the raw data, from which this table is drawn, are reorganized to consider all changes, and not just whether or not the respondent mentioned financial rewards three times, the following picture emerges:

	1966 Entry	*1962 Entry*
Increased mention of financial rewards	15	19
Same number of mentions	13	20
Reduced number of mentions	9	13
	37	52

In each case about a quarter of the apprentices appeared to place less emphasis on financial rewards at the end of the two and a half years than they did at the start, but the majority of apprentices either had a strongly "calculative" orientation to work early in their training or acquired one as apprenticeship proceeded.

TABLE 5

FUTURE PROSPECTS

(What kind of things do you look for in a good job?)

(a) 1966 Entry	*After 3½ years training*			
After one year	*(per cent)* *Not* *Mentioned*	*Mentioned*	*Total*	*N*
Not mentioned	65	3	68	25
Mentioned	27	5	32	12
Total	92	8	100	37
N	34	3	37	
(b) 1967 Entry	*After 2½ years training*			
At start of training	*(per cent)* *Not* *Mentioned*	*Mentioned*	*Total*	*N*
Not mentioned	46	10	56	29
Mentioned	35	10	44	23
Total	81	19	100	52
N	42	10	52	

Two further sets of answers can be taken as evidence of such an orientation insofar as they both relate to "extrinsic" rewards which might be derived from work: future prospects (Table 5) and job security (Table 6). As has already been noted, the pattern here is in both cases the opposite to that observed for financial rewards, a marked decline in the proportion of respondents who mentioned these characteristics as desirable in a job. This overall decline is only accompanied by a negligible minority swing in the opposite direction.

The fourth item selected for special attention, an emphasis on interesting and varied work, can be taken as indicating a less

TABLE 6

A SAFE AND STEADY JOB
(Which three of the following are most important in a job?)

(a) 1966 Entry	*After 3½ years training*			
After one year	*(per cent)* Not Mentioned	*Mentioned*	*Total*	*N*
Not Mentioned	35	16	51	19
Mentioned	38	11	49	18
Total	73	27	100	37
N	27	10	37	

(b) 1967 Entry	*After 2½ years training*			
At start of training	*(per cent)* Not Mentioned	*Mentioned*	*Total*	*N*
Not Mentioned	31	2	33	17
Mentioned	43	23	66	35
Total	74	25	100	52
N	39	13	52	

"instrumental" orientation. In the case of both cohorts there was a trend towards increasing emphasis on these "intrinsic" characteristics of a job as desirable, with only just over one in ten of the apprentices changing in the opposite direction.

Thus these data provide a clear indication of the changes in attitudes to work which took place in a fairly uniform way for these two cohorts of apprentices. They also illustrate the point that such attitudes or orientations can become both more instrumental and more concerned with the intrinsic characteristics of a job at the same time. Certainly on this evidence it would be difficult to regard the changes taking place in the apprentices' attitudes as representing a straightforward shift either towards or away from an instrumental orientation to work.

TABLE 7

INTERESTING AND VARIED WORK
(What kind of things do you look for in a good job?)

(a) 1966 Entry	*After 3½ years training*			
After one year	*(per cent)* *Not* *Mentioned*	*Mentioned*	*Total*	*N*
Not Mentioned	27	27	54	20
Mentioned	11	35	46	17
Total	38	62	100	37
N	14	23	37	

(b) 1967 Entry	*After 2½ years training*			
At start of training	*(per cent)* *Not* *Mentioned*	*Mentioned*	*Total*	*N*
Not Mentioned	21	42	63	33
Mentioned	12	25	37	19
Total	33	67	100	52
N	17	35	52	

4. Attitudes to the Firm and to Management

The experience of employment appears to be associated with an increasingly critical or hostile attitude to management (Tables 8a-c). Schools and the Training Centre can be expected to suggest a "teamwork" view of the firm, though even before they start work the apprentices will have been aware of alternative definitions of the situation. The evidence suggests that such a consensus view begins to change even during the first year of apprenticeship, but at least in terms of the "football team" question (8c), changes much more markedly after starting work in the yard.

Unfortunately for these purposes, exactly comparable questions were not put to adult shipbuilding workers, and this is an area where the precise wording can be crucial. There is some evidence, however, to indicate that apprentices become more hostile to management

TABLE 8

ATTITUDES TO THE FIRM AND TO MANAGEMENT
Which statement do you agree with most?

Years of Apprenticeship	(per cent) 0	1	2/2½	3½	5-15*
a)					
The good worker is interested in his job and loyal to his firm	1966	—	22	11	(38)
	1967 (49)54	17	21		
The good of the firm is management's worry: all that matters to the worker is his pay packet	1966	—	22	19	(18)
	1967 (5) 2	12	25		
The good worker is loyal to his mates and interested in his trade but as long as he has a job it doesn't matter which firm he works for	1966	—	57	70	(37)
	1967 (29)29	69	52		
b)					
Management are only interested in profits	1966		(39)41	81	81
	1967 (25)21	56	67		
Management are interested in the good of the firm and of all workers	1966		(59)59	14	16
	1967 (68)75	42	29		

c)
It has been said that: A firm is like a football team, in which management and workers are on the same side, because good teamwork means success — and is to everyone's advantage. Do you —

	(per cent) 0	1	2/2½	3½	5-15*
Definitely agree	1966		(49)46	19	16
	1967 (50)50	42	10		
Agree on the whole	1966		(46)54	16	19
	1967 (40)42	37	29		

TABLE 8 CONTINUED

Years of Apprenticeship Apprenticeship	(per cent) 0	1	2/2½	3½	5-15*
(c) cont.					
Disagree on	1966		(3)—	41	51
the whole	1967	(4) 4	15	42	
Definitely	1966		(1)—	24	14
disagree	1967	(5) 2	6	19	

Shipbuilding Workers Aged 21-30

(d)
Someone once said — a firm is like a football team in which management and workers are on the same side, because good teamwork is to everyone's advantage. Would you generally agree, or generally disagree? Does it work like this here?

Agree, and works like this	39
Agree, but does not work like this	34
Disagree	24

* Answers not strictly comparable as the marking differed considerable

than older workers (see, for example, Table 8a). The "football team" question was asked in the form shown in Table 8d; the proportion who felt their own firm was like a football team was similar to the proportion of positive replies among the older apprentices, but almost as many again appeared to take a teamwork view of firms in general.

5. Attitudes to Trade Unions

The answers to a question about the reasons for being a member of a Trade Union did not vary very much over the period of apprenticeship and gave most emphasis to instrumental reasons (for example, to get better conditions, to help prevent redundancy, etc.) rather than to more solidaristic ones (for example, support for workmates, all workers should belong, etc.). More general attitudes towards Trade Unions and their place in society, however, did change markedly for both cohorts in a very similar way. There was a decline in the proportion who thought Trade Unions too powerful (Table 9a), and an increase in support for compulsory union membership though not to the extent to which this view was held by adult shipbuilding workers (9c). Trade Union functions were defined increasingly narrowly in one respect — being for the benefit of members only rather than all workers (9b); but much more widely in another — the desirability of getting workers "a say in management" (Table 9d and e).

TABLE 9

ATTITUDES TO TRADE UNIONS AND INDUSTRIAL RELATIONS
Which statement do you agree with most?

Year of Apprenticeship	(Per cent) 0	1	2/2½	3½	5-15
(a)					
Trade Unions have too much power — 1966		[(42)51]	5	5	18
1967	(23)13	17	10		
Trade Unions have enough but not too much power — 1966			38	62	61
1967	(50)58	63	58		
Trade Unions do not have enough power — 1966		[(56)46]	54	30	17
1967	(24)27	19	31		
(b)					
A Trade Union should only be concerned with the interest of its own members — 1966		(34)38	46	57	—
1967	—	37	44		
A Trade Union should be concerned with the welfare of the workers, whether they are members or not — 1966		(60)62	54	41	—
1967	—	62	54		
(c)					
It should be compulsory for every worker to be a member of a Trade Union — 1966		(29)24	32	51	(80)
1967	—	17	27		

TABLE 9 CONTINUED

Year of Apprenticeship	(Per cent) 0	1	2/2½	3½	5-15
(c) cont.					
No worker should be forced to join a Union — 1966		(70)76	65	43	(17)
1967	—	81	71		
(d)					
Trade Unions should try to get workers a say in management — 1966		(60)65	73	70	—
1967	(33)31	58	73		
Trade Unions should *only* be concerned with wages and conditions for members — 1966		(38)35	24	27	—
1967	(53)48	40	25		
(e)					
Workers should have some say in the running of the firm — 1966		(64)68	81	73	—
1967	(50)50	75	77		
The job of managers is to manage; of workers to work — 1966		(34)32	16	27	—
1967	(39)35	23	19		

6. Social Perspectives

It is notoriously difficult to devise and interpret closed-ended questions about images of society, of the class structure, and so on. In the context of the apprentice questionnaires very little was possible, and the questions used were varied when earlier formulation appeared inadequate. The data available do suggest, however, that, as expected, views in this area change relatively little during apprenticeship, and are very similar to those of adult shipbuilding workers (Table 10). Such changes as are apparent are towards a more "proletarian" imagery and away from acceptance of an ideology of opportunity (that is, some increase in support for "two-class" views of society and decline in support for "getting ahead with ability and hard work"), though the position of the majority is not to support such supposedly working class views.

TABLE 10

SOCIAL PERSPECTIVES

Which statement do you agree with most?

Year of Apprenticeship:	*(Per cent)* 0	1	2/2½	3½	5-15
(a) In Britain most people are the same class nowadays; the only important difference is how much money they earn 1966		(36)27	16	19	—
Broadly speaking, there are still two main classes, bosses and workers 1966		(63)73	84	78	—
(b) In Britain today there are basically two main classes, bosses and workers, and these classes have opposing interests 1967	(23)29	21	27		30
Most people in Britain today belong to the same class; the only important difference is how much money they earn 1967	(61)52	58	65		56
There are several classes in Britain today: the upper classes run the country and industry and this is as it should be 1967	(5)10	19	8		8

TABLE 10 CONTINUED

Year of Apprenticeship:		*(Per cent)* 0	1	2/2½	3½	5-15
(c) Anybody can get to the top if they have ability and are prepared to work hard	1967	(64)65	75	56		68
Some people are born to rule: ordinary people cannot hope to become bosses	1967	(5)10	6	10		10
Basically the people at the top are no better than anyone else but they try not to give the ordinary man a chance	1967	(15)15	19	33		21
(d) What happens to you depends a lot on luck: otherwise you have to learn to put up with things	1966 1967	(5) 6	(4) 3 –	19 8	27	24
You can get ahead if you have ability and initiative and are prepared to work hard	1966 1967	(86)87	(94)97 98	78 90	73	75

It is possible at this stage to comment on the first three "hypotheses" outlined earlier. There is evidence in the data presented so far to support the claim that the experience of work will bring about changes of attitudes on matters such as promotion, and management and Trade Union functions, towards a more "working class" position. There is no clear pattern as to when the changes take place, all three possibilities being observable on different questions:

change after starting work at all; change after moving from the Training Centre to work in the yard; and change over the whole period. There is some evidence to suggest that there is less change in general social perspectives than in relation to work related issues.

In addition, there is an indication of the importance of also taking into account the current situation when the questions were asked, as recent events appeared to have influenced answers to the questions about job priorities.

FURTHER ANALYSIS: SOCIAL CHARACTERISTICS

Two main tasks now remain: to explore the relationship between the social characteristics of the two cohorts of apprentices and their attitudes and expectations; and to explore the relationship between these social characteristics and the changes which took place in the replies to our questions over the two and a half years. To simplify the analysis, attention will be concentrated on those attitudes to work, to the firm and to the Trade Unions which showed the most marked changes. This is essential for the second task, and the items on which changes took place should also provide sufficient indication of any relationship between social characteristics and attitudes and social perspectives at a single point in time.

The main social characteristics for which we have data are shown in Table 11. As mentioned earlier the apprentices form a relatively homogeneous population in terms of age, area of residence and educational experience. It is however possible to subdivide them in terms of whether or not their relatives or father work in shipbuilding and repairing; the extent to which they have friends in the industry; and the sort of occupation they themselves are training for. These will be the main factors referred to in the discussion which follows. There is no relationship between kinship connections with the industry and friendship networks for either sample.

For the 1967 cohort of apprentices at the very start of their training contact with the industry through their father or other relatives does appear to have some influence on orientations to work. Those with such contacts are more likely to mention financial rewards *and* interesting and varied work as desirable characteristics of a job, and to be somewhat more hostile to management than the sample as a whole (Tables 12 & 13). This is in line with the expected attitudes of adult shipbuilding workers. Having friends in the industry

TABLE 11

SOCIAL CHARACTERISTICS

		1966 Entry		1967 Entry	
	N	*126*	*37*	*204*	*52*
Area of Residence		*(per cent)*		*(per cent)*	
Wallsend (location of Yard)		(21)	30	(24)	46
Hebburn		(21)	11	(9)	
Jarrow	Tyneside	(8)	3	(7)	4
North Shields	Shipbuilding	(17)	16	(28)	19
Walker	Towns	(6)	8	(5)	10
South Shields		(2)	3	(4)	
Newcastle, Gateshead, etc.		(23)	30	(18)	21
Father's Occupation & Industry					
In Shipbuilding		(18)	19	(18)	25
In Ship Repair & Marine Engineering		(13)	14	(14)	10
Other Industries		(68)	68	(68)	65
Skilled manual worker (shipbuilding)		(19)	16	(20)	21
Non-skilled manual worker (shipbuilding)		(3)	3	(7)	10
Other skilled workers		(40)	41	(29)	25
Supervisory, White Collar		(13)	11	(18)	27
Others		(24)	30	(27)	17
Relatives other than father					
In same firm		(36)	43	(38)	33
In other shipbuilding firms		(45)	27	(43)	42
Type of School					
Secondary Modern		–		(89)	94
Grammar		–		(5)	2
Other		–		(5)	4
Friends in Shipbuilding					
Friends seen regularly who work in shipbuilding/repairing		(68)	76	(64)	58
Number of 6 best friends who	0	(n.a.)	22	(n.a.)	42
work in shipbuilding/repairing	1		22 44		12 54
	2		14		15
	3		16		10
	4		14		12
	5		8		4
	6		5 57		6 47

TABLE 11 CONTINUED

		1966 Entry		1967 Entry	
N		*126*	*37*	*204*	*52*
Occupation of Apprentice		*(per cent)*		*(per cent)*	
Steelworking Trades:		(41)	33	(38)	56
Caulker/Burner		(2)	–	(2)	–
Welder		(21)	11	(13)	25
Shipwright		(10)	11	(13)	21
Plater		(8)	11	(7)	8
Riveter/Driller		–	–	(1)	2
Other		–	–	(2)	–
Outfitting Trades:		(59)	69	(54)	44
Electrician		(12)	16	(11)	19
Joiner		(17)	26	(8)	8
Plumber		(9)	8	(10)	2
Fitter		(20)	19	(21)	13
Coppersmith		(1)	–	(2)	2
Other		–	–	(2)	–
Draughtsmen (who leave Training Centre after 3 months)				(7)	–

NOTE: Figures in brackets refer to the total cohort of apprentices in the respective years; the other figures to the sub-samples who responded on all three occasions.

TABLE 12

KINSHIP, OCCUPATION AND CHANGES IN ATTITUDES[4]

			Relatives in Shipbuilding			*Occupation: Steel-working Trades*
		1967 Entry*				
		Total	*None*	*Some*	*Father*	
N		*52*	*17*	*35*	*18*	*29*
Changes in emphasis on:		%	%	%	%	%
Financial Rewards						
(3 mentions)		46/62	29/53	54/66	62/78	55/83
Increase		37	47	31	28	38
Stable all mentions		38	24	46	56	48
Decrease		25	29	23	17	14
Interesting & Varied work		37/67	24/71	43/66	50/56	45/55
Increase		42	53	37	28	31
Stable		46	41	49	50	48
Decrease		12	6	14	22	21

TABLE 12 CONTINUED

		1967 Entry*				
			Relatives in Shipbuilding			Occupation: Steelworking Trades
	N	Total 52	None 17	Some 35	Father 18	29
Changes in emphasis on: cont.		%	%	%	%	%
Future Prospects		44/19	47/24	43/17	28/11	38/21
Increase		10	12	9	11	10
Stable		56	53	57	61	62
Decrease		35	35	34	28	28
Safe and Steady Job		67/25	71/12	66/31	72/39	66/35
Increase		2	–	3	6	3
Stable		54	41	60	56	62
Decrease		44	59	37	39	35
Want promotion to Foreman		63/56	65/47	63/60	61/67	59/48
Increase		13	6	17	17	14
Stable		65	71	63	72	62
Decrease		21	24	20	11	24
Attitudes to Firm, etc.						
Firm like a team		92/38	94/29	92/43	88/44	90/41
Change to agree		–	–	–	–	–
No change		46	29	52	56	48
Change to disagree		54	65	49	44	48
Management only interested in profits		19/65	12/58	26/69	17/72	17/69
Change to agree		48	47	49	61	55
No change		42	41	43	28	34
Change to disagree		4	–	6	6	3
Workers should have say in running firm		50/65	35/58	57/71	50/67	48/66
Change to agree		19	18	20	22	24
No change		60	65	57	56	48
Change to disagree		4	–	6	6	7

TABLE 12 CONTINUED

	Total	None	Some	Father	Occupation: Steelworking Trades
		Relatives in Shipbuilding			*Occupation: Steelworking Trades*
N–	*52*	*17*	*35*	*18*	*29*
	1967 Entry *				

	Total	None	Some	Father	Trades
Attitudes to Trade Unions	%	%	%	%	%
T.U. should try to get workers a say in management	31/56	–	–	39/56	35/55
Change to agree	33			33	28
No change	37			33	45
Change to disagree	8			16	7
Should join T.U. for solidaristic reasons	52/56	47/59	54/40	28/50	48/48
Change to agree	13	18	11	11	14
No change	60	66	55	44	62
Change to disagree	19	6	26	33	14

* In Tables 12, 13, 14 and 15 the format is as follows:
   Positive response in 1967/positive response in 1970
   Change to positive response
   No change in response
   Change to negative response.

makes less difference, though those with one or none of their six best friends in shipbuilding place less emphasis on interesting and varied work as a desired feature of a job, and are less likely than average to want to be promoted foreman. Those training for one of the steelworking trades also emphasize financial rewards, and interesting and varied work, more than average, but otherwise do not differ from the rest of the sample at this stage in their careers.

For the apprentices who entered the Training Centre in 1966 these questions came after a year's experience at work. Somewhat surprisingly those with no kinship connections with the industry were more likely to emphasize interesting and varied work (but so were those whose fathers worked in shipbuilding), and less likely to look for future prospects. They also wanted workers to have some say in running the firm, and Trade Unions to have more power, so that they appeared to be relatively more 'proletarian' than their

TABLE 13

FRIENDSHIP NETWORKS AND CHANGES IN ATTITUDES

	1967 Entry					
		Friends in Shipbuilding (1967)			(1970)	
		(of 6 best friends)				
	Total	Yes	0 or 1	2 or more	0 or 1	2 or more
N	52	30	28	24	21	31
Changes in emphasis on: Financial Rewards	%	%	%	%	%	%
(3 mentions)	46/62	47/60	50/68	42/54	57/71	39/55
Increase all	37	37	32	42	33	39
Stable mentions	38	33	50	24	48	32
Decrease	25	30	18	33	19	29
Interesting & Varied Work	37/67	43/67	29/68	46/67	27/62	42/71
Increase	42	40	46	37	33	45
Stable	46	43	46	46	57	39
Decrease	12	17	7	17	5	16
Future Prospects	44/19	40/23	46/11	42/29	43/19	45/19
Increase	10	13	4	17	14	6
Stable	56	57	57	54	48	61
Decrease	35	30	39	29	38	32
Safe and Steady Job	67/25	70/27	75/32	58/17	76/24	61/26
Increase	2	3	4	–	–	3
Stable	54	50	50	58	48	48
Decrease	44	47	46	42	52	39
Want promotion to Foreman	63/56	63/57	50/57	79/54	67/62	61/52
Increase	13	13	21	4	10	16
Stable	65	67	64	67	76	58
Decrease	21	20	14	29	14	26
Attitudes to Firm, etc. Firm like a team	92/38	97/53	100/43	83/33	90/52	94/29
Change to agree	–	–	–	–	–	–
No change	46	57	43	46	62	35
Change to disagree	54	43	57	50	38	65

TABLE 13 CONTINUED

	1967 Entry					
		Friends in Shipbuilding (1967)			(1970)	
			(of 6 best friends)			
	Total	Yes	0 or 1	2 or more	0 or 1	2 or more
N–	52	30	28	24	21	31
Attitudes to Firm etc. cont.	%	%	%	%	%	%
Management only interested in profits	19/65	23/60	21/75	21/54	33/86	13/52
Change to agree	48	43	57	38	62	39
No change	42	43	36	50	29	52
Change to disagree	4	7	4	4	10	0
Workers should have say in running firm	50/65	63/77	50/68	50/62	57/57	45/71
Change to agree	19	17	18	21	5	29
No change	60	67	61	58	62	58
Change to disagree	4	3	–	8	5	3
Attitudes to Trade Unions T.U.s should try to get workers a say in management	31/56	27/47	29/54	33/58	52/62	16/51
Change to agree	33	33	36	29	29	36
No change	37	23	32	42	43	32
Change to disagree	8	13	11	4	19	–
Should join T.U. for solidaristic reasons	52/46	57/40	43/29	63/67	67/47	42/45
Change to agree	13	10	7	21	5	19
No change	60	53	65	54	62	58
Change to disagree	19	27	21	17	24	16

fellows. Those with one or no good friends in shipbuilding appeared slightly less hostile to management but also more critical of trades unions, as did those training for a steelworking trade. (Tables 14 & 15).

These findings provide only slight support for the hypotheses that kinship connections and/or friendship networks would be

TABLE 14

KINSHIP, OCCUPATION AND CHANGES IN ATTITUDES

		1966 Entry				
				Relatives in Shipbuilding		*Occupation: Steel-working*
	N	*Total* 37	*None* 12	*Some* 25	*Father* 12	*Trades* 12
Changes in emphasis on:		%	%	%	%	%
Financial Rewards						
(3 mentions)		41/65	42/67	40/64	42/50	33/75
Increase	all	41	33	44	33	42
Stable	mentions	35	50	28	33	42
Decrease		24	17	28	33	17
Interesting & Varied Work		46/62	58/75	40/56	67/67	50/50
Increase		27	33	24	8	8
Stable		62	50	68	83	83
Decrease		11	17	8	8	8
Future Prospects		32/8	17/–	40/12	42/8	17/–
Increase		3	–	4	–	–
Stable		70	83	64	67	83
Decrease		27	17	32	33	17
Safe and Steady Job		49/27	67/16	40/32	25/33	33/25
Increase		16	8	20	33	25
Stable		45	33	52	42	42
Decrease		38	58	28	25	33
Want Promotion to						
Foreman		54/27	58/25	52/28	67/33	67/58
Increase		5	8	8	–	17
Stable		57	50	60	67	68
Decrease		35	42	32	33	25
Attitudes to Firm, etc.						
Firm like a team		100/35	100/33	100/36	100/25	100/33
Change to agree		–	–	–	–	–
No change		35	33	36	25	33
Change to disagree		65	67	64	75	67
Management only						
interested in profits		41/81	42/83	40/80	33/75	17/75
Change to agree		43	42	44	42	58
No change		51	58	48	58	33
Change to disagree		3	0	4	–	–

TABLE 14 CONTINUED

	N	Total 37	*Relatives in Shipbuilding* None 12	Some 25	Father 12	*Occupation: Steel-working Trades* 12
Attitudes to Firm etc. *cont.*	%	%	%	%	%	
Workers should share in running firm		68/73	83/75	60/72	50/67	50/75
Change to agree		22	8	28	17	42
No change		62	75	56	67	42
Change to disagree		16	17	16	8	17
Attitudes to Trade Unions T.U. should try to get workers a say in management		65/70	—	—	58/58	58/75
Change to agree		19			17	33
No change		65			67	50
Change to disagree		14			17	17
T.U. Membership should be compulsory		24/51	33/50	16/52	25/67	33/67
Change to agree		38	25	44	50	33
No change		49	67	40	42	67
Change to disagree		8	8	8	8	—

significantly related to differences in attitudes and expectations. In the case of the 1967 entrants the differences are what might have been expected; for the other cohort this is not so with regard to kinship connections where the difference is unexpected. In this latter case, however, the apprentices already had work experience which is probably more influential.

The analysis of the relationship between these differences in social characteristics and *changes* in attitudes and expectations is rather more complex. In order to simplify it attention will be concentrated on the overall changes in the 2½ year period, ignoring the second set of replies to the questionnaires completed in 1968.

TABLE 15

FRIENDSHIP NETWORKS AND CHANGES IN ATTITUDES

		1966 Entry				
		Friends in Shipbuilding *(1967)*			*(1970)*	
			(of 6 best friends)			
	Total	*Yes*	*0 or 1*	*2 or more*	*0 or 1*	*2 or more*
N	37	28	16	21	14	23
Changes in emphasis on:	%	%	%	%	%	%
Financial Rewards						
(3 mentions)	41/68	42/65	44/50	38/76	50/57	35/70
Increase all	41	46	25	52	21	52
Stable	35	33	38	33	50	26
Decrease mentions	24	14	38	14	29	22
Interesting & Varied Work	46/62	50/61	56/75	38/52	36/64	52/61
Increase	27	25	25	29	36	22
Stable	62	61	69	56	57	65
Decrease	11	14	6	14	7	13
Future Prospects	32/8	29/7	25/—	38/14	29/7	35/9
Increase	3	3	—	5	—	4
Stable	70	71	75	67	79	65
Decrease	27	25	25	29	21	30
Safe and Steady Job	49/27	50/25	50/25	48/29	50/29	48/26
Increase	16	17	25	10	14	17
Stable	45	39	25	62	50	43
Decrease	38	43	50	29	36	39
Want promotion to						
Foreman	54/27	47/37	56/38	52/14	57/28	52/22
Increase	5	7	6	5	14	—
Stable	57	68	63	52	36	70
Decrease	35	21	31	43	43	30
Attitudes to Firm etc.						
Firm like a team	100/35	100/36	100/25	100/43	100/36	100/35
Change to agree	—	—	—	—	—	—
No change	35	36	25	43	36	35
Change to disagree	65	64	75	57	64	65

TABLE 15 CONTINUED

	1966 Entry					
		Friends in Shipbuilding (1967)			*(1970)*	
			(of 6 best friends)			
	Total	*Yes*	*0 or 1*	*2 or more*	*0 or 1*	*2 or more*
N	37	28	16	21	14	23
Attitudes to Firm etc. *cont.*						
Management only interested in profits:	41/81	36/75	25/75	52/86	36/77	44/83
Change to agree	43	43	50	38	43	44
No change	51	50	50	52	50	52
Change to disagree	3	4	—	5	—	4
Workers should share in running firm:	68/73	64/70	63/69	71/76	64/86	70/65
Change to agree	22	25	25	19	36	13
No change	62	57	56	67	50	70
Change to disagree	16	18	19	14	14	17
Attitudes to Trade Unions T.U. should try to get workers a say in management	65/70	71/71	63/69	67/72	43/64	78/74
Change to agree	19	18	19	19	29	13
No change	65	64	63	67	57	69
Change to disagree	14	18	13	14	7	17
T.U. membership should be compulsory	24/51	21/54	6/63	33/43	21/50	22/52
Change to agree	38	39	56	24	36	39
No change	49	50	38	57	50	48
Change to disagree	8	7	—	14	7	9

Considering first the 1967 cohort of apprentices, who were first questioned at the very start of their training, there is some indication that those most likely to change their attitudes to work were those who had no previous contact with the industry through relatives (Table 12), and that the pattern of changes in the 2½ years results in there being somewhat smaller differences between the kinship categories than at the earlier date. Those with fathers in the industry differ most from the average, placing more emphasis on financial rewards and job security and less on job interest or prospects (though not promotion to foreman). The differences are, however, slight, as are those between steelworkers and the rest, except for a very marked emphasis on financial rewards. This absence of other occupational differences is interesting in view of the existence of such differences among adult shipbuilding workers; it may reflect the fact that this group of apprentices were only half way through their apprenticeship at this time, and therefore not yet strongly identified with their trade and union; or it may reflect the greater emphasis in recent years on common elements in the training of all apprentices.

Differences in friendship "networks" appear to be largely unrelated to replies to questions about attitudes to work in 1970, or to the likelihood of changes in the pattern of replies between the start of training and that date (Table 13). This is so when one takes into account the degree to which friends work in the industry as recorded both at the earlier and at the later date. Those with more friends in the industry are, however, less likely to emphasize financial rewards as an important element in their jobs, and in this respect, contrary to hypothesis, they differ from what we know about adult shipbuilding workers. The absence of other differences may reflect the greater influence of the work situation itself on attitudes than any participation in an "occupational community" of shipbuilding workers outside work.

With regard to attitudes to the firm, management and trade unions, there is little difference between friendship, kinship or occupational categories in the distribution of replies or changes in replies to the two questions concerning worker "participation" (Tables 12 and 13). The variations are greater in the answers to questions about management and the unions in relation to friendship and kinship, though not occupational, categories, though the overall pattern does not conform to any simple hypothesis (such as, for example, that those most closely integrated into the industry through kin and friends will be more hostile to management and more favourable to the union). Those without kinship connections are more hostile to management and less likely to view the firm as a team, and *more* likely to agree that one should join a trade union for "solidaristic" (rather than "instrumental") reasons. Those with fewer friends in shipbuilding are more likely to see management as solely concerned with profits, but *less* likely (1967) or only equally likely (1970) to justify union membership on "solidaristic" grounds. There is no general tendency for those with kinship or friendship connections with shipbuilding to be more stable in their replies over the 2½ years than those without such connections.

This rather confused picture, which is, of course, based on the answers to a small number of questions of a relatively small number of apprentices, is paralleled by the very complex pattern of attitudes and "images of society" which we have already reported for adult shipbuilding workers (Cousins and Brown 1972). Preliminary analysis indicates that, in the case of apprentices, as in that of adult shipbuilding workers, certain typical clusters of attitudes can be discerned, but these require further analysis and have not so far been related to differences in social situation or social characteristics.

The analysis of the attitudes of the 1966 cohort of apprentices is based on a smaller sample so that small absolute changes can emerge as relatively large percentage changes. There is no general tendency for those with greater kinship or friendship connections with the industry to show more stability in their replies; and, as in the case of the 1967 cohort, occupational differences have little effect, though those in the steelworking trades in this group too place more emphasis than average on financial rewards (Tables 14 and 15). Surprisingly, those with fathers in the industry place less rather than more emphasis on such rewards. In other respects neither kinship nor friendship connections (especially as recorded in 1970) appear to be related to any significant differences in the pattern of replies to questions about attitudes to work. This may reflect a growing homogeneity of outlook amongst the apprentices as their experience of the industry increases. Such differences as remain may well be related to differences in their social situations (for example, more detailed occupational differences) which are not tapped by these questionnaires.

This tendency (if that is not too strong a word) towards a growing similarity in the pattern of replies as between categories (and on some items at least, a growing homogeneity in the replies generally) is reflected in the answers to questions about the firm, management and the Trade Unions. Only on the question of compulsory trade union membership (a particularly controversial issue in 1970) is there no clear majority point of view, and no close similarity of replies in the different kinship, friendship and occupational categories. On that issue, surprisingly, those with few or no close friends in the industry are more likely to favour compulsory membership. There is no general relationship between the propensity to change attitude over the two and a half year period and these distinctions in terms of social characteristics.

DISCUSSION AND CONCLUSION

Whilst it was possible to claim earlier that there was definite evidence to support the hypothesis that attitudes would change during the period of apprenticeship towards a more "working class" position, and that this would be particularly the case on work related issues, the relationship is much less clear cut between "orientations to work" and attitudes towards the firm, management and the unions, and the apprentices' kinship and friendship networks and occupations. Though kinship connections did appear to be weakly related to differences in attitudes in the first year of training, friendship patterns did not. Occupational differences (in terms of the simple dichotomy between steelworking and outfitting trades) were not of much apparent importance either, except with reference to the emphasis on financial rewards; as this particular occupational division is reinforced by the difference in union membership between the Amalgamated Society of Boilermakers and other craftsmen's unions, it is of some importance that it is not reflected in these replies. The patterns of change and the resultant pattern of attitudes at the end of two and a half years are even less clearly related to differences in social characteristics.

We know from our studies of adult shipbuilding workers that there is a good deal of diversity of attitude and opinion amongst them as well as a general homogeneity of culture and outlook on other issues. We have argued elsewhere that this reflects the many cross-cutting ways in which the shipbuilding labour force is differentiated at work and in their home localities (see Brown *et al.* 1972, 1973). It can be suggested that underlying these replies are two related processes: a tendency, perhaps particularly noticeable in the 1966 sample who had spent longer in the industry, for there to be increasing support for the majority point of view and a more widely shared orientation to work; and a tendency for non-work related differences to be less important as explanatory variables. In other words the growing integration of these apprentices into the world of shipbuilding is associated with a decline in the importance of pre-existing differences between them. The differences which do remain may be related to aspects of their situation at work (and this can vary widely), or perhaps also outside work, about which we have no information.

One attempt to pursue this line of argument further could be made with available data, to see whether there was a consistent relationship between the apprentices' attitudes and orientations, and whether or not they felt committed to the industry (in terms of answers to two questions: Do you think you will stay in shipbuilding?; Do you now wish you had taken a job outside shipbuilding?). There does not appear to be any relationship between these either at the start of apprenticeship or after several years training. This is not altogether surprising in that differences in the processes of socialization into the status of adult shipbuilding worker, and of integration into the "occupational culture" of shipbuilding, to which reference has just been made, are not adequately reflected in answers to questions of this sort.

Indeed the period of apprenticeship does include a number of rather different processes. It takes place in the years between 16 and 21, during which boys come to be accepted, and to see themselves as belonging, in the fully adult world. It involves the acquisition of quite considerable knowledge and experience, and in some cases at least relatively complex skills. Neither of these processes, however, is unique to apprenticeship and neither was the focus of our research. The chief significance of apprenticeship in the modern world lies in the fact that it offers the main route to a particular and relatively privileged position in the labour market, that of skilled craftsman (see Williams 1957; Liepmann 1960). We have been able to show how in the course of acquiring this status the attitudes, expectations and social perspectives of apprentices in shipbuilding do undergo some important changes, in particular losing the more obviously "middle class" emphases on work as a career with prospects and the firm as a team; and how the pre-existing contacts with, and (presumed) knowledge of, the industry through kin and friends does affect the initial attitudes of the new apprentice. We cannot say from our data how far such changes have occurred in other contexts, but it is obviously important to recognize such changes as an integral part of the apprenticeship process. For the employer, the trade union and the apprentices themselves the most important aspect of apprenticeship may be the ways in which it socializes boys into a distinct occupational status and leads to the internalization of particular norms and values.

With the exception of a few items we have been less successful in showing any marked relationship between the pattern of changes and/or the later pattern of attitudes and expectations and the social characteristics of the apprentices. This was not one of the original intentions behind this part of our research, but became a relevant aim in the context of an attempt to exploit more fully available social survey data. What can be argued is that the absence of any relationship between attitudes, etc. and what are mostly characteristics of the apprentices' non-work situation does lead to the conclusion that any attempt to explain the differences of outlook of older apprentices (and adult shipbuilding workers) should start with sources of variation in their work situations, about which more detailed information would be needed than was available for this study. This emphasis on the importance of the work situation reinforces the criticism which was mentioned earlier of other approaches to the study of orientations to work. Finally it can be argued that the general assumption behind this paper — of a relationship between men's immediate social context and their perceptions of society and of their own place in it — has in part been supported; and that the more negative findings at most leave the issue open for further enquiry.

NOTES

1. The other members of the research team were Peter Brannen, Jim Cousins and Michael Samphier. The project was a joint effort but I am entirely responsible for this account of this part of it. I am, however, very much indebted to Pat Gore for some invaluable help retabulating much of the data, and to Eric Tanenbaum for advice and assistance with computer analysis.

2. The notion of "expectations and social perspectives held by adult shipbuilding workers" is of course very problematic; as we have outlined elsewhere they tend to be highly differentiated in terms of both social situations and social perspectives (see Brown *et al.* 1972). For present purposes I have taken this phrase to mean a similar distribution of replies to that found among adult skilled shipbuilding workers in the next oldest (20-30) age bracket.

3. In Table 1b I have taken extrinsic factors to be: good wages, safe and steady job, good chances of promotion and being near home; and intrinsic: having good workmates, good conditions, interesting work, and having responsibility for one's own work. I realise that this classification is somewhat arbitrary and not the only way in which the data might be organised. The results of this arrangement, however, are:

Years:		0	1	2/2½	3½	5-15
Extrinsic	1966		(153)165	159	149	182
	1967	(174)183	184	155		
Instrinsic	1966		(119)116	127	141	106
	1967	(113)118	112	126		

4. All figures in Tables 12-15 are percentages to the nearest whole number. Non-respondents at *either* date have been excluded and this means that the figures do not always tally exactly with those in earlier tables.

REFERENCES

BROWN, R.K., BRANNEN, P., COUSINS, J.M., SAMPHIER, M.L., (1972). "The Contours of Solidarity: Social Stratification and Industrial Relations in Shipbuilding", *Brit. J. Industrial Relations*, Vol.10, No.1.

BROWN, Richard, (1973). "Sources of Objectives in Work and Employment", in J. Child (ed.), *Man and Organization,* London: Allen and Unwin.

BROWN, R.K., BRANNEN, P., COUSINS, J.M., SAMPHIER, M.L., (1973). "Leisure in Work: the Occupational Culture of Shipbuilding Workers" in M.A. Smith *et al.* (eds.), *Leisure and Society in Britain,* London: Allen Lane.

BULMER, Martin (ed.), (1972). *The Occupational Community of the Traditional Worker,* Proceedings of an SSRC Conference, Durham.

COUSINS, J.M. & BROWN, R.K. (1972). *Patterns of Paradox: Shipbuilding Workers' Images of Society,* Working Paper No.4, University of Durham, Department of Sociology and Social Administration, and in M. Bulmer, *op. cit.*

GOLDTHORPE, J.H. *et al.*, (1968). *The Affluent Worker: Industrial Attitudes and Behaviour,* Cambridge University Press.

LIEPMANN, K., (1960). *Apprenticeship,* London: Routledge and Kegan Paul.

LOCKWOOD, D., (1966). "Sources of Variation in Working Class Images of Society," *Sociological Review,* Vol.14, No.3.

WILLIAMS, G. (1957). *Recruitment to Skilled Trades,* London: Routledge and Kegan Paul.

Chapter 5

ORGANIZATIONAL FACTORS IN WHITE-COLLAR UNIONISM

Michael White

INTRODUCTION

This analysis concerns an organizational survey conducted during 1972. The population for the survey comprised the employees of a single organization, and the original purpose was to assess employees' preferences concerning unionism. All the employees were non-manual. An unusual characteristic of the survey was that it measured opinions at a choice-point, for the employees believed, as indeed was the case, that their opinions would influence organizational decisions concerning staff representation. The original purpose of the survey was essentially a practical one, directed towards determining the company's policy on staff representation. However, sufficient data were collected to make a wider theoretical analysis possible.[1]

The question to which the re-analysis is addressed is as follows: what factors internal to the organization lead white-collar employees to favour unionization? The theory of bureaucracy provides the main focus for re-analysis. It has also proved useful to introduce an additional perspective, which we have called that of "rational conflict;" in this formulation unionism is considered to be stimulated by processes which are set in train by conflicts between any of a wide range of individual aspirations and the perceived situation at work. The survey data, which include employees' opinions of various aspects of the work situation and expressions of their support for or opposition to union representation, have been recast to provide an assessment of the relative contribution of the two theories towards explaining white-collar unionism in this organization.

THEORETICAL PERSPECTIVE

The most obvious limitation of single-organization studies is that they are not generalizable to other organizational situations. How then can the results of such studies be related to theories which are essentially general? One reply is that an accumulation of single studies, provided they are appropriately analyzed and compared, may lead to progressive confirmation of a theory, through induction rather than statistical inference. Indeed, the availability of theory should help to systematize single studies and achieve comparability.

The study of single organizations is also important if one wishes to apply theory to the interpretation of specific problems. If the relationships anticipated by a theory can be shown to hold in single organizations, in the midst of all the complicating features which beset such studies, it is a strong demonstration of the theory's sufficiency.

But above all the value of single-organization studies is that they require the broad concepts of a theory to be operationalized in a way which is appropriate for the particular situation being investigated. In doing this, the concepts may be clarified, extended and differentiated. The modified concepts may then be tested in yet different situations. This is perhaps particularly important in the case of theories developed on broad, qualitative grounds, such as the classical theory of bureaucracy.

Much of the research stimulated by the theory of bureaucracy[2] has been in the form of studies of one organization, or at most a small number of organizations. These empirical studies, however, have not been concerned with the growth of unionism or at most have mentioned it as a subsidiary issue, as in Crozier's study (1963). Nevertheless, in the most comprehensive theoretical discussion of white-collar unionism to date, Lockwood (1958) attributed an important role to the effects of the bureaucratic process.

Lockwood, using evidence from historical sources, largely from the nineteenth and early twentieth century, created a picture of clerical work in the pre-bureaucratic or minimally bureaucratic organisation. There the clerk enjoyed a relatively privileged position, based on paternal, personal and particularist treatment by his employer, and carrying special opportunities for upward social and economic movement. This position arose from the small size of the typical business, the informal and often idiosyncratic ways of working, the close contact between employer and clerk, and the development of a real dependence of the employer on the clerk as the latter accumulated a fund of highly personal administrative knowledge.

The development of the modern bureaucratic form of organization, employing large numbers of white-collar workers in relatively standard tasks, undermines this special relationship. It is replaced by formal and impersonal treatment, bound by rules and procedures, and limiting personal, economic and social opportunity. The bureaucratic process disposes white-collar workers to unionization partly because of these shifts in opportunity relative to expectation. Also, perhaps, the loss of the personal and particularist relationship and the submission to a set of impersonal rules may be disliked by the individual irrespective of the immediate effects on his economic or social situation. This point is clarified by Crozier's (1963) analysis of the bureaucratic process, where he shows how rules and formal relationships regulate power between work groups. As the employee loses his personal relationship with the employer or "boss," so also he loses his personal influence over the latter's actions. Individual powerlessness in a rule-bound situation (however benevolent the rules) may provide the basic link between bureaucracy and unionism.

To apply Lockwood's account of the historical growth of unionism to current developments in white-collar unions, it is of course necessary to adjust the focus. Most employees now work for organizations which would have been large and bureaucratic by the standards of the pre-bureaucratic organizations which Lockwood considered. Nevertheless the processes of rationalization, standardization, and formalization continue in many large but still growing organizations. Office work has been and continues to be systematized and mechanised. Salary structures and pay review procedures have become widely accepted in large organizations. Welfare provided formerly on an *ex gratia* basis has been progressively codified. And many of the "management techniques" widely introduced during the past decade — such as job evaluation, performance appraisal, and management-by-objectives — could be described as bureaucratic innovations, serving particularly to increase the objectivity and rationality of rules and relationships.

Gouldner (1955) has shown that even a quite limited growth of rules and rationalization can have a considerable impact on an already substantially bureaucratic organization. So it appears to be reasonable to extend Lockwood's theory, which originally related to change over a long time-period, and apply it to situations in single organizations over a short time-period.

Derived from the theory of bureaucracy, our main hypothesis is that as administrative particularism in the organization gives way to formalization of relationships, individuals affected by this change will have an increased disposition towards unionism. This should be true whether or not the change involves any direct material disadvantage. We can put this hypothesis in concrete terms by predicting an association between unfavourable opinions of bureaucratic policies and positive support of unionism.

While Lockwood's discussion is generally acknowledged as a major theoretical contribution, it has not greatly influenced empirical investigations. Much of the empirical work seeks to link unionism directly with individuals' disadvantage or dissatisfaction concerning pay, promotion or status. In a recent review of this evidence, Bain (1970) concluded that such "economic factors" do not help to explain the growth of white-collar unionism. An equally appropriate conclusion might be that it is impossible to evaluate most of these studies' results due to the lack of an explicit theoretical perspective. The question of what constitutes an "economic factor" in the employment situation is not trivial. Without a position being stated on this issue, it is difficult to decide whether a particular result supports the view that economic factors influence unionism. Another important question is whether economic factors should be given separate theoretical consideration, or be treated as part of the wider concept of rationality.

What is required, therefore, is a theoretical perspective within which one might pose "common-sense" questions about the influence of such matters as pay. One approach is provided by certain aspects of the organization theory of March and Simon (1958). March and Simon did not directly discuss the decision to join a union; but they provided a theory of rationality and a theory of organizational conflict, from which we can sketch a number of propositions about white-collar unionism.

Drawing on findings from psychology, they emphasize that an individual within an organization will normally be pursuing a variety of personal goals and aspirations. Which goals an individual decides to pursue depends on his "definition of the situation", and rationality is, therefore, fundamentally subjective and relative. Moreover, limitations on his intellectual capacity make it impossible for him to integrate his goals within a process of optimal decision making. Instead, goals remain fragmentary, diverse and shifting, and they are conceptualized in terms of satisfactory rather than optimal levels of attainment. The processes of goal selection and modification are guided by attention-focusing mechanisms, including identification with the goals of organizations or groups.

The March and Simon view of organizational conflict was as broad as their concept of rationality: thus, "conflict occurs when an individual or group experiences a decision problem." What we have called dissatisfaction with pay, for instance, could be described as a conflict situation; the individual does not know how to attain the level of pay which he has adopted as his goal. This would be just one of a very large class of conflict situations which arise in organizations.

A number of straightforward propositions relevant to the issue of unionism can be derived from the March and Simon perspective. First, when the individual experiences conflict (in the sense just described), he initiates a search to find some way round the problem. The greater the number of individual goals which are obstructed, the more extensive will be the process of search and, other things being equal, the greater the likelihood of union membership being focused upon as a potential solution. Another way in which the disposition to unionism may develop is through processes of identification. Given that the employing organization is perceived as a source of conflict, identification with its goals will tend to diminish, and there will be an increased identification with some other group or organization, such as a union.

The March and Simon theory of organization does not suggest which are the most important sources of conflict leading to unionism; on the contrary, the theory is open-ended and suggests that there may be many different sources of conflict, varying from one individual to the next even within an apparently uniform situation. The common-sense questions concerning pay or promotion are legitimate within this framework, but one would expect them to have an influence on unionism in some circumstances while having no influence in others. One would, however, hypothesize that the total number of individually perceived conflicts will have a general relationship with unionism. It is apparent from March and Simon's discussion of the decision to participate in or leave the organization that they consider attitudinal measures of satisfaction and dissatisfaction to be relevant to their discussion of conflict. We can, therefore, operationalize our second hypothesis by predicting an association between the sum of employees' dissatisfactions with the employment situation and their disposition towards unionism.

Of the two theoretical perspectives which have been advanced, that derived from the theory of bureaucracy leads to more specific propositions about white-collar unionism. It also differs from the March and Simon position in that it attributes to unionism a regulative or protective function, rather than a problem-solving or goal-directed function. It might be possible to analyse the regulation of power relationships, and thus to demonstrate that the March and Simon position included this as a special case. However, so little is said about the issue of power by March and Simon, and their presentation of issues is in general so heavily rationalist, that we will adopt the view that the theories are separate. We must then also suggest in what respects the two positions lead to different expectations.

If we press to its conclusion the viewpoint developed from the theory of bureaucracy, we would expect that only adverse reactions to the bureaucratic process would predispose employees to unionism, while factors which were more widely concerned with rational self-interest would have only a chance relationship with unionism. Conversely, the viewpoint derived from March and Simon suggests that the factors connected with bureaucratization will have an influence on unionism, if at all, in no different sense from the other sources of organizational conflict.

Another distinction between the two positions can be identified by introducing the additional concept of morale in the organization. This concept is given extended treatment by March and Simon, in terms of decisions to participate in or withdraw from the organization. The desire to withdraw from the organization is identified by them with measures of the individual's overall dissatisfaction. In the March and Simon perspective, it is reasonable to assume that the factors which increase the desire to withdraw also incorporate those which increase the probability of unionism. It is expected that there should be if anything an even stronger relationship of these factors with morale than with unionism[3], since they influence the desire to withdraw directly but are only indirectly associated with unionism, through the supposed intervening processes of search and identification. In relating the theory of bureaucracy to unionism, however, one does not make use of the concept of morale or desire to leave. If one found that there was an association between employees' reaction to bureaucratization and overall morale, one would feel less confident of the distinctness of this position from the more general theory of March and Simon.

It is now possible to summarize the propositions arising from this discussion of the two theoretical approaches:

(1) Propositions derived from the theory of bureaucracy:
    unfavourable reaction to bureaucratic developments are *positively* associated with support of unionism;
    other sources of conflict (for example, those related to issues of rational self-interest) are unrelated to support of unionism;
    reactions to bureaucratic developments are unrelated to employees' morale.
(2) Propositions derived from the March and Simon organizational theory:
    the sum of conflicts or dissatisfactions is positively related to support of unionism; reactions to bureaucratic developments can be represented as part of this sum of conflicts or dissatisfactions;
    the sum of conflicts or dissatisfactions is negatively related with morale, or positively related with the desire to withdraw from the organization.

These are the propositions to be considered in the empirical analysis, to which we now turn. First, however, it may be worth repeating that only within-organization factors are being considered in this analysis. This is not because the factors outside the organization are considered unimportant; there are indeed points of contact in the present analysis with broader across-organization studies of unionism.[4] The different levels of analysis, and different forms of measurement, should be considered complementary rather than conflicting.

THE ORIGINAL SURVEY

The Background

The survey can only be fully understood in the context of some major background developments. The first and perhaps central event leading to the survey was the introduction of new legislation to regulate the conduct of collective bargaining: the Industrial Relations Act, 1971. This legislation provided machinery for union recognition disputes which had previously not existed. Moreover the Commission on Industrial Relations (CIR), whose functions were prescribed in the Act but which had come into being in advance of it, had by its early activities given many people the impression that the Act must stimulate the process of union recognition.

Another major factor leading up to the survey was the period of considerable growth, during the late 1960s and early 1970s, experienced by the financial services sector: building societies, insurance companies, banking, credit finance, and various more specialized concerns. This provided two opportunities for white-collar unions. First, it increased the numbers of potential members in traditional types of finance service businesses, and often the increase in size went with technological change in the direction of mechanization. Second, it opened up new types of occupation around the fringes of the established finance industries, which again could be tapped for membership.

The survey arose from an initiative for recognition by the National Union of Bank Employees (NUBE) in the financial services sector but outside the traditional banking occupations. The company concerned had no tradition of staff representation whatever; indeed, until three years previously it had had very little in the way of formal personnel policies. At that stage, however, a personnel function had been set up (bringing in personnel specialists from manufacturing industry) and there had been a rapid development of more formal personnel policies and administration. This development included such things as the writing of job specifications, the creation of grading structures with associated salary bands, formal salary review procedures, a staff appraisal system, and a review of welfare and benefit provisions. Largely to evaluate the effect of these policies, the company planned to carry out an internal staff opinion survey. While this was being planned, however, NUBE made its request for recognition, based on membership that it had rapidly built up in one of the company's large central offices. The company wished to avoid a case in the National Industrial Relations Court, which might lead to a reference to the Commission on Industrial Relations. It therefore invited the research institution to conduct a dual-purpose survey, partly to evaluate personnel policies and partly to measure the amount of support among staff for a system of formal representation. This approach met with the approval of NUBE. It should be noted that the survey had the character in part of a ballot, because the company was committed to using the results for policy decisions. But it also provided an opportunity for studying the relationships between unionization choices and opinions of the employment situation.

Survey Procedures and Descriptive Results

The type of questionnaire used in the survey, and the data
collection procedures, were largely governed by the balloting
requirements of maximum participation and unambiguous
quantification. A structured and reasonably simple self-completion
form was used. The survey was planned as a census, not a sample
design. Staff in larger offices completed the questionnaire in
company canteens or conference rooms, under the supervision of
a researcher. Those in smaller offices (for example, branches)
completed questionnaires privately and singly in the local manager's
office or interview room, in accordance with a pre-arranged schedule.
The questionnaires were anonymous. These formal procedures were
preceded by preliminary investigations consisting of semi-structured
interviews, collection of documentary evidence, and pre-testing of
questionnaires by interview methods.

The structured questionnaire used in the survey included six main
types of item, which are outlined below. (The items which are
relevant to the theoretical issues will be discussed in more detail at
a later point.)

(1) Demographic items (age, sex, tenure, job grade — which is related to
    salary, and place of employment).
(2) Employment satisfaction items: these asked the employee to state
    whether or not he felt satisfied with various broad aspects of pay,
    promotion opportunities, training, job security, job interest, work
    pressure, working conditions, fringe benefits, and company
    reputation.
(3) Personnel policy items: these were a series of opinion questions
    concerning details of the company's policies relating to training, job
    grades, salary structures, holiday entitlements, staff appraisal, and
    so on. Many of these items were occasioned by new schemes which
    the company had introduced during the previous two years.
(4) Managerial relationship items: four items were included to assess the
    individual's perceptions of relationships with his manager.
(5) Unionization choice items: here individuals stated their support for
    or opposition to introducing staff representation through a union,
    with or without the development of a staff consultative committee
    system.
(6) Overall satisfaction rating: this was a single 6-point scale, on which
    the individual rated his overall satisfaction as an employee.

A total of 2,436 individuals, 94 per cent of the organization's employees, returned usable questionnaires. The major result of the survey was that the expressed support for unionization was at a much higher level than the existing union membership. NUBE had claimed a membership of about 8 per cent, but in the survey nearly a third of all the staff (31 per cent) declared themselves in favour of staff representation by means of a union. This result led to a rapid resolution of the basic practical issue: a procedural agreement was concluded between the company and NUBE, with clauses allowing for further development to a full bargaining relationship.

Remaining within a limited descriptive and practical approach, one next considered whether the support for unionization came particularly from any sectors of the company's employees. The overall results were, therefore, broken down in the customary way by various demographic classifications. Tabe 1 shows the results of such an analysis, for one of the central items evaluating support for union representation. It will be seen that there were *prima facie* differences in the amount of support from different job-grade levels, different locations in the company, and different age-groups. The stronger support for unionism came from the clerical rather than the professional and managerial job-grades, and from the under-30 age group rather than those aged 30 or over. Moreover, two large central offices, concerned mainly with routine paper-work functions, and also the large central computer department, were more favourable towards unions than staff in branch offices and in two central offices where the specialists and professionals tended to be concentrated. Men and women, however, showed the same level of support for unionism.

These results, it must be remembered, do not come from a stratified sample but from a population in which the various demographic classifications tend to be correlated. To allow for this, questions of central importance for the survey were analysed as large multi-way tables, in a series of 2×2^4 factorial designs; the factors, dichotomized on the basis of marginal distributions, were in each case location, job-grade, sex and age. The analysis method for such tables (Cox, 1970) takes account of the intercorrelations among variables and produces estimates of main and interaction effects.

When we considered in this way the item concerning support for union representation (see Table 1), we found that all four demographic factors had large effects, while the interactions were not significant. With age, grade and location held constant, men were

TABLE 1

SUPPORT FOR UNIONISM

Item: "I would like to see staff represented by a Union"

Per cent of row total answering:

Group	N	"Yes"	"No"	'Need more information' (that is, don't know)	No reply
Total survey	2,436	31	48	20	2
Clerical grades	1,586	34	43	21	2
Intermediate grades	460	33	49	17	0
Senior grades	390	17	65	17	1
Branch office staff	1,013	26	51	21	2
Central offices (mainly specialist)	544	25	58	16	1
Central offices (mainly clerical)	734	42	36	20	2
Computer centre	145	41	39	21	0
Men aged under 30	294	41	39	18	2
Men aged 30 or over	839	28	54	17	1
Women aged under 30	704	35	41	22	2
Women aged 30 or over	599	28	48	22	2

significantly more favourable towards union representation than were women. The effects of job-grade and of age, suggested by the analysis of Table 1, were also confirmed. Finally, the most important conclusion, the different locations in the company were shown to vary in their support for unionism, even when one had controlled statistically for the varying proportions of female, relatively young, and relatively low-paid staff in the different locations. Location of work was, therefore, confirmed as a variable in its own right, rather than merely a composite one reflecting the other demographic factors.

Another question which was considered at this stage was whether the different levels of support for union representation in different parts of the company might be related to different attitudes to their employment situation, as measured by the other groups of items which have been outlined above. The broad picture emerging from the survey was one of a rather high degree of expressed satisfaction with the employment situation. Of the total of employees, 86 per cent expressed themselves either satisfied, very satisfied, or completely satisfied in overall terms (this might be compared with Blauner's (1960) suggestion of an 80 per cent satisfaction norm), and none of the demographic subgroups of employees departed much from this result. At a rather qualitative level of description, one might point out that each of the three most pro-Union locations was relatively less satisfied in a number of specific aspects than the employees as a whole. For instance, at one of the three locations there were particularly frequent criticisms of lack of prospects for promotion; in one of the three, there were particularly frequent complaints of excessive work pressure; and in two of the three, there was particular dissatisfaction concerning physical working conditions. However, there was no one major source of dissatisfaction that was common to all three of the more pro-Union locations.

To summarize the descriptive results, then, we can say that the survey recorded a rather striking movement towards unionism within a situation of generally high satisfaction or morale. While the respondent's age, sex and job-grade were all related to support for union representation, so too was the location in the company which he or she worked within. This suggested that variations in the work situation, as perceived in different locations, might help to explain the degree of union support. However, no simple difference in attitudes to the work situation emerged from inspection of the descriptive results.

RE-ANALYSIS OF THE SURVEY

Operationalization of Variables

An outline description has been given in the previous section of the six main types of items contained in the original questionnaire. The first step in the re-analysis was to consider how these items might be recast and combined to form variables that could represent the theoretical issues of interest.

Let us first consider the main *dependent* variable arising from the theoretical discussion: disposition to unionism. This is the dependent variable of concern to both theoretical approaches. It was operationally defined by a combination of three items taken from the "unionization choice" items described in the previous section.

If an individual stated that he would like to see staff represented by a Union, he was scored +1. If he stated that he wanted the existing situation to continue (that is, no representation), and if consistent with this he supported neither a Union nor a staff committee form of representation, he was scored −1. Any intermediate position on these three items was scored 0. The empirical distribution across these categories was approximately uniform. Although other measures of disposition to unionism could be derived from the questionnaire, the measure selected is considered to be an intrinsically important one.[5]

A dependent variable of secondary importance in the theoretical discussion was "morale" or the desire to withdraw from the organization. The measure to be used for this is the "overall satisfaction rating." That this measure is generally related to labour turnover, to absenteeism, and to other measures of morale is attested by a wide range of empirical evidence (Argyle, 1972); it is also referred to by March and Simon as a suitable operational measure for their analogous concept of desire to withdraw from the organization.

We can now turn to the *independent* variables which represent the two different theoretical positions. Our development of the theory of bureaucracy suggests that where bureaucratic policies have been adopted within an organization, adverse reactions to these policies will be related to unionism. A number of items in the questionnaire referred directly to specific changes introduced during the previous two years in the direction of more formalized personnel policies. For example, there were a number of items concerning perceived repercussions of the introduction of job grading structures. On the basis of prior knowledge obtained from preliminary interviews with staff, we selected from the section concerned with "personnel policies" the seven items which appeared to be most directly linked in employees' thoughts with the new formalized methods of personnel administration. To this we added one item from the section concerning aspects of "employment satisfaction;" this item concerned work pressure, and although expressed in general terms we believed that it was connected in employees' thoughts with currently proceeding work rationalization and work measurement programmes. Thus there were eight items altogether in this group, which we now re-label "formalization of personnel policies."

A second variable suggested by the theory of bureaucracy concerned the impersonality of relationships between employees and their managers. All four items from the group we have previously called "managerial relationships" appeared to reflect the degree of impersonality in the organization. Since formalization and impersonality appeared to be distinct concepts, it was decided to keep this group separate from the previous one for purposes of analysis, even though both variables were derived from the same theory.

A more difficult problem arose when trying to operationalize the propositions drawn out from March and Simon's theories of rationality and conflict. These could be represented by a large number of items in the questionnaire. Any item reflecting a potential conflict between individual goals and what is available in the employment situation could be considered eligible for inclusion. It was decided, however, to represent this variable by an *a priori* selection of items giving a broad coverage of the main aspects of the employment situation, using the same number of items as that used in defining formalization of personnel policies. Two considerations were helpful in making this selection. First, one could draw from a large body of research into work satisfaction, which generally suggests that to most individuals the employment situation presents about half-a-dozen salient aspects (Hinrichs, 1968). Second, where one of the finer details of the situation is a source of conflict, we would expect that this would be at least reflected also among the individual's more general attitudes. For example, if the individual feels that the employer gives an inadequate canteen subsidy, and this is an issue of real concern to himself, then there will be an increased probability that he will also express dissatisfaction with the employer's provision of fringe benefits in general. In our selection of items, accordingly, we have included an item concerning the satisfactoriness of fringe benefits in general, but we have not included items concerning specific fringe benefits. By following these principles, we arrived at a selection of seven rather broad items, defining a variable which we label "employment conflict." This label is intended to convey that measures of employment satisfaction are being used to reflect the extent of conflict between the individual's goals and the employment situation.

The demographic items form the last class of variables to be considered. Demographic factors have no systematic role in either of the theoretical positions which have been described, but their actual effects on the data must not be ignored. Let us first review the nature of the demographic variables in this survey. Each demographic item might be called an organizational background variable, rather than a social background variable. In fact the demographic items were included in the questionnaire because they concerned real distinctions in the treatment of employees.[6] For example, in this organization as in many others, women have different pension rights from men; employees under the age of 21 are paid on different principles from those over 21; senior grades of staff enjoy special social privileges, as well as higher salaries than junior grades; different locations perform different types of task; and so on. Because the demographic groups differ in this way, it is not inconsistent with either of the theoretical viewpoints to find demographic effects on disposition to unionism. At the same time, however, one should be aware that these organizational background factors possibly also incorporate social background differences of the more familiar type. If they do, then they may introduce sources ·- of variation beyond those to be expected from the theoretical propositions. For this reason, each of the demographic variables was included in the re-analysis, as well as the theoretically defined variables. What we would hope, of course, is that the demographic effects will be much attenuated when the more powerful (as we assume) theoretical variables enter the analysis.

Specification of Hypotheses

Now that the operational variables have been described, it may be useful to restate the main theoretical propositions in terms of these variables:

(1) Propositions derived from the theory of bureaucracy, operationally modified:
    positive "disposition towards unionism" will be associated with adverse opinions concerning "formalization of personnel policies" and with perceived "impersonality of relationships with management;" "disposition towards unionism" will not be associated with any other variables relating to the employees' situation in the organization; "formalization of personnel policies" and "impersonality of relationships with management" will have no association with "overall satisfaction."
(2) Propositions derived from the March and Simon theory, operationally modified:
    "disposition towards unionism" will be associated with the number of individually perceived "employment conflicts;" opinions concerning any aspect of the employment situation, including

"formalization of personnel policies" or "impersonality of relationships with management" could be represented as part of the sum of "employment conflicts;" a large number of perceived "employment conflicts" will be associated with low levels of "overall satisfaction."

To complete the operationalization of the theories, we have to introduce some additional assumptions about the causal ordering of the variables. First, we assume that "formalization of personnel policies" and "impersonality of relationships with management" are not causally related, but co-related. This is because both are derived from the same theory by a similar process of reasoning and there are no grounds for placing one in a prior position to the other. Second, we assume that both these variables are causally related to "disposition to unionism," they may influence it but not be influenced by it. Third, and fourth, we assume that the "employment conflicts" variable is causally related to both "disposition to unionism" and "overall satisfaction." Fifth, we assume that "disposition to unionism" and "overall satisfaction" may be co-related but not causally related.

These assumptions, together with the preceding propositions, enable us to specify precisely which are the permissible models under the two theories. These are shown in Figure 1(a) and (b). Figure 1(a) illustrates the two variables drawn from the theory of bureaucracy influencing additively the disposition to unionism. Figure 1(b) shows how, in accordance with the propositions derived from March and Simon's theories, "employment conflicts" influence both unionism and overall satisfaction. It is also permissible for the other variables to enter the model, but only in the specific ways shown.

Methods of Analysis

The analysis procedure was: first, to form appropriate combinations of items to represent the variables; second, to assess and if necessary adjust for the effects of demographic variables; and third, to conduct a series of multiple and partial correlation analyses to examine the plausibility of the various models which have been discussed above. Statistical testing procedures have not been used, since this survey concerned a population rather than a sample, and rather a substantial population at that (2,436 respondents). Inferences have been based on the relative magnitude and stability of relationships rather than "significance" in the limited statistical sense.

(a) Unionism influenced by bureaucratic process

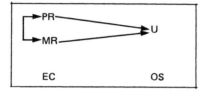 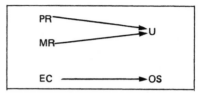

(b) Unionism influenced by the individual's experience of conflict between his goals and the employment situation

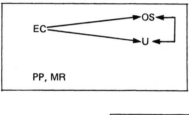 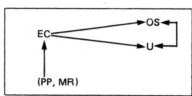

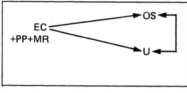

Figure 1. MODELS CONSISTENT WITH THE THEORETICAL PROPOSITIONS
Key: EC: "employment conflicts" PP: "formalization of personnel policies"
MR: "impersonality of managerial relationships", U: "disposition to unionism",
OS: "overall satisfaction".

The matrix of simple correlations among all the items discussed above was obtained in order to check the satisfactoriness of the groupings. The intra-group correlations were in all cases sufficiently large relative to extra-group correlations to confirm the original pattern of groupings. On the other hand they were in no case so large that one could consider elimination of an item on grounds of redundancy. Accordingly, each of the variables ("formalization of personnel policies," "impersonality of managerial relationships," "employment conflicts") was formed as the unweighted sum of the items originally selected.

The categories within each demographic variable were treated as binary. The correlations of these classes with the other items were generally small. More important, perhaps, was the question of whether the demographic items interacted with the other variables. This was checked by searching for any marked change in correlation from one class of demographic variable to another. There was only one case where this appeared to be potentially a problem: the "place of employment" or location variable. Certain items correlated more highly with some locations than with others. It was, therefore, decided to carry out three types of analyses:

(1) multiple and partial correlation, including demographic variables;
(2) multiple and partial correlation, excluding demographic variables;
(3) multiple and partial correlation, excluding demographic variables, but with separate analyses for each of the places of employment.

The analyses showed that the system of relationships between the five variables of theoretical interest changed little when the demographic variables were partialled out. However, the relationships did differ quite markedly in some respects when separate analyses were obtained for the different places of employment. In the following section, therefore, attention will be focused on the analyses in which the effects of demographic variables have not been partialled out, but the picture for each location will also be separately presented.

RESULTS OF THE RE-ANALYSIS

The simple correlation matrix for the five variables of theoretical interest is presented in Table 2. All the correlations are substantial, especially if one bears in mind the size of the population. The bottom row of the table shows the simple correlations between disposition to unionism and the other four variables. All the signs are negative, which is consistent with the central hypothesis from both theories. Another feature of the results is that "employment conflicts" is more highly correlated with each other variable than is any other variable. Therefore, this variable is likely to occupy a central position in the structure of relationships.

The corresponding partial correlation matrix (that is, pairwise correlations, with the other three variables held constant) is given in Table 3. This shows that there are substantial correlations between both "employment conflicts" and "disposition to unionism" and between "formalization of personnel policies" and "disposition to unionism." However, there is a very small correlation between "impersonality of managerial relationships" and "disposition to unionism." So the central hypothesis that disposition to unionism is influenced by the bureaucratic process is partly confirmed, because

TABLE 2

SIMPLE CORRELATIONS BETWEEN MAJOR VARIABLES

N = 2,436				
	EC	PP	MR	OS	U
EC	1				
PP	0.5092	1			
MR	0.4393	0.4107	1		
OS	0.4415	0.2885	0.3053	1	
U	−0.3079	−0.3040	−0.2031	−0.2247	1

KEY: EC: "employment conflicts," PP: "formalization of personnel policies,"
MR: "Impersonality of Managerial Relationships," OS: "overall satisfaction,"
U: "disposition to unionism."

TABLE 3

PARTIAL CORRELATIONS BETWEEN MAJOR VARIABLES

N = 2,436				
	EC	PP	MR	OS	U
EC	1				
PP	0.3345	1			
MR	0.2319	0.2260	1		
OS	0.3000	0.0360	0.1193	1	
U	−0.1338	−0.1623	−0.0267	−0.0871	1

KEY: as Table 2.
For each entry in the above Table, the remaining three variables are held constant.

employee attitudes rejecting formalized personnel policies tend to be connected with pro-union dispositions. On the other hand, perceived impersonality of relationships with management does not seem to be connected with pro-union dispositions; this other aspect of the first main hypothesis is not confirmed. The hypothesis derived from the rational conflict theory is confirmed by the substantial correlation of "employment conflicts" with "disposition to unionism."

The fact that both of the central hypotheses are supported by these results entails that the secondary propositions, which claim for each theory that it is a complete explanation of unionism, are not

supported. The other subsidiary propositions, concerning the
relationships of the theoretically derived independent variables to
overall satisfaction, are, however, supported by the partial
correlations. The partial correlation of "formalization of personnel
policies" with "overall satisfaction" is small, as expected; the partial
correlation of "employment conflicts" with "overall satisfaction"
is large, also as expected.

It appears that although a number of the original propositions are
supported by these analyses, no one of the models presented in
Figure 1 is appropriate. Figure 2 summarises the chief observed
relationships between the variables, for purposes of comparison.

At this stage it might seem tempting to develop a full path model
of the relationships. However, as is apparent on inspection of the
correlations, the amount of residual variation is large. In this
circumstance it is difficult to see how one can justify making the
very strong assumptions required for causal modelling. The partial
correlations are close to the values of the coefficients one would
enter in a path model developed from Figure 2. Moreover, they have
a limited and straightforward interpretation.

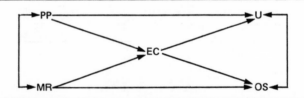

Figure 2: MODEL BASED ON OBSERVED RELATIONSHIPS
Key: as Figure 1.

A criticism which could be made of the analysis represented by
Table 3 is that the effects of the overall satisfaction variable have
been partialled out from the other relationships, whereas it should
perhaps be excluded from consideration on the grounds that it is at
a higher level. Tables 4 and 5 show the results when the 5 x 5 matrix
of partial correlations is reduced to two 4 x 4 matrices, overall
satisfaction being omitted from the first and disposition to unionism
from the second. These analyses show that the general pattern of
results established by the 5 x 5 table is preserved in the sub-tables,
although as one would expect the coefficients are now in general
a little larger. These comparisons show the high degree of stability in
the analyses.

TABLE 4

PARTIAL CORRELATIONS OMITTING "OVERALL SATISFACTION"

	EC	PP	MR	U
	N = 2,436			
EC	1			
PP	0.3622	1		
MR	0.2827	0.2321	1	
U	−0.1683	−0.1661	−0.0375	1

Key: as Table 2

TABLE 5

PARTIAL CORRELATIONS OMITTING "DISPOSITION TO UNIONISM"

	EC	PP	MR	U
	N = 2,436			
EC	1			
PP	0.3643	1		
MR	0.2377	0.2335	1	
OS	0.3157	0.0510	0.1222	1

Key: as Table 2

As already mentioned, it was considered necessary to repeat the correlational analysis for each of the main "places of employment" in the company. These locations were (1) the branch offices of the organization, providing 1,013 respondents; (2) the specialist central offices, with 544 respondents; (3) a central office carrying out mainly clerical functions for the main part of the company's business, with 475 respondents; (4) a similar clerical office, but physically situated some distance apart and dealing with a different segment of business, with 259 respondents; (5) the company's computer centre, physically situated at location (3) but servicing the whole organization, with 145 respondents. Locations (3), (4) and (5) were the most pro-union.

Table 6 shows the five tables of partial correlations, one for each location, derived from 4 x 4 correlation matrices (overall satisfaction

TABLE 6

PARTIAL CORRELATIONS, OMITTING "OVERALL
SATISFACTION," FOR STAFF AT VARIOUS
LOCATIONS IN THE ORGANIZATION

		EC	*PP*	*MR*	*U*
(i)					
N = 1,013	EC	1			
	PP	0.3464	1		
	MR	0.2504	0.1920	1	
	U	−0.1547	−0.1276	−0.0244	1
(ii)					
N = 544	EC	1			
	PP	0.3490	1		
	MR	0.3279	0.2070	1	
	U	−0.1031	−0.1872	−0.1038	1
(iii)					
N = 475	EC	1			
	PP	0.4094	1		
	MR	0.2746	0.2035	1	
	U	−0.1641	−0.1588	−0.0176	1
(iv)					
N = 259	EC	1			
	PP	0.4272	1		
	MR	0.1958	0.2578	1	
	U	−0.2026	−0.2088	−0.0295	1
(v)					
N = 145	EC	1			
	PP	0.4716	1		
	MR	0.1548	0.3414	1	
	U	−0.1252	−0.2703	−0.1754	1

Key: as Table 2
Groups: (i) branch staff, (ii) central office, mainly specialist, (iii) and (iv) central offices,
mainly clerical, (v) computer centre.

now being omitted from all). The important similarity between these
tables is that in each case there is the expected negative correlation
between "formalization of personnel policies" and "disposition to
unionism," and also between "employment conflicts" and
"disposition to unionism." There is in each case too a large positive
correlation between the "personnel policies" and "employment
conflict" variables. Thus the main features of the analysis for the
whole population are preserved in the locational analyses.

Where the locational results differ appreciably, however, is in the
"managerial relationships" variable. In three locations the relation of

this variable to union disposition is negligible, but in one group, group (2), it is of moderate size and in the expected direction, while in the case of computer staff, group (5), it is substantial and in the opposite direction to that expected. Among these, staff who feel their managers have preserved personal relationships with them are more likely, rather than less likely, to be in favour of union representation.

SUMMARY OF FINDINGS

The results which have been described can now be compared with the theoretical propositions that were initially advanced. They fall into three classes: findings that are in accord with theoretical propositions, findings that are contrary to theoretical propositions, and findings which are not related to any theoretical propositions.

First, the main hypothesis concerning unionism from each of the two theoretical positions is supported by the findings. The partial correlation between "attitudes to personnel policies," the major variable representing reaction to the bureaucratic process, and disposition to unionism, is quite substantial, and is consistently maintained for subgroups of employees in different parts of the organization. "Employment conflicts," the variable representing the March and Simon rational conflict theory, has a very similar partial correlation with disposition to unionism, and this relationship is also stable across subgroups. It should be noted that one has obtained this result with the composite "employment conflicts" variable even though none of the component items within it, such as satisfaction with pay, has a substantial correlation with disposition to unionism.

The subsidiary hypotheses, which distinguish the two theoretical positions by postulating different relationships of their independent variables with overall satisfaction or morale, are also supported by the results. We expected to find the sum of conflicts or dissatisfactions at least as strongly related to morale (as measured by overall satisfaction), as it is to unionism; we actually find that it is more strongly related to morale than it is to unionism. We did not expect to find a relationship between reactions to bureaucratisation and morale, and there is none.

The propositions which are not consistent with the results of the analyses are those which assert the completeness of one theoretical explanation to the exclusion of the other. The proposition asserting the completeness of the theory of bureaucracy as an explanation, implies that the rational conflict variable should have zero correlation with unionism when the bureaucratization variable is held constant. This, as we have seen, is not the case. The proposition asserting the completeness of the rational conflict formulation, implies that if the bureaucratization variable is related to unionism, then it will also be related to morale; and this is not so.

One of the results which does not fit into the original set of propositions is the substantial positive relationship of "formalization of personnel policies" with "employment conflicts." This can most simply be interpreted as the result of the difficulty of operationalizing the two theories in a way which is completely distinct. As defined in our variables, adverse attitudes to specific personnel policies representing bureaucratization were themselves, it appears, components of the more general dissatisfactions representing rational conflict. But the relationship is not so large as to invalidate the distinction between the two concepts. Their distinctness is independently supported by the results already summarized, concerning the pattern of partial correlations with unionism and with morale.

The other group of results which does not fit the original propositions concerns the variable "managerial relationships." It was expected that this variable would reflect reaction to bureaucratization, would be correlated with attitudes to formalized personnel policies, and would have the same relationships as the latter with other variables. But although it is positively related with attitudes to formalized personnel policies, it has a quite different pattern of relationships with the other variables from what was expected, and these relationships are not wholly stable across the various subgroups of employees working in different parts of the company. This discordant set of results will be discussed further in the concluding section which follows.

IMPLICATIONS OF THE STUDY

The factual results of the re-analysis have now been presented, and we can consider to what extent they have contributed towards the theoretical understanding of white-collar unionism, or towards the practical issues of industrial relations policy.

The first requirement is to assess how well the two sets of

theoretical propositions have fared in the re-analysis. The neatest result would have been for one or the other theoretical position to have been strongly supported to the exclusion of the other. In fact, however, both sets of propositions have received a moderate amount of support. It is necessary to consider separately the support which each theoretical approach has obtained, but also whether the two can be in some sense combined.

Each of the two theories has pointed towards relationships which are neither trivial nor easily predicted. The situation analyzed was one of incipient but rapidly developing union support. It was found that employees' opinions about a number of newly formalized personnel policies, such matters as the fixing of holiday entitlement on the basis of job grading, were associated with their views on unionism, even though the former had no direct relationship with their overall satisfaction or "morale." A common-sense viewpoint would surely be that these issues were too minor to have an effect on such an important development as unionism. Because the theory of bureaucracy has focused attention on these otherwise easily neglected factors, its fruitfulness has been confirmed.

A similar point can be made concerning the other set of propositions, derived from the March and Simon theories of rationality and conflict. In no one area of the employment situation did individual dissatisfaction correlate substantially with support for unionism; for instance, whether or not an individual was satisfied with his earnings was a poor predictor of his position concerning union representation. However, by summing the dissatisfactions across all the main aspects of the employment situation, we obtained an index which was related to union support, and was also related to overall satisfaction or "morale." So, while the still widely held viewpoint that economic advantage lies behind unionism can not be supported by these results, a wider concept of subjectively rational advantage, derived from March and Simon, can be re-introduced as an explanation.

Insofar as the two theoretical positions are supported, therefore, we can advance the view that two factors within the organization increase the disposition to unionism. One is the factor of power relationships, which are altered or put under stress as bureaucratization advances; unionism may be seen as a means of regulating power within the organization. The second factor is the individual's desire to achieve his own subjectively rational advantage; to the extent that this is frustrated, he scans his environment for alternative means of pursuing it, of which unionism may be one.

The question arises as to whether these two factors are completely distinct or whether they might be integrated by reference to some more general concept. The existence of a substantial correlation between the two sets of operational measures should not be given undue prominence in assessing this question, since this could reflect more on the operations used than on the underlying concepts. In other words, we may have impure or overlapping measures even though the concepts are logically distinct. In this case, we have two types of empirical evidence to offset against the correlation of the main independent variables. One point is that these variables have separate relationships with disposition to unionism, even when all other influences have been statistically controlled, and these relationships are stable across subgroups of the population. The other point is that the variables have quite different relationships from one another with the "morale" variable. These points help to put into perspective the correlation between the two independent variables.

Returning to the conceptual level, one can point to underlying similarities and meeting-points between the theory of bureaucracy, especially in some of its later developments, and the March and Simon theory of organizations; a discussion along these lines has been provided by Mouzelis (1967). Our view, however, is that the concepts of power and power regulation have implications which are not adequately dealt with in the theoretical tradition concerned with rational, goal-directed behaviour. In the field of white-collar unionism it appears reasonable to preserve these two points of view. In particular, the theory of bureaucracy suggests that unionism is a defensive response by employees to the developing processes in their organization; the March and Simon viewpoint allows to the goal-pursuing individual the chance to take the initiative.

So far we have concentrated on interpreting the positive features of the results, but there was one main variable for which the expected relationships did not obtain. This was the variable labelled "impersonality of relationships with management." In some accounts of the bureaucratic process, a great deal of attention has been given to the factor of impersonal relationships between superior and subordinate; in Crozier's account, for instance, the need for this impersonality is presented as one of the mainsprings of bureaucracy. Moreover, in the present survey a large proportion of the employees gave critical replies to each of the questions concerning the relationships with their manager. The failure to find any relationship between the variable and disposition to unionism points to the need for further differentiation of this concept. One possibility is to investigate not the individual's relationships with his personal superior, but his perceptions of the norms in the organization as a whole. Possibly it is the norm of impersonal relationships, rather than the character of a specific relationship, which may influence disposition to unionism. If, however, it is not possible to find a path connecting impersonality of relationships with unionism, then one would have to accept a narrower application of the theory of bureaucracy to this field.

Another feature which might be considered a limitation of the results is that only a modest proportion of the variance of "disposition to unionism" has been accounted for by the relationships with the theoretical variables. But if one relates the measures which have been used to the theoretical positions from which they have been derived, one may feel that the magnitude of the relationships is more impressive than at first sight. In particular, one should take the time factor into consideration. Through the organizational survey, one has assessed the effects of easily identifiable aspects of the formalization of policies and procedures, selected on the basis of events in the organization during the previous two years. But this process of formalization is likely to be a continuing one. If one integrated the effects of the bureaucratic process over a longer time period, they should cumulate to a much larger factor. This of course is the advantage of the historical perspective used by Lockwood, Bain and others. By focusing on the details of a specific situation, the present survey has provided a relatively direct demonstration of a relationship of moderate size rather than an indirect argument for a relationship of considerable size.

The same point may also hold for the measure of "employment conflicts." Only the immediately present areas of conflict are measured by the survey, in the form of statements of dissatisfaction, but the whole employment history of the individual may have a cumulative effect on his disposition to unionism. For instance, we can imagine that an individual's receptivity to unionism is progressively changed by his experience of dissatisfactions in the organization, so that the total effect from this source might be greater than the effect obtained by measuring only his attitudes to the present situation.

Finally, one should consider whether the re-analysis of the survey (which was originally conducted for practical ends) has contributed to policy issues as well as to theoretical questions. In the context of this study the main participants in policy issues would be employers and unions.

It has already been noted that in this particular situation, the level of employees' satisfaction or morale was high, yet unionism was rapidly developing. This represents a paradox for a widely popular viewpoint in industrial circles, which believes that an increase in unionism is indicative of a deteriorating situation within an organization. This belief is part of a general position which Fox (1966) has called the "unitary" view of industry. According to this, employers and employees share overriding common interest and conflict therefore stems from pathological or irrational behaviour by one or other of the parties. Another aspect of this viewpoint, which Fox also discusses, is the belief that the function of unions is confined to wage bargaining. This also is not supported by the present survey, where little relationship is found between attitudes to earnings and disposition towards unionism.

Probably the main policy contribution of the re-analysis, therefore is in adding further evidence of the misleading nature of the "unitary" viewpoint, and providing an alternative viewpoint which suggests that a different set of attitudes and beliefs would be more realistic.

The theory of bureaucracy presents white-collar unionism as a natural accompaniment to the type of organization which is characteristic of our society, and suggests that the sharing and regulation of power will be a basic concern of unionism. The March and Simon notion of subjective and relative rationality leads to a broad view of what individuals may seek from unionism, and suggests that individuals may follow many different paths to goal fulfilment, of which unionism may be only one. Industrial relations may best be conducted on the understanding that unionism is a natural development and most useful when the scope of its role is wide.

APPENDIX

WORDING OF ITEMS USED IN THE ANALYSIS

Below are given, first, the name by which a variable is referred to in the text, and then the wording of the item or items used to measure the variable.

Variable: "disposition to unionism"

I would like to see staff represented by a Union.
I would like to see a staff committee system set up.
I would like to see staff representation continue as it is.
(Each of these items could be answered "Yes", "No", "Need more information.")

Variable: "overall satisfaction"

Taking the overall view, how would you rate your satisfaction as an employee of the XYZ Co? (Completely satisfied, very satisfied, satisfied, dissatisfied, very dissatisfied, completely dissatisfied).

Variable: "formalization of personnel policy"

The company expects more work from its staff than most companies
More information about job grades should be given to all the staff
Holiday entitlement should depend on job grade.
There is not enough reward for extra responsibility
My job grading gives me too little scope to improve my salary
Everyone doing the same job should get the same salary increase
From your own point of view, how would you rate your last appraisal interview. (Very helpful, satisfactory, little help, did more harm than good, not applicable).
(With the exception of the last item, for which the rating scale is given above, the response categories were "definitely agree," "agree," "disagree," "definitely disagree;" scoring was based on whether the reply indicated a positive or adverse opinion concerning recent known changes in policy).

Variable: "employment conflicts"

The company has a good reputation with outside people
I am not satisfied with my working conditions
The company provides good fringe benefits for staff
I am often bored with my job
I am happy about the chances I have for promotion
On the whole, my present salary is fair
I feel secure about my future with the company
(The response categories were "definitely agree," "agree,"
"disagree," "definitely disagree;" scoring depended on whether the
response indicated a satisfied or a dissatisfied attitude).

Variable: "impersonality of managerial relationships"

My boss does little to develop my skills and abilities
My boss is friendly and willing to talk
My boss often asks staff what they think before making a decision
which affects them
My boss keeps closely in touch with the views of staff
(The response categories were "definitely agree," "agree,"
"disagree," "definitely disagree.)"

NOTES

1. This re-analysis was part of a broader research project concerning the analysis of employee attitudes, supported by a grant from the Social Science Research Council.

2. The term "bureaucracy" in this paper is always used in the technical sense of an ideal type of administration towards which organizations tend, as originally described by Weber.

3. In neither position is it suggested that there should be a relationship between unionism and morale, but from the March and Simon view-point one might expect a spurious correlation between unionism and morale, due to common antecedent factors.

4. Bain (1970) presented a model of white-collar union growth which he called "strategic" because it concerned itself only with variables affecting unionism on an industry-wide, indeed a national and historical, scale and not with variables at the local or organizational level. One variable in this model is, however, connected with the present within-organization analysis: what Bain calls employment concentration. At the strategic level, employment concentration is important because it facilitates union recruitment, which is

necessarily directed to organizations employing large numbers of potential members. However, as Bain recognises, employment concentration also reflects the size and specialization of organizations — factors associated with the bureaucratic process. The facilitative effects of employment concentration on union recruitment should be carefully distinguished from the supposed effects of the bureaucratic process in predisposing employees to unionism. The facilitative effects can reasonably be assessed at the strategic level chosen by Bain. The influence of bureaucratization on dispositions to unionism can be directly assessed only by looking within organizations, as in the present analysis.

5. A complete listing of the items used in the re-analysis is provided in an Appendix.

6. This point may be clarified by referring to some social background variables not included, for example, father's occupation or locality of home. These variables are unrelated to organizational policies and so were not included.

REFERENCES

ARGYLE, M., (1972). *The Social Psychology of Work*. Penguin Books.
BAIN, G.S., (1970). *The Growth of White-Collar Unionism*. Oxford.
BLAUNER, R., (1960). Work Satisfaction and Industrial Trends in Modern Society, in GALENSON, W. and LIPSET, S. (eds.), *Labour and Trade Unionism*. Wiley.
COX, D.R., (1970). *Analysis of Binary Data*. Methuen.
CROZIER, M., (1963) *The Bureaucratic Phenomenon*. Tavistock.
FOX, A. (1966). *Industrial Sociology and Industrial Relations*. Research Papers 3, Royal Commission on Trade Unions and Employers' Associations. HMSO.
GOULDNER, A.W., (1955). *Patterns of Industrial Bureaucracy*. Routledge and Kegan Paul.
HINRICHS, J.R., (1968). A Replicated Study of Job Satisfaction Dimensions. *Personnel Psychology*, Vol. 21, 479-503.
LOCKWOOD, D., (1958). *The Black-Coated Worker*. Allen and Unwin.
MARCH, J.G., and SIMON, H.A., (1958). *Organizations*. Wiley.
MOUZELIS, N.P. (1967). *Organizations and Bureaucracy*. Routledge and Kegan Paul.

Chapter 6

MANAGEMENT STYLE AND ECONOMIC SUCCESS IN INDUSTRY[1]

Timothy Leggatt

INTRODUCTION

This study is concerned with the loosely defined area shared by the sociology of organizations and management theory. On the theoretical side its object is to identify models of management (also more colloquially referred to here as management styles), taking discussions in the literature as a starting point. On the empirical side it seeks to relate management styles with measures of economic success.

The theoretical assumptions of the study may be stated in the following two general propositions:

(1) variations in technological and commercial environment (that is, in sector of industry) together with variations in size, are associated in industrial organizations with the development of different styles of management.
(2) variations in styles of management are associated with variations in economic success beyond that attributable to differences between sectors of industry.

These assumptions, and the relationships which it is the purpose of this chapter to explore, are illustrated in Figure 1.

Figure 1. KEY VARIABLES IN THE ANALYSIS

The plan of the analysis that follows is to specify, operationalize and test these propositions, first by identifying types of management style and, second, by exploring the relationships of these styles to economic success measures and to other relevant variables.

THE NATURE OF THE DATA

The opportunity to examine these issues has arisen for the writer out of a survey research project undertaken in 1970 with quite other aims in view.[2] At that time, he undertook a study concerned to identify the country's need and demand for management education and training throughout the decade of the 1970s, and the research aimed (a) to provide a descriptive account of what management education and training were being undertaken or made use of by employers of managers or their equivalents and were being experienced by these same managers, and (b) to assess the extent to which the real management education and training needs of employing organizations and their managers were being, and could be, met.

The policies that the research brought under review were the management training policies of organizations employing managers and those of agencies, such as Industry Training Boards, concerned to maintain the activities and to encourage the development of management training courses and practices. The conclusions of the research were that

(1) no across-the board prescriptions about management training could reasonably be made since
(2) the management training needs of organizations and their managers varied according to the size and economic sector of the organization and the age, education, position, level, function and prior training of the manager. However, it was estimated that
(3) the demand for management training would be maintained and even increased at least up to 1975 owing to the continuing growth of the managerial labour force. It was also noted that
(4) too little systematic attention was being paid to identification of the real management training needs of managers.

This research was carried out by means of two social surveys. These were neither guided nor their results interpreted within a framework of sociological theory.

Material on firms employing managers was collected in 1970 by means of an interview survey. These data have now been reconceptualised for use in the analysis of management styles. Data used to indicate commercial success were freshly gathered for the purpose of the present paper.[3]

The 1970 sample of 278 industrial companies included those active in the following areas of manufacturing industry: food, oil and petroleum, chemicals and allied products, mechanical engineering (including motor vehicle manufacture), electrical and instrument engineering, clothing, printing and publishing. Also included were firms in the following non-manufacturing fields: construction, retail and wholesale distribution, road transport, banking, insurance and building societies. The sample was a national sample stratified according to the size of the firm's labour force, using the following categories:

(1) firms with 10,000 or more employees
(2) firms with 1,000–9,999 employees
(3) firms with 500–999 employees
(4) firms with 100–499 employees

The geographical locations accepted as being highly industrialized, such that clustering would naturally occur as the sector samples were drawn, and therefore readily accessible, were as follows: Birmingham; Cardiff/Bristol; Edinburgh/Glasgow; Home Counties (accessible from London); Hull; Leeds/Bradford; Liverpool; London; Manchester; Newcastle and the North East; Nottingham/Derby; Sheffield.

It was evident from the outset of the earlier study that even stratified random sampling of the selected sectors would not provide an adequate number of organizations in the largest size category. In this case, therefore, either all the organizations in the sector with over 10,000 employees were chosen or the largest organizations and those most widely recognized to be dominant in the sector. On the basis of early enquiries and soundings, it was decided also to over-represent (in terms of their incidence in the total population of organizations) the 1,000–9,999 employee category on the ground of the much greater activity in management training of organizations with 1,000 or more employees.

In view of the difficulties encountered in obtaining an adequate sampling frame the sample of organizations drawn for the 1970 study could not be considered representative of the sub-populations of organizations in each of the chosen sectors of industry. Its relationship to all organizations of the relevant size either in the country as a whole or in the selected sectors and regions was unknown. However, from the viewpoint of the present study this is not of great consequence since what is here required is that the sample adequately represents

(1) the range of sizes of firm in which a recognizable management structure exists (thus, firms with less than 100 employees are excluded), and
(2) sectors of industry exemplifying employment variations, in this case in (a) the employment of scientists and technologists and (b) distribution of employment between establishments of different size.

In any event, there was and is no firm reason to believe that the sample is not representative of the universe of samples (of unknown bias) that might have been drawn in a similar manner from a frame constructed from available published sources.

THEORETICAL PERSPECTIVE

Models of Management

Throughout much of the writing in the sociology of organizations and in much of the management literature runs the theme that there are two or three clearly recognizable models of management. These are ideal types, and, although mixed types are admitted as possible, normally it is suggested that the majority of real organizations approximate to the ideal or polar types.

The first model, variously called Weberian, bureaucratic or mechanistic, embodies the characteristics first identified by Max Weber: a clear-cut division of labour, a hierarchical structure of authority, a consistent system of abstract rules of procedure, the exercise of impersonal, impartial, rational standards, and the employment of qualified personnel in secure careers.[4] This model in origin is mechanistic. It likened organizations to machine-like structures designed to achieve optimal performance in stable conditions; whose members were aiming to behave with the discipline and impersonality of cog-wheels going through repetitious and routine motions; and the prime criteria of whose working were efficiency and rationality. At one time the analogy was very possibly apt for the majority of industrial concerns (though it was in fact derived from analysis of the working of public administration) and even today it may be apt for those least affected by environmental change.

However, for very many organizations it has long since been seen to be or to have become inappropriate. The environment of business administration is far from stable when each enterprise's transactions with its environment have multiplied through government interventions, market shifts, international events, and so forth. There is often an acute need for great internal flexibility and for ready and quick responsiveness to the environment. The goals of an organization, seldom if ever as rationally formulated and clarified as the traditional theory implied, not infrequently poorly understood and even to some degree irreconcilable, are far from static. They are likely to require constant scrutiny and modification in the light of internal resource factors or external turbulence. And once goals or at least sub-goals are subject to revision, the same inevitably holds for internal structures, unit goals, individual targets and job specifications, and routine rules and procedures.

Hence alternative models of management have been conceptualized. Of these the principal model is one in which the organization is treated as analogous to an organism or an open system rather than a machine; in which conflict and bargaining are seen as normal and legitimate internal processes as much as is smooth running consensus. This second model exemplifies fluidity of communications, looseness of structure, diffuseness of authority and informality of interaction. Under this model organizations are expected to be able to respond to critical or ambiguous situations, for example, to sudden developments in technology or the market, and to redeploy resources accordingly; the prime criteria of their workings are flexibility and adaptability to the environment and humane responsiveness to employees.[5]

These two models still hold the centre of the field of organizational sociology despite the attempts of various writers to proffer a third, mediating or mixed, model.[6] And they are directly echoed by writers on management who in their concern with management styles, philosophies and values still maintain the distinction enshrined in McGregor's Theory X and Theory Y; between the traditional philosophy of management by direction and control and the newer, social scientifically respectable and apparently more humanly sympathetic philosophy of management by integration of individual and organizational goals and by self-control.[7]

The first main aim of the present study, approached from this theoretical context, is to identify empirically the types and dimensions of management style actually exemplified by industrial firms in this country. It was further hypothesized that the two principal factors influencing the management style adopted by a firm were (a) its size and (b) its sector of industry, given that sector of industry is a summary indicator of, first, the market situation in relation to its product or service and, second, its technology. Variation of management style is therefore analyzed by treating style as a dependent variable in relation to size of firm and industrial sector.

Economic Success: The Management Gap

Although fashions and fads come and go in the management education and training field, one assumption is steadfast: that commercial and industrial success is at least partly dependent on a management factor. Hence if this country lags behind others in economic growth, it could in part be due to a "management gap." Hence also, when some firms are more successful (whatever the criterion) than other comparable firms, some recognition is due to superior management.

This study converts this assumption into a hypothesis by examining the association of management style and economic success. Firms have been differentiated according to a scale based on three linked measures of economic success; (i) profitability, (ii) the stability of profits, and (iii) growth in assets, all calculated over a five year period. The association is then examined between management style and economic success.

IDENTIFICATION OF MANAGEMENT STYLES

Consideration of discussions about management systems and management philosophies to be found in the literature suggested that two dimensions underlay the distinction between the mechanistic and organic styles of management.[8] The first dimension appeared to be that of the fluidity-rigidity of the management system in terms of who is a manager, how he becomes one and what he does. At one end of the spectrum the definition of who is a manager is conservative and restricted; recruitment and promotion opportunities are precise and narrowly channelled, and qualifications are not necessarily thought about but are rigid; jobs are defined by tradition. At the other end all these definitions and processes are more open and fluid, and issues relating to them are tackled in a professional managerial, rather than traditional, manner. This we term the *flexibility* dimension.

Seven questions from the 1970 survey have been taken to tap management flexibility:

A. whether foremen or supervisors were considered to be managers (inclusive, open) or not (exclusive, restricted),

B. whether senior specialists of rank equivalent to managers were considered to be managers (inclusive, open) or not (exclusive, restricted),

C. where junior managers were recruited from outside as well as inside the company (inclusive, open) or not (exclusive, restricted),

D. where senior managers were recruited from outside as well as inside the company (inclusive, open), or not (exclusive, restricted),

E. whether higher educational or professional qualifications were required of some managers (open-minded) or not (limited vision, conservative),

F. whether managers were thought not to need technical skills so much as management skills (broad view) or were though to need technical (rather than management) skills (limited view),

G. whether job specifications for managers were used for performance appraisal or assessment of training needs (alert, flexible) or for other purposes (intermediate) or not used at all (traditional).

The second dimension underlying traditional typologies appeared to be that of manager-centredness: of readiness to involve a manager directly in the making of decisions affecting himself, to allow a measure of manager autonomy. This dimension, which we call the *autonomy* dimension, varies from the allowance of autonomy through traditional paternalism (benevolent or otherwise) to virtual neglect. It is taken to have been tapped by four questions asked in the 1970 survey:

H. the mode of appraising managers' performance: whether discussions were held with the managers themselves or some other method not involving discussion was used or no appraisal at all was carried out,

I. the mode of assessing managers' training needs: whether discussions were held with the managers or some other method not involving discussion was used or no assessment at all was made,

J. the mode of evaluation of management training carried out within the company: whether discussions were held with the manager or another method used or no evaluation was carried out,

K. the mode of evaluation of management training undergone outside the company: whether discussions were held with the manager or another method used or no evaluation was carried out.

The first part of the analysis was the examination of all possible relationships between pairs of these eleven variables in order to identify those that were significant. The two hypothesized clusters of related variables do indeed emerge.[9] The relationships and their significance are shown graphically in Figures 2 and 3. Figure 2 demonstrates the existence of the *flexibility* dimension and Figure 3 that of the *autonomy* dimension. In these figures the sign ** indicates a relationship significant at the .001 level, the sign * indicates significance at the .01 level, while for other relationships the actual significance level found has been given.[10]

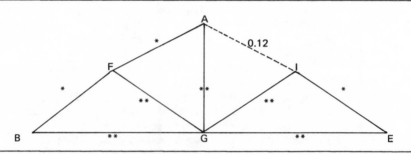

Figure 2. MANAGEMENT FLEXIBILITY
Key: A = inclusion/exclusion of supervisors/foremen. B = inclusion/exclusion of specialists. E = need for educational/professional qualifications. F = need for technical skills. G = use of job specifications. I = mode of training need assessment

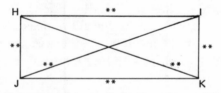

Figure 3: MANAGER AUTONOMY
Key: H = mode of performance appraisal. I = mode of training need assessment J = mode of evaluation of internal training. K = mode of evaluation of external training.

The figures full confirm the reality of the dimensions of management flexibility and manager autonomy as discriminants between managerial and traditional styles of management. We may also note differences in the nature of the two clusters of variables. In the case of management flexibility it seems clear that the operational questions are indeed about different, though related, matters. The questions have therefore cumulated to identify a common style showing itself in different policy areas. In the case of manager autonomy, by contrast, it is not so clear how much more than covert translations of one question the four questions are; or to what extent some underlying factor gives rise to the answers to them. Nonetheless, it remains certain that the varied answers reflect an aspect of management style quite distinct from flexibility.

Derivation of Scales

On the basis of this analysis scales have been built up using the variables found to be related, measuring respectively manager autonomy and management flexibility. In each case, answers to questions have been converted into numerical scores; scores on related questions have been summed so as to give a distribution of firms on the particular dimension; and finally firms on this continuum have been grouped in what seemed the most meaningful way for further analysis.

ANALYSIS OF MANAGEMENT STYLES

We have now reached the first of the two goals of this study: to seek from theoretical premises to identify management styles that actually exist; and to relate these to organizational size and to characteristics of industrial sectors.

Dimensions of Management Style

Having identified two dimensions of management style, manager autonomy and management flexibility, and constructed scales to measure these, we then looked for a correlation between them. The appropriate correlation coefficient (Spearman's r_s) was 0.48, significant at the .001 level.[11] In other words the greater the flexibility of management, the greater is the likelihood of manager autonomy. The relationship is apparent in Table 1.

TABLE 1

MANAGER AUTONOMY X MANAGEMENT FLEXIBILITY (%)

		Degree of Flexibility					
		High	*Medium-High*	*Inter-mediate*	*Medium-Low*	*Low*	*(N)*
	High	51.9	31.7	11.6	9.7	–	(44)
Degree of Autonomy	Medium-High	29.6	43.3	34.9	29.0	12.9	(71)
	Medium-Low	11.1	18.3	44.2	43.5	48.4	(75)
	Low	7.4	6.7	9.3	17.7	38.7	(33)
	(N)	(27)	(60)	(43)	(62)	(31)	(223)

The data directly confirm the reality of the two models of management. Further, they show that the polarity of the two is base upon at least the two dimensions identified.

Management Style and Size of Firm

The next relationship to be examined was that between size of fir and management style factors. The evidence, in Tables 2 and 3, show that size is negatively related to both factors and significantly so. The correlation coefficient (using Spearman's r_s) for size and autonomy i -0.26; that for size and flexibility is -0.36. Both relationships are significant at the .001 level. In other words, as Table 2 shows, the larger the firm the less frequently is the manager accorded autonomy With its increased complexity and greater bureaucratization (in the sociological not the derogatory sense) the large firm can involve its managers less in decisions concerning themselves. This interpretation is directly supported by Table 3 which demonstrates that the larger is the firm the less flexible is the management.

Management Style and Sector of Industry

More characteristic of a firm even than its size is its sector of industry. Yet different sectors of course have like features and we can therefore use industrial sector as a discriminating factor in the analysis by breaking it down into the component features that

TABLE 2

SIZE OF FIRM X MANAGER AUTONOMY (%)

| | | Size of Firm (No. of Employees) | | | |
		10,000 or more	1,000-9,999	500-999	Up to 499
Degree of Autonomy	High	4.1	19.8	25.6	35.7
	Medium-high	24.5.	35.2	34.9	28.6
	Medium-low	49.0	31.9	25.6	26.2
	Low	22.4	13.2	14.0	9.5
	(N)	(49)	(91)	(43)	(42)

TABLE 3

SIZE OF FIRM X MANAGEMENT FLEXIBILITY (%)

| | | Size of Firm (No. of Employees) | | | |
		10,000 or more	1,000-9,999	500-999	Up to 499
Degree of Flexibility	High	5.7	15.6	10.9	26.4
	Medium-High	17.0	20.8	43.5	43.4
	Intermediate	18.9	18.7	19.6	15.1
	Medium-low	34.0	30.2	19.6	13.2
	Low	24.5	14.6	6.5	1.9
	(N)	(53)	(96)	(46)	(53)

determined the original selection of sectors for the 1970 survey. Comparable information is only available (as in 1970) for sectors of manufacturing industry.

The two features used in 1970 were

(1) the proportion of scientists and technologists in the industry's labour force; which ranged from 0.06 per cent in the clothing industry to 3.7 per cent in the chemicals and allied products manufacturing industry,

(2) the distribution in the industry of establishments of different size; varying from the electrical and instrument engineering industry with 11.3 per cent of its establishments among those with 500 or more employees and 63.4 per cent among those with less than 100 employees to the printing and publishing industry with 2.3 per cent of its establishments among those of the largest size and 82.5 per cent among the smallest.[12]

In looking for relationships between sector of industry and the management style factors, therefore, each of these two components has been examined. We first looked at direct relationships between industrial sector characteristics and management style dimensions. None was found. This raised the question as to whether indirect relationships were being concealed behind the association between firm size and management style, notwithstanding the fact that no relationship was found between size of firm and industrial sector characteristics.

In the case of manager autonomy what emerges is that the relationship between autonomy and size of firm varies in strength and significance according to the industry. Table 4 gives the correlation coefficients (Spearman's r_s) and the significance levels of all the statistically significant relationships. When we look at the science base of the industry (as measured by the proportion of scientists and technologists in the labour force), we find the strongest relationship ($r_s = -.46$) between autonomy and firm size occurring among the least scientific industries. That is, the association of increasing size and diminishing autonomy is strongest here. A lesser association ($r_s = -.36$) is found for the most science-based industries (employing over 3 per cent scientists and technologists in the labour force).

When we examine the industries' concentration into large or small establishments, we again find the stronger and more significant relationships at either end of the scale — in industries more concentrated into large establishments ($r_s = -.44$) and in industries most distributed among small establishments ($r_s = -.47$). In other words, in these industries the association is strongest between increasing size of firm and decreasing manager autonomy.

We may speculate upon the interpretation of these findings. First, it would appear likely that in the industries with the least reliance upon science senior managers are able to direct a company's affairs on the basis of accumulated experience and expertise, without dependence on technical specialists. This would result, in larger firms, in all but the most senior managers having a low degree of autonomy. Surveillance and co-ordination of those below would be unproblematic and traditional. In smaller firms, where co-ordination would be readily achieved, management would be on a basis of colleagueship and co-operation; and hence autonomy would be normal. In contrast, in industries relying most heavily upon science dependence upon technical expertise would be prevalent. However, in smaller firms the line managers would themselves be the technical experts; and hence their autonomy could be maintained. In contrast, in larger firms the scientists would be independent experts in staff positions. The co-ordination of disparate specialities and numerous departments would present major control problems; and their solution would again lead to centralized management and a low degree of autonomy for individual managers.

TABLE 4

RELATIONSHIP OF SIZE OF FIRM AND MANAGER AUTONOMY
ACCORDING TO SECTOR OF MANUFACTURING INDUSTRY

A. According to Proportion of Scientists and Technologists in the Labour Force

	Proportion Over 3%	*1-3%*	*Up to 1%*	*All*
Correlation coefficient (r_s)	−.36	*	−.46	−.38
Significance level	.01	*	.001	.001

NOTES: (i) Industries in the "over 3%" category are the oil and petroleum, the chemical and allied products, and the electrical and instrument engineering industries; in the middle category are the mechanical engineering and the vehicle manufacturing industries; in the "up to 1%" category are the food, the textile, the clothing, and the printing and publishing industries.[13]
  (ii) * indicates that the relationship found was not significant.

B. According to the Distribution of Establishments by Size

	Size of Establishment			
	Mainly Large	*Inter- mediate*	*Mainly Small*	*All*
Correlation coefficient (r_s)	−.44	−.28	−.47	−.39
Significance level	.01	.05	.01	.001

NOTE: Sectors whose establishments are mainly of large size are the chemical and allied products, the electrical and instrument engineering and the textile industries; of intermediate size are the oil and petroleum, the mechanical engineering and the food industries; of small size are the clothing and the printing and publishing industries.[14]

Second, it would seem likely that in industries that are more concentrated into large establishments the need for managerial co-ordination within and between establishments is of paramount importance. In larger firms, whose activities span many establishments, this would result in a high degree of centralization and correspondingly a low degree of managerial autonomy. In smaller firms, with their activities concentrated into one establishment or at any rate a small number of establishments that are homogeneous and geographically closely knit, co-ordination could be on a face-to-face basis with all managers continuing to know each other. Likewise in industries distributed mainly among small establishments, co-ordination needs would have the same outcome: co-ordination would be problematic and require centralization in larger firms, while it would be solved in smaller firms on a face-to-face basis.

This hypothesis — that co-ordination is managed on a face-to-face basis in smaller firms — would not hold, we suggest, for establishments of intermediate or mixed size either because the establishments would be too numerous (the difference from the large establishment case) or because they would be too separate or specialized (the difference from the small establishment case).

We now turn to management flexibility. The relationship between flexibility and size of firm again varies in strength and significance according to the industry. The relevant correlation coefficients with their levels of significance are given in Table 5. If we look at the science base of the industry (again measured by the proportion of scientists and technologists in the labour force), we find the strongest and most significant relationship ($r_s = -.67$) occurring in the intermediate group of industries. In other words, the association of increasing firm size and diminishing management flexibility is strongest in the industries with a medium reliance upon science.

If we look at the industries' distribution among establishments of different size we again find the strongest relationship ($r_s = -.51$) in the middle group, in those industries more distributed in establishments of intermediate size. In this group of industries the association is strongest between increasing size of firm and decreasing management flexibility.

These findings are not easy to interpret. However, if we examine the science base of the industries, we may return to our earlier hypothesis that the use of technical expertise requires co-ordination and that the style of co-ordination varies according to whether the technical specialists are staff managers or the line managers themselves. The findings in Table 5A for management flexibility would confirm this hypothesis. But why is the relationship strongest for the middle group of industries? Here we suggest that the explanation lies in the distribution of specialists; these may be (i) individuals scattered throughout an enterprise or (ii) groups working in small units in each establishment or (iii) constitute

TABLE 5

RELATIONSHIP OF SIZE OF FIRM AND MANAGEMENT FLEXIBILITY
ACCORDING TO SECTOR OF MANUFACTURING INDUSTRY

A. *According to Proportion of Scientists and Technologists in the Labour Force*

	Proportion Over 3%	1-3%	Up to 1%	All
Correlation coefficient (r_s)	−.28	−.67	−.38	−.42
Significance level	.05	.001	.01	.001

NOTE: See notes to Table 4A

B. *According to the Distribution of Establishments by Size*

	Mainly Large	Inter- mediate	Mainly Small	All
Correlation coefficient (r_s)	−.29	−.51	*	−.42
Significance level	.05	.001	*	.001

NOTE: See notes to Tables 4A and B.

a separate department or division of a company. It seems plausible that the association of size and flexibility grows weaker as the proportion of scientific specialists rises to the point where the third type of distribution becomes possible. The association may likewise be weaker when the first type of distribution is the most prevalent and specialists are scattered throughout the enterprise.

To examine the association of size and flexibility in industries differing in establishment distribution, we may again return to an earlier hypothesis: that problems of co-ordination are solved by centralization in larger firms and on a face-to-face basis in smaller firms. Dealing now with management flexibility we suggest that in small establishments all firms are able to be flexible (according to the criteria used in this study) regardless of size. It also seems possible that in larger firms large establishments win for themselves more autonomy than do establishments of medium size and hence are freer to pursue flexible policies of management definition, recruitment and training.

In sum, we clearly need to specify what lies behind the overall finding that manager autonomy and management flexibility are negatively related to size of firm. We put forward the following hypotheses:

(1) manager autonomy and management flexibility vary according to *style of management co-ordination* (from a high degree of, formalised, centralization to direct, face-to-face co-ordination).
(2) style of co-ordination is dependent upon:
    (a) degree of reliance upon scientific and technical specialists;
    (b) distribution of technical expertise among staff managers, line managers and specialists; and of specialist groups and departments;
    (c) number, size and homogeneity of establishments;
    (d) geographical distribution of establishments.

CORRELATES OF ECONOMIC SUCCESS

We now turn to the second main object of the study: to test for an association between aspects of management style and economic success.

Measures of Success

The measures chosen to assess the companies' economic success were inevitably crude since they were based on published accounts relevant to the five-year period 1965-1966 to 1969-1970, 1970 being the year in which the survey of organizations was carried out. Using these figures the following indicators of commercial success were calculated:

L. Profitability (the ratio of pre-tax profits to total assets) over the five-year period,
M. Profit stability over the same period: whether profitability had been steady (varying over a range of no more than 4.9 percentage points during the period), fluctuating (varying over a range of from 5 to 14.9 percentage points), or erratic (varying over a range of 15 or more points),
N. Economic growth, as measured by per cent growth in assets over the same period.

Analysis established that these three indicators were in fact highly significantly related, as shown in Figure 4.[15]

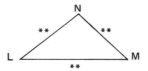

Figure 4. ECONOMIC SUCCESS
      Key: L = Profitability over 5 years. M = Profit stability over 5 years
      N = Economic growth over 5 years.

NOTE: The sign ** indicates a relationship significant at the .001 level

Using these three indicators, a further scale was calculated to measure economic success. As with the other scales, firms were allotted numerical scores for each indicator; the scores were summed to give an overall distribution of firms on the economic success dimension; and finally the resulting continuum was divided discretely to facilitate further analysis.

Correlates of Success

The finding here is perhaps disappointing to students of management and to proponents of modern management methods and of management education and training. However, it is that there is no significant direct relationship between either of the two aspects of management style and our measure of economic success. Indeed success is more closely related to size of firm (inversely, at a significance level of .026) than to any management style factor.

Hidden by this finding is a problem concerning the direction of causation. If there is no relation between management style and success, it does indeed imply that there is no action of style upon success. But it also implies that there is no effect of success upon management style, which is a result every bit as interesting. We are examining a relationship where it is not possible to be precise about the time-order of the variables. This is so not because observation is faulty but because it is not always clear what should count as identification of an aspect of management style or a feature of economic success. From this it would seem likely that there could be an interaction of factors, mutual influence. But the findings indicate that these factors do not influence each other in any way at all.

In contrast to this, some relationship is to be found between success and each of the industrial sector characteristics. In the case of the industries' employment of scientists and technologists the coefficient of correlation has a value of $r_s = -.2$, significant at the .05 level. The relationship is admittedly weak, but it is there. It would seem that the least technologically based industries are somewhat more likely to achieve economic success. When we try to specify this association, we find only one significant relationship: that for the most science-based industries (employing over 3 per cent scientists and technologists in the labour force) the correlation coefficient between success and size of firm has a value of $r_s = -.32$, significant at the .05 level. In other words, in the most science-based industries the larger the firm the less likely it is to be successful.

In the case of the industries' distribution among establishments of different size, the coefficient of correlation with economic success is $r_s = -.22$, significant at the .02 level; indicating that the small establishment industries are more likely to show success.

These relationships are too weak for weighty interpretation, but we may make three comments. First, it seems likely that small firms, which are usually small establishment firms, would have to be moderately successful in order to come into the sample for which data were collected at all; while larger firms can at least survive even if they go through a bad business period. Second, science-based firms (and large firms) are *prima facie* likely to be heavily capitalized and hence (a) they may be at greater risk and (b) "success" may require a longer time period for just estimation. Third, overall caution in interpretation is necessary because the criteria for grouping industries are crude, and the measures of commercial success, used because they were most available, may not be those preferred by either economic analysts or businessmen.

Nonetheless, the measures are pertinent to an analysis using a short time-scale, and the sector criteria do indeed discriminate clearly between the firms in the survey. Questions are thus raised about the uncertainties of industries with a heavy investment in scientific research and its applications, about the real economies of scale deriving from the large establishment, and about the economic merits of the large firm.

SUMMARY AND IMPLICATIONS OF THE RESEARCH

At the theoretical level the study has confirmed the existence of the two management models, the traditional and the managerial. But it has moved beyond ideal types. It has shown that the two styles of management lie at opposite ends of a continuum and that this is underpinned by at least two discriminatory dimensions, manager autonomy and management flexibility, which are significantly related.

Analysis next revealed both these dimensions to be negatively associated with size of firm; and also to be related in a complex manner to two industrial sector characteristics — the proportion of scientists and technologists in the labour force and the distribution in the industry of establishments of different size. Our interpretation of these findings led us to put forward the following explanatory hypotheses:

(1) manager autonomy and management flexibility vary according to *style of management co-ordination* (from a high degree of, formalized, centralization to direct, face-to-face co-ordination).
(2) style of co-ordination is dependent upon:
  (a) degree of reliance upon scientific and technical specialists;
  (b) distribution of technical expertise among staff managers, line managers and specialists; and of specialist groups and departments;
  (c) number, size and homogeneity of establishments;
  (d) geographical distribution of establishments.

The study is thus a contribution to the development of organizational theory but further research is obviously called for both in the search for further dimensions of management style and in seeking to specify and test the hypotheses that have arisen from the analysis. More detailed study on a case-study basis should permit the examination of internal structural features and internal management processes that the data available from the 1970 study unfortunately did not allow.

At the policy level the study's implications are also clear. It is more than ever apparent, as the NEDO Report maintained, that management styles and structures vary, and do so systematically, This reinforces the demand for the flexible and self-critical approach to management development, education and training put forward in the Report. And this is given emphasis by the lack of relationship between management style factors and economic success. The finding that the industrial sector characteristics and in some circumstances size of firm are negatively associated with success and with autonomy and flexibility raise urgent questions about organizational size and structure and about economic matters, such as investment policy, that are every bit as urgent for the practical businessman as for the economic or management analyst.

At the same time a caveat is called for. It would be a false conclusion on the basis of these findings to abandon modern management development approaches because they have not yet shown economic pay-off. On the one hand, this may occur in the long term and only in the long term. On the other, the pay-off may be non-economic but real; it may accrue primarily to the manager himself and only secondarily to the firm that employs him. The allowance of autonomy, the demonstration of concern, the openness of the organization, the flexibility of management — these may be essential moves toward the development of greater managerial responsibility and self-respect; and these may in turn lead to improved co-operation and colleagueship, with sure social, and possibly also economic, benefits in the long term.

Such a judgement leads to one final point. In this study firms and their managers have been treated as if they were cocooned within their industries away from forces in the wider society. This served the purposes of this analysis. But of course they are not so cocooned, and it must be emphasized that each organization provides a context for the tension of competing values at large in the outside world: in this case for the tension between efficiency, sought through rationalization and bureaucratization, and humanity, sought through the care and development of men.

FOOTNOTES

1. The bulk of the data upon which this study is based is derived from research carried out for the Institute of Manpower Studies at the University of Sussex and commissioned by the Management Education, Training and Development Committee of the National Economic Development Office. The author wishes to thank both organizations for permission to make further use of these data.

2. Full details of this earlier research can be found in the research report. See T.W. Leggatt, *The Training of British Managers: A Study of Need and Demand* (London: HMSO, 1972).

3. The sources of these data were the annual reports deposited by companies by statutory requirement at the Department of Trade and Industry. I am grateful to Peter Allen for much assistance in collecting these data.

4. See *From Max Weber: Essays in Sociology,* trans. H.H. Gerth and C. Wright Mills (London: Routledge & Kegan Paul, 1964) and Max Weber, *The Theory of Social and Economic Organization,* trans. A.M. Henderson and Talcott Parsons (Glencoe: Free Press, 1947).

5. For a variety of approaches see, for example, T. Burns & G.M. Stalker, *The Management of Innovation* (London: Tavistock, 1961), A. Etzioni, *A Comparative Analysis of Complex Organizations* (Glencoe: Free Press, 1961), A.W. Gouldner, *Patterns of Industrial Bureaucracy* (Glencoe: Free Press, 1954), E. Litwak, "Models of Bureaucracy which Permit Conflict," *American Journal of Sociology,* Vol. 69 (1961), pp. 177-184, J.G. March & H.A. Simon, *Organizations* (New York: Wiley, 1958), P. Selznick, "Foundations of the Theory of Organizations," *American Sociological Review,* Vol. 13 (1948), pp. 25-35, and Talcott Parsons, *Structure and Process in Modern Society* (Glencoe: Free Press, 1960), Chapter 1.

6. See, for example, Litwak, *op. cit.*

7. See Douglas McGregor, *The Human Side of Enterprise* (New York: McGraw-Hill 1960).

8. These terms are those used by Burns & Stalker, *op. cit.*

9. These clusters are identified by inspection on the basis of two-variable cross-tabulations.

10. All tests to determine the significance of these relationships were X^2 tests. The variables involved were neither continuous nor ordinal, and most tests were of 2 x 2 tables.

11. Spearman's r_s is a coefficient of rank-order correlation appropriate where the relationship between the ordinal measures is monotonic increasing or decreasing but where linearity cannot be assumed.

12. Establishments were grouped into three size categories: those with up to 99 employees, those with 100-499 employees, and those with 500 or more employees.

13. Source: *Employment & Productivity Gazette* (January, 1969). Figures relate to May, 1968.

14. Source: Department of Employment communication. Figures relate to June, 1961. No more recent figures were available in 1970.

15. The coefficients of correlation between the indicators were as follows: for LM, $r_s = .58$; for LN, $r_s = .72$; for MN, $r_s = .61$.

Chapter 7

THE SOCIAL CONSTRUCTION OF LOCAL COMMUNITIES

Morris Janowitz and John D. Kasarda

POLICY ISSUES IN THE ORIGINAL SURVEY

In the process of formulating recommendations for restructuring local government, the Royal Commission on Local Government in England commissioned a large scale sample survey. The survey focused on the public's contacts with local administrative agenices and elected bodies, as well as on attitudes toward these institutions. The survey also collected detailed sociological information on community participation and local social networks and probed the strength of home area attachments. The Royal Commission apparently believed that public preferences as to the size and structure of local government should be taken into consideration. But they were concerned with more than attitudes and preferences; they assumed, of course, that the structure of local government should articulate with the social organization and social fabric of the local community. They were, in essence, concerned with themes of central interest to sociologists – namely, the ecological and symbolic boundaries of the daily life space of community residents in an advanced urban society.

It remains a relevant task to investigate the extent to which, if at all, the findings collected by the Royal Commission on Local Government entered into their final recommendations. Some of the evidence gathered indicated that local residents – to the extent that they had preferences – wanted very localistic and decentralized services and agencies – if only because of accessibility. However, the general thrust of the Royal Commission's recommendations pointed toward larger units of local government. The Commission assumed that these larger units of local government would be more efficient, both technically and administratively. Moreover, one can infer that the Royal Commission anticipated that larger units — especially in the case of elected councils — would create new and stronger aggregates of political power and influence. No doubt parliamentary leaders estimated which political party would be assisted by such a consolidation movement. But there was a general expectation that these enlarged centres might well serve as focal points for local initiative and as a counterweight to the powerful trends toward the overcentralization of agencies of national government.

The articulation of these larger centres of local government which have been created with the social organization of the local communities and home areas remains to be assessed. Nevertheless, the Royal Commission survey collected "basic" sociological data — data thus far unavailable on a national basis — which threw new light on the social organization and patterns of participation in local community life in Great Britain. These findings presented a more detailed picture than previously available of the manner in which local residents through their day-to-day activities, including their informal social network and associational ties, were responding to and fashioning the social order.

Thus, the design of reform for local government leads to an examination of the underlying issues of the social construction of the local residential community. In essence, the analysis of the underlying factors which in advanced industrial societies facilitate or retard community participation and attachments is not only a potential contribution to the academic literature on urban community, but is a central concern for those persons concerned with reorganizing local government. While the Royal Commission had at its disposal a report which presented the basic findings without extensive statistical and conceptual analysis, the purpose of this paper is to present a reanalysis which seeks to examine the available data in a systematic framework.

CENTRAL THEORETICAL ISSUES

Sociologists have approached the study of community organization in terms of the consequences of urbanization and industrialization.[1] One problem that has generated a substantial amount of scholarship is the influence of population size and density on people's social participation and attachment to their local community.[2] In this paper we plan to explore, by means of survey research data, some of these basic sociological issues of local community participation, especially those factors which account for strong or weak community attachments.

The theoretical point of departure is the two competing models of the local community in "mass society" which have come to dominate the thinking and work of contemporary social researchers. First is the linear development model, or population growth approach. This orientation has its intellectual roots in the philosophical writings of Ferdinand Toennies, which postulate the transformation of society from *Gemeinschaft* to *Gesellschaft*.[3] In this view, urbanization and industrialization alter the essential character of society from that based on communal attachments to that derived from associational relationships. The writings of Louis Wirth of the Chicago school of sociology gave strong impetus to contemporary formulations of this approach. In his article, "Urbanism as a Way of Life," Wirth saw the essential character of urban society as resulting from (a) increased numbers of population, (b) density of settlement, and (c) heterogeneity of inhabitants and group life.[4] The outcomes of these variables were said to include the substitution of secondary for primary contacts, the weakening of the bonds of kinship, and the declining social significance and eventual disappearance of the local community.

Other members of the Chicago school of urban sociology resisted this formulation, in particular W.I. Thomas, Robert E. Park, and Ernest W. Burgess.[5] Their formulations sought to account for the range of "social worlds" and social solidarities which emerged in the urban metropolis. For them the local community was not a residue but a social construction which had its own life cycle and reflected ecological, institutional and normative variables. The constituent elements which they and subsequent urban sociologists utilized supply the basis for our alternative model of community participation and attachment. This model, which we call the systemic model, reflects continuing criticisms of the notions which flow from the linear development approach. These criticisms are based on historical and anthropological materials which call into question the existence of *Gemeinschaft* in pre-industrial societies because of their internal discontinuities and complexity, and especially because of the dependence of these societies on some variant of bureaucratic or associational institutions.

In good measure, the theoretical formulations of Toennies and those of many of his disciples are incomplete and tautological at essential points. Much of the Toennies tradition is a normative value treatment of modern life which reflects a reasoned moral position, but is not the basis for empirical research. The fundamental problem, however, with the *Gemeinschaft-Gesellschaft* approach is that it fails to explain the variety of forms of community organization found in modern society. Research on the social structure of urbanized Western societies is rich in those empirical observations which cannot be accounted for by this sociological traditon.

In the alternative model, community organization is viewed as an essential aspect of modern society. It is a structure which has its ecological, institutional, and normative dimensions. The local community is a complex system of friendship and kinship networks and formal and informal associational ties rooted in family life and the needs of personal socialization. At the same time it is fashioned by the large scale institution of mass society. Indeed, it is a generic structure of modern society, whose form, content, and effectiveness vary over a wide range and whose defects and disarticulations are inherent consequences of the social problems of the contemporary period.

Community — that is the geographically based community — manifests varying and diffuse boundaries and reflects different intensity and scope of participation depending, among other factors, on a person's position in the social structure and his locus in his life cycle. One can identify the social fabric of communities in systemic terms by focusing on the daily networks of the populations and analytically abstracting those that are directly linked to the occupational system. The remaining social relations, to the extent that they have a geographical base, are manifestations of the social fabric of human communities, be they neighbourhoods, local communities, or metropolitan areas.

To explore adequately hypotheses about the social fabric of communities derived from the linear development and systemic models, more than case study data are required; sample surveys become essential. However, we are aware of the limitations inherent in survey research data for examining local social networks. There is obviously an element of arbitrary delimitation both in the questions asked and the sampling procedures utilized in survey research. Social networks require investigation by careful and detailed participant observation. Moreover, frequency of community contact and participation must take into consideration available opportunities. For example, frequency of visiting patterns with relatives could be an arbitrary measure if the data are not standardized by availability and location of relatives and alternative means of contact. However, survey research strategies have been developed to recognize these complex issues and to produce still meaningful measures of social participation and local community attachment.

We equally recognize various cultural and normative definitions of community participation in different historical periods and different societies. Furthermore, persons will attribute alternative meanings to the questions in a standardized survey research interview. In particular, we recognize that community participation and attachment in an advanced industrial society has its own and various cultural and normative meanings. In the context of contemporary mass society, and for the purposes of quantitative analysis of survey research data, the notion of community of "limited liability" has been formulated by Janowitz.[6] It is designed to prevent mechanical comparisons with other historical periods and cultural areas or stereotyped assessments.

> In this regard, the individual, responding to the general cultural norms is likely to demand more from his community than he will invest. But more significantly, his relation to the community is such — his investment is such — that when the community fails to serve his needs, he will withdraw. Withdrawal implies either departure from the local community or merely lack of involvement.

A body of research literature has emerged on community participation — informal and formal — and on community attachments since the publication of *The Community Press in an Urban Setting*, which roughly supports the systemic model.[7] However, the measures which have been employed are often incomplete and the sample design and size limited so as to prevent adequate statistical analysis. The large scale and detailed survey from the Royal Commission on Local Government in England permits us to explore more comprehensively than has been the case in the past the impact of increased population size, density and residential mobility on these issues of local community organization.[8]

DESCRIPTION OF THE DATA

The fact that the sample was drawn from Great Britain has certain advantages for the purposes at hand, especially in that it reflects a relatively high degree of cultural homogeneity and we are therefore able to highlight the particular variables in which we are interested. The population is living under a single unified system of central and local government, although there is administrative variation according to the size of the local government unit. The regional differences to be found in Wales and Scotland are excluded, and England at the time of the sample had a relative absence of racial and ethnic enclaves, although the concentration of foreign-born was increasing. We expected that the findings would converge with those already encountered in other industrial nations, including the United States, but because of these factors that the relations would be more clear-cut and pronounced.

The sample survey we are utilizing was conducted by Research Services, Ltd. in March 1967. It was designed to assist the Royal Commission on Local Government in England in making recommendations to restructure the size and format of local government units. In this survey 2,199 adults were interviewed. The sample was drawn from 100 local authority areas throughout England (excluding London) in numbers "correctly proportionate to the population which is contained within three main types of local authority of different population sizes within the Registrar General's Standard Regions." The focus of the survey was on information collected from individuals about their social position, their attitudes, and their social behaviour both within and outside their local community. Data were also gathered on the demographic characteristics of the local jurisdiction in which they resided.

As stated, the purpose of our reanalysis of this body of survey data is to examine empirically some of the sociological factors which influence the character of local community participation and attachment. However, the main thrust of the reanalysis is not based on a direct search for multivariate findings of the highest aggregate explanatory value. Instead, the strategy is to explore a series of interrelated propositions which seek to examine the implications of the two competing models of the local community.

Our initial expectation, derived from the rejection of the linear development model, was that population size and population density would not be associated with important and significant differences in community participation and attachments. Under the Toennies-Wirth approach, the larger the population size and density of an area, the more attenuated would be community participation and attachments. Of course, some differences would be expected, especially between the very largest and very smallest population concentrations, but the overall relevance of size and density as explanatory variables should be limited.

By contrast, the systemic model focuses on length of residence as the key independent variable influencing community behaviour and attitudes. The major intervening variables are friendship and kinship bonds and formal and informal associational ties within the local community. The local community is viewed as an ongoing system of social networks into which new generations and new residents are assimilated, while the community itself passes through its own life-cycle. Assimilation of newcomers into the social fabric of local communities is necessarily a temporal process and residential mobility operates thereby as a barrier to this process of socialization. The development of extensive friendship and kinship bonds and widespread local associational ties might well require a generation or more. Once established, though, these local bonds tend to foster community attachments.

This is not to suggest that length of residence is the only independent variable affecting community behaviour and attitudes. The available literature leads us to investigate whether a person's social position and stage in his family life cycle likewise influence his friendship, kinship and associational ties within the community.[9] Moreover, the influence of population size and density on community participation and attachments must also be determined and controlled if we are to compare the relative merits of the linear development and systemic models. We have therefore sought to construct and analyze a model of community organization which will examine the impact of five basic independent factors — population size, density, length of residence, socio-economic status, and family life cycle — on friendship, kinship, and associational ties within the community and the influence of all these eight factors on local community attitudes and sentiments.

It is first appropriate to identify the key variables and the operational measures.

Dependent Variables (Community Attitudes and Sentiments)

The survey contains three items which may be used as measures of community attachment. These items are:

(1) Is there an area around here where you are now living which you would say you belong to, and where you feel "at home?"

(2) How interested are you to know what goes on in . . . (Home Area)? (NOTE: In the actual interview questionnaire, the phrase "home area" was replaced, in all questions using it, with the *name* of the given local community.)

(3) Supposing that for some reason you had to move away from (Home Area), how sorry or pleased would you be to leave?

Item 1, dealing with the respondent's statement as to whether there was a local community to which he belonged or felt at home, was scored as a dichotomized yes-no response. Item 2 about his community interest had four ordinal categories: very interested, quite interested, only a little interested and not at all interested. Item 3 on sentiments about leaving the local community had five ordinal categories: very sorry, quite sorry, neither sorry nor pleased, quite pleased, and very pleased to leave the local community.

Intervening Variables (Participation in Local Social Networks)

To measure friendship and kinship networks within the local community, an additional series of questions was asked. These questions included:

(1) How many people would you say you know who live in (Home Area)?

(2) How many adult friends do you have who live within ten minutes' walk of your home?

(3) How many adult relatives and in-laws do you have who live within ten minutes' walk from your home?

(4) Taking all your adult friends that you have now, what proportion of them would you say live in (Home Area)?

(5) Taking all your adult relatives and in-laws, except the very distant ones, what proportion of them live in (Home Area)?

Responses to item 1, number of people known in the local community, were scored into five ordinal categories: none, only one or two people, a few, many or very many. Items 2 and 3, number of friends who live within 10 minutes' walk of respondent's home were recorded as absolute numbers. Items 4 and 5, relative proportion of friends and relatives who live in the local community, were scored as four ordinal categories ranging from none to all friends/relatives residing within the local community.[10]

To measure the degree of the respondent's participation in formal associations within the local community, an extensive question was asked regarding participation in the following types of associations:

(1) Organizations connected with the respondent's work, such as trade unions, business clubs, and professional associations.

(2) Public bodies or committees concerned with community affairs.

(3) Organizations connected with politics.

(4) Organizations connected with education and training.

(5) Associations connected with churches or other religious groups.

(6) Charitable organizations.

(7) Civic or community groups such as a rentpayers association or parent-teacher association.

(8) Formal social clubs such as a sports team, dance club, automobile club, hobby club, or fraternal organization.

(9) Any other formal association not described above.

For each of the formal associational memberships listed by the respondent it was noted whether the locus of participation was inside or outside the designated local community. The total number of local affiliations was noted and scored as a summated index of local formal ties.

Likewise, a question was asked regarding informal participation in local social activities. Included under this item were visits to cinemas, live theatre, concerts, recitals, football, rugby or cricket matches, race tracks, bingo sessions, ten-pin bowling, public dances, swimming pools, golf clubs, tennis clubs, public parks or gardens, or drives into the countryside. Again it was noted whether or not participation in such informal social activities occurred within or outside the local community.

Independent Variables

Population size was measured in terms of the size of the respondent's local authority. Five size categories in terms of a rural-urban continuum were employed. The continuum consisted of (1) rural districts; (2) municipal boroughs and urban districts up to 30,000; (3) municipal boroughs and urban districts 30,000-60,000; (4) municipal boroughs and urban districts 60,000-250,000; and (5) municipal boroughs and urban districts over 250,000, including connurbations. Population density was measured in terms of persons per acre in the local ward or parish where the respondent resided. Six density categories were obtained ranging from under 1 person per acre to over 20 persons per acre. Length of residence in the local community was scored into six categories ranging from less than one year to over 20 years/born there. Socio-economic status was also scored into six categories ranging from unskilled to professional. Non-working housewives and retired persons were classified according to last job held. Finally, family life-cycle was a constructed variable containing seven categories ranging from married, between the ages of 21 and 44 with children present to over age 65, living alone.

Our statistical analysis will be in two stages. First, we shall carry out a cross-tabular analysis of the independent, intervening, and dependent variables to establish their zero-order correlations. Since the majority of our data are ordinal, gamma coefficients are used as the basic measure of association. Second, we shall dichotomize all variables to equalize variances and apply regression analysis to deduce the direct effects of each factor on community behaviour and attitudes and measure their statistical significance.

SUBSTANTIVE FINDINGS

In Table 1 are presented the relationships between the independent variables and social network variables.[11] The results indicate that population size and density have relatively little association with the extent of people's friendship, kinship and associational ties within their local community. On the other hand, length of residence exhibits fairly strong and consistent positive relationships with participation and involvement in community social networks. Particularly noteworthy is the steep gradient between length of residence and percentage responding that they know many people in their local community. Whereas only 18 per cent of those who had lived in the local area under one year claimed that they knew many people, over 83 per cent of those who had lived in the community over 20 years or were born there responded that they knew many people. Other marked increments in percentage involved in local social networks by length of residence include number of friends, number of relatives, and percentage of friends and relatives living within the local community.

Socio-economic status and family life cycle have some specific and limited linkages with particular social network variables. As was to be anticipated, a higher incidence of membership in formal organizations was found in the upper socio-economic status groups, and conversely S.E.S. had a negative gradient with the variable of

TABLE 1
ZERO-ORDER ASSOCIATIONS BETWEEN INDEPENDENT VARIABLES AND INTERVENING SOCIAL NETWORK VARIABLES

Local Social Networks: Percentages

	Know many people	6 or more friends	3 or more relatives	Over 50% of friends in community	Over 50% of relatives in community	Belong to 2 or more formal organizations	Participate in 2 or more social activities
Size							
Rural District	71.8	53.4	25.9	38.8	14.5	20.3	15.1
U.D. to 30,000	73.1	56.5	35.1	47.9	27.2	17.3	23.8
30-60,000	67.7	53.8	24.7	37.2	17.0	19.1	25.0
60-250,000	61.4	46.6	24.9	38.6	18.6	15.8	18.8
Over 250,000	64.8	47.0	27.4	37.3	13.7	12.4	16.2
Gamma =	-.11	-.09	-.02	-.04	-.06	-.15	.00
Density (Persons per acre)							
Under 1	72.9	57.2	22.5	39.2	12.7	21.2	16.0
1-5	71.0	53.3	29.5	41.5	21.7	18.8	19.2
5-10	66.8	49.9	25.4	38.7	16.2	15.4	18.5
10-15	67.2	51.2	27.1	38.9	20.7	17.2	19.8
15-20	63.8	49.2	33.8	39.5	13.6	11.7	19.6
Over 20	64.2	45.3	28.8	40.3	17.3	14.0	19.9
Gamma =	-.10	-.09	.06	.00	.00	-.13	.04

TABLE 1 CONTINUED

Local Social Networks: Percentages

	Know many people	6 or more friends	3 or more relatives	Over 50% of friends in community	Over 50% of relatives in community	Belong to 2 or more formal organizations	Participate in 2 or more social activities
Length of Residence							
Under 1 year	18.2	34.5	9.1	12.7	7.5	9.1	12.7
1-3 years	47.3	47.3	12.9	22.4	5.8	11.5	15.1
4-5 years	56.6	40.6	18.9	23.3	5.5	8.6	20.6
6-10 years	57.9	46.2	17.7	33.0	8.0	18.0	17.7
11-20 years	65.8	48.0	21.8	30.9	9.3	14.9	18.4
Over 20/born here	83.5	58.5	41.1	56.2	30.9	20.6	20.8
Gamma =	.48	.18	.44	.44	.60	.20	.09
S.E.S.							
Unskilled	63.7	45.2	28.0	51.0	20.8	9.6	14.0
Partly skilled	70.0	49.6	33.8	42.3	22.5	13.9	18.3
Skilled manual	69.6	53.4	32.9	43.6	20.3	15.8	19.2
Skilled non-manual	64.8	52.3	28.8	32.1	12.7	19.2	19.7
Intermediate	70.5	51.1	21.0	31.2	10.8	23.2	22.9
Professional	62.8	59.1	6.8	20.5	7.5	34.1	18.2
Gamma =	.02	.05	-.11	-.12	-.15	.21	.08

TABLE 1 CONTINUED

Local Social Networks: Percentages

	Know many people	6 or more friends	3 or more relatives	Over 50% of friends in community	Over 50% of relatives in community	Belong to 2 or more formal org-anizations	Participate in 2 or more social activities
Family life cycle*							
Stage 1	69.9	51.0	33.3	37.3	19.3	16.9	23.6
Stage 2	69.2	47.9	28.4	37.7	15.2	22.3	24.2
Stage 3	58.8	53.9	23.0	32.5	14.6	20.0	17.6
Stage 4	71.5	52.7	30.2	41.6	17.7	17.8	14.8
Stage 5	67.3	49.0	25.0	35.6	20.0	8.7	23.1
Stage 6	67.0	57.4	23.5	44.9	15.8	14.2	14.2
Stage 7	60.5	42.2	19.7	50.3	16.4	8.8	6.8
Gamma =	−.04	.00	−.12	.09	.04	−.10	−.21

* Family life cycle stages:
1. age 21-44, married, children present
2. age 45-64, married, children present
3. age 21-44, married, no children
4. age 45-64, married, no children
5. age 21-64, single
6. age 65 and over, married
7. age 65 and over, alone

[219]

relatives in the home area. Both of these linkages reflect the greater mobility of higher socio-economic status groups and their more extensive reliance on formal and secondary social networks. Participation in informal social activities in the local community declines with advanced life cycle stage, reflecting the impact of family composition and age. However, for comparative purposes, two main points emerge. First, neither S.E.S. nor family life cycle are powerful and consistent and pervasive variables in explaining the patterns of social network; and second, neither population size nor population density influences any of the seven intervening social network variables as much as does length of residence.

Let us now consider the zero-order relationships between the independent and dependent variables of community attachment and sentiment in the overall model. That is, we shall examine the relationships of population size, density. length of residence, S.E.S., and family life cycle to (1) whether or not a person feels a sense of belonging to his local community, (2) how interested he is in what goes on in his community, and (3) whether or not he would be sorry to leave his community if he had to leave. These relationships are presented in Table 2.

Again we observe that population size and density manifest relatively little association with local community sentiments. Examining individually the three different types of community sentiments, we observe that whether or not a person feels a sense of belonging to his local community is clearly a function of length of residence. Barely one-half of those who had lived in their community for less than one year felt a "sense of belonging" compared with almost 90 per cent of those who were either born in the community or had lived there for over 20 years. Likewise, length of residence exhibits the highest degree of association with the extent to which a person would be sorry to leave his local community.

Expressions of interest in the affairs of the local community appear to be primarily influenced by a person's socio-economic status. Only 40.4 per cent of persons in the lowest S.E.S. category expressed a high degree of interest in what goes on in their community compared with over 72 per cent of those in the highest S.E.S. group.

Amount of interest in the affairs of the local community also exhibits a consistent negative gradient with population size. Sixty-two percent of the residents of rural districts are interested in what goes on in their local community, whereas only 49 per cent of the

TABLE 2

ZERO-ORDER ASSOCIATIONS BETWEEN INDEPENDENT VARIABLES
AND LOCAL COMMUNITY SENTIMENTS

	(Approx.) *(Base)*	*Sense of Community*[a]	*Sorry to Leave*[b]	*Interested in Community*[c]
Population Size				
Rural District	(533)	76.0	68.6	62.1
Urban to 30,000	(416)	81.9	71.3	60.3
30-60,000	(288)	79.9	65.5	54.5
60-250,000	(340)	75.0	66.8	53.5
Over 250,000	(611)	77.6	55.5	49.1
Gamma =		−.01	−.13	.12
Density				
(Persons per acre)				
Under 1	(305)	78.7	71.8	66.0
1-5	(514)	80.4	69.5	56.5
5-10	(368)	76.3	67.7	53.9
10-15	(373)	78.6	59.4	51.5
15-20	(240)	76.7	61.3	52.1
Over 20	(379)	75.9	57.0	55.3
Gamma =		−.05	−.16	−.09
Length of Residence				
Under 1 year	(55)	51.9	58.2	58.2
1-3 years	(278)	69.4	56.7	53.2
4-5 years	(175)	68.0	67.2	52.0
6-10 years	(315)	67.6	54.9	53.3
11-20 years	(435)	73.4	59.6	50.6
Over 20/born here	(930)	89.4	72.8	60.4
Gamma =		.40	.20	.09
S.E.S.				
Unskilled	(156)	76.9	64.1	40.4
Partly skilled	(585)	78.7	63.4	52.5
Skilled manual	(556)	82.5	64.6	54.1
Skilled non-manual	(386)	71.8	60.1	59.1
Intermediate	(318)	76.2	68.6	69.2
Professional	(44)	77.3	64.3	72.7
Gamma =		.03	.04	.21

TABLE 2 CONTINUED

	(Approx.) (Base)	Sense of Community[a]	Sorry to Leave[b]	Interested in Community[c]
*Family Life Cycle**				
Stage 1	(625)	76.5	60.9	58.5
Stage 2	(211)	73.9	65.2	59.2
Stage 3	(165)	66.1	51.5	51.5
Stage 4	(493)	79.9	68.3	57.4
Stage 5	(104)	78.8	63.5	51.0
Stage 6	(204)	82.4	73.1	57.1
Stage 7	(146)	81.5	73.3	40.7
Gamma =		.09	.13	−.08

a. percentage responding that they feel a sense of belonging to their local community
b. percentage responding that they would be quite sorry or very sorry to leave their local community
c. percentage responding that they are very interested or quite interested in what goes on in their local community

*   See Table 1 for definitions of stages

residents of places over 250,000 or connurbations express as much interest. However, variation in community interest within different size categories is nearly as large as variation between size categories resulting in a relatively low degree of association between population size and community interest.

Examination of the linkage of locus in family life cycle to community sentiments reveals that younger married persons without children have the least feelings of attachment to their local community. Older age has opposing effects on feelings of attachment and degree of interest in the local community. While people over age 65 have a high "sense of belonging" and strong aversion to leaving their local community, they express the least amount of interest in the affairs of their local area. However, as was the case with population size noted above, there is almost as much variation of these sentiments with each stage of the family life cycle as there is between stages, which, of course, attenuates the gamma coefficients.

The next step is to examine the relationship of local social networks to community sentiments. Our working hypothesis as derived from the systemic model is that the more extensive a person's friendship, kinship and associational bonds within the local community, the stronger will be his feelings of attachment to the community. Table 3 presents the gamma coefficients from a cross-tabular analysis between the social network variable and the three indicators of local community sentiments.

TABLE 3

GAMMA COEFFICIENTS FROM CROSS-TABULATION OF
SOCIAL NETWORK VARIABLES AND COMMUNITY SENTIMENTS

Within Local Area	*Sense of Community*	*Sorriness to Leave*	*Interest in Community*
Number of people known	.59	.42	.48
Number of friends	.39	.38	.35
Number of relatives	.17	.26	.11
Percent of friends	.52	.37	.28
Percent of relatives	.48	.26	.17
Formal association ties	.23	.21	.56
Informal social activities	.31	.12	.39

The gamma coefficients provide clear empirical support to the proposition that local community sentiments in mass society are substantially influenced by a person's involvement in local social networks. Each of the three indicators of local community sentiments correlates positively with each indicator of friendship, kinship, and associational bonds. Looking first at the determinants of sense of community belonging, number of people known in the local community exhibits the highest association. We found that 86 per cent of those who knew many people in the home area felt that they "belonged" to the neighbourhood against just over 60 per cent of those who knew few or less people. Next in importance in feelings of attachment is percentage of friends living in the local community, followed by percentage of relatives living there. Ninety percent of those who had over one-half of their relatives living in the local community expressed a sense of belonging, compared to 76 per cent of those who had less than one-half of their relatives residing in their local community. The corresponding percentages of respondents having a "sense of belonging," based on under and over one-half of their friends living in the local community, were 71.1 per cent and 88.5 per cent respectively.

Expressions that one would be "sorry to leave" the local community are likewise closely associated with number of people known. Less than one-half of the respondents who knew few people in their local community said that they would be sorry to leave, compared to nearly three-quarters of those who knew many people in the local community. Number of friends and percentage of friends residing in the local community were also found to have a relatively strong association with feeling "sorry to leave."

Interest in the affairs of the local community exhibits the strongest relationship with participation in local formal associations. Nearly 80 per cent of those who participated in two or more local associations expressed high interest in their local community, while only approximately 50 per cent of those participating in less than two associations expressed interest in what goes on in their local community. Number of people known in the neighbourhood likewise exhibits a strong positive association with local community interest. Only 38 per cent of those who knew but a few people expressed much interest in the community as compared to nearly 65 per cent of those who knew many people.

In sum, the results presented in Tables 1 to 3 provide consistent support for the systemic model based on a three-stage linkage from length of residence to friendship, kinship and associational bonds to community sentiments. Very little support could be found for the linear development model based on population size and density. However, we have thus far only examined zero-order associations between the exogenous, intervening and dependent variables. We have not controlled for the possibility of spuriousness or suppressor effects masking functional relationships among the variables. Our next step, therefore, will be to standardize variances and introduce statistical controls among the independent and intervening variables to determine the direct effects of each social and structural factor.

To standardize variances, all dependent factors were converted to dichotomized variables. The seven intervening network variables and three dependent variables of community attachment and sentiment were maintained in the dichotomized form presented in Tables 1 and 2.[12] Population size was divided into local authorities containing fewer than 30,000 people (including all rural districts) and local authorities (including connurbations) above 30,000. Approximately 45 per cent of the sample resided in places under 30,000. Population density was dichotomized at under and over 10 persons per acre. Again, approximately 45 per cent of the sample resided in local areas (wards) with population density less than 10 persons per acre. Length of residence was dichotomized into those who lived in the local community for over one generation (or were born there) and those who lived in the local community for less than one generation.

Approximately 43 per cent of the respondents either had lived in their local community for more than one generation (that is, 20 years) or had been born there. Socio-economic status was divided into lower and higher status. Lower includes those classified as unskilled, partly skilled, and skilled manual. Higher status includes the skilled non-manual, intermediate and professional categories. Thirty-six per cent of the respondents were in the higher status categories. Family life cycle was dichotomized as married, under age 65, with children present in the household and others. Forty-three per cent of the respondents were in the former category.

With all independent, intervening, and dependent variables in standardized form, the model was examined through the use of stepwise multiple regression. Standardized partial regression coefficients (that is, path coefficients) were computed to determine the direct effects of each independent variable on the intervening variables and the direct effects of each intervening variable on the dependent variables.[13] The direct effects of each independent variable on the intervening network variables are presented in Table 4.

When length of residence, socio-economic status, and family life cycle are held constant, neither population size nor density exhibits a statistically significant relationship with any of the seven indicators of participation in local community social networks. However, with population size, density, S.E.S., and family life cycle held constant, length of residence exhibits significant direct effects on all but one indicator of participation in local social networks. These results indicate that population size and density are relatively unimportant factors as compared with length of residence in affecting friendship, kinship, and local associational bonds.

In addition, socio-economic status and family life cycle each have significant direct effects on four of the seven indicators of participation in local community social activities. *Ceteris paribus*, as socio-economic status increases, the percentage of friends living in close proximity declines, as do local kinship ties, while participation in local formal associations increases. Similarly, married persons under age 65 with children present tend to know more people in their local community, have stronger kinship ties and participate in a greater number of local social activities. Note, however, that the only social network variable that either S.E.S. or family life cycle affects as much as does length of residence is participation in informal social activities. This provides further evidence that length of

TABLE 4

STANDARDIZED PARTIAL REGRESSION COEFFICIENTS BETWEEN INDEPENDENT VARIABLES AND INTERVENING SOCIAL NETWORK VARIABLES

(N = 1,648)

	Within Local Community						
	Number of People Known	Number of Friends	Number of Relatives	Percent of Friends	Percent of Relatives	Formal Association Memberships	Informal Social Activities
Population Size	−.08	−.04	−.06	−.06	−.05	−.05	.03
Population Density	.01	−.04	.07	.02	.03	−.03	.04
Length of Residence	.29*	.12*	.33*	.28*	.33*	.11*	.07
Socio-economic Status	.03	.02	−.11*	−.09*	−.09*	.08*	.05
Family Life Cycle	−.10*	−.01	−.13*	−.04	−.10*	−.05	−.11*

* Statistically significant at p<.001 based on ratio of regression coefficient to its standard error with 1 and 1,647 degrees of freedom.

residence is the key independent variable on which to focus in examining determinants of community participation.

Having examined the relative impact of each independent variable on participation in local social networks, we now wish to determine the effects of the intervening social network variables on local community attachments and sentiments. Table 5 presents the results of a regression of each of the three attitudinal variables on the seven indicators of social networks within the local community.

TABLE 5

STANDARDIZED PARTIAL REGRESSION COEFFICIENTS
BETWEEN INTERVENING SOCIAL NETWORK VARIABLES
AND COMMUNITY SENTIMENTS

(N = 1,648)

Network Variables	Sense of Community	Sorriness to Leave	Interest in Community
Number of people known	.19*	.13*	.16*
Number of friends	.07	.12*	.09*
Number of relatives	.09*	.07	−.04
Per cent of friends	.11*	.10*	.03
Per cent of relatives	.00	−.02	−.02
Formal association ties	−.01	.01	.14*
Informal social activities	.05	−.01	.08*

* Statistically significant at p<.001 based on ratio of regression coefficient to its standard error with 1 and 1,647 degrees of freedom.

The standardized partial regression coefficients indicate that of these social network variables, number of people known in the local community is the most important in shaping community attitudes and sentiments. Friendship bonds appear to be the next most important. Examining separately the three components of community sentiments, "sense of belonging" to the local community is independently influenced by number of people known in the local community, percentage of all friends living in the local community, and by number of relatives living in close proximity. Sentiment to remain in the home area (that is, "feel sorry to leave") is independently affected by number of people known in the local area and by both measures of friendship networks in the community. Neither formal nor informal participation in local community associations and activities appears to have an independent effect on sentiment to remain in the local community.

On the other hand, interest in the affairs of the local community is significantly related to both formal participation in community associations and informal participation in local social activities. Furthermore, expressed interest in what goes on in the local community is independently influenced by relative number of people known in the local community and by number of friends living in close proximity. As was the case with both measures of feeling of attachment to the local community, percentage of relatives living in the local community exerts no independent influence on a person's interest in what goes on in his local community.

Parenthetically, in analyzing the effects of the social network variables, it was found that rather than replacing primary contacts, formal associational ties fostered greater numbers of local primary contacts. The zero-order gamma coefficients between participation in local formal associations and relative number of people known in the local community and number of friends living in close proximity were +.64 and +.36 respectively. Even when controls were instituted for population size, density, length of residence, S.E.S., and family life cycle, participation in local formal associations had a positive impact well beyond the .001 level of significance on both relative number of people known in the local community and number of adult friends residing in close proximity.

The final step in the analysis was to examine the relationship between the independent variables — especially population size, population density, and length of residence — and the three community sentiment variables, controlling for the intervening social network variables. These findings are presented in Table 6.

Three specific relations emerge as statistically significant and each of these help to explicate the systemic model of the local community. First, with respect to the variable "sense of community," only one independent variable, length of residence, has a direct and positive effect when all other intervening social network variables are controlled. The fact that length of residence has this direct effect in addition to its relatively strong indirect influence via strengthening local social networks provides clear support for the systemic model.

Second, the variable "sorry to leave the local community" exhibits a significant relation only with population density when other intervening social network factors are controlled. This relationship is negative and is an extension of the findings presented in Table 2, namely the zero-order negative association between density and "sorry to leave." These findings imply that attachment to a community does not preclude conditions under which a person is prepared to leave — which is the implication of the idea of "community of limited liability." It appears likely that in high density areas the housing conditions and the quality of schooling are such as to have a limiting and weakening effect on community attractiveness.

TABLE 6

STANDARDIZED PARTIAL REGRESSION COEFFICIENTS BETWEEN
INDEPENDENT VARIABLES AND COMMUNITY SENTIMENTS
CONTROLLING FOR INTERVENING SOCIAL NETWORK VARIABLES

(N = 1,648)

Independent Variables	Sense of Community	Sorriness to Leave	Interest in Community
Population Size	.03	.00	−.05
Population Density	.00	−.10*	−.02
Length of Residence	.14*	.07	−.01
Socio-economic Status	−.02	.01	.10*
Family Life Cycle	.00	.06	−.02

* Statistically significant at p<.001 based on ratio of regression coefficient to its standard error with 1 and 1647 degrees of freedom.

Third, the attitudinal variable, the degree of interest in the affairs of the local community, is influenced directly only by socio-economic status, when the other intervening social networks variables are controlled. In other words, higher social status produces greater interest in community affairs, both directly and indirectly, through more extensive and expanded formal associational ties. Such a finding was to be expected; higher status persons have the skills and tastes required for such associational involvements and the educational background for greater interest. Their social position implies a greater stake in the community or at least a greater ability to articulate their interests. But we are dealing not only with a set of rational self-interests, but rather with a pattern of concerns which are embedded to some degree in local social attachments and which, even for higher socio-economic persons, is strengthened first by longer residence and second by both informal and formal social networks.

IMPLICATIONS OF THE ANALYSIS

The data collected by the Royal Commission on Local Government in England by means of a sample survey supply an opportunity to explore basic issues in community organization and urban sociology, issues directly related to the interests and goals of the Royal Commission. Using data from a large scale survey of residents of English communities, we have shown that community sentiments were substantially influenced by participation in social networks. Whether or not a person experienced a sense of community, had a strong interest in the affairs of the community, or would be sorry to leave the community was found to be strongly influenced by his local friendship and kinship bonds and formal and informal associational ties.

Participation in these local social networks, in turn, was found to be influenced primarily by length of residence in the community. The longer the length of residence, the more extensive were friendship and kinship bonds and local associational ties. Even when population size, density, S.E.S., and family life cycle were held constant, length of residence exhibited a significant direct effect on participation in local friendship, kinship and associational networks.

On the other hand, neither population size nor density exhibited a significant relationship with participation in local friendship, kinship or associational networks when length of residence, S.E.S., and family life-cycle were held constant. The most general inference to be drawn, therefore, is that the systemic model of community organization based on length of residence is a more appropriate model than the linear development model (based on population size and density) for the study of community participation in mass society.

In drawing inferences from these data about the inadequacy of the *Gemeinschaft-Gesellschaft* orientation and of Wirth's reformulations, it is necessary to underscore that we are dealing with a cross-sectional sample. But three conclusions continue to emerge and re-emerge from this sample survey study of the social fabric of the local community in the mass society. First, location in communities of increased size and density does not weaken networks of kinship and friendship. Instead, length of residence is a central and crucial factor in the development of these social networks. Second, location in communities of increased size and density does not result in a substitution of secondary for primary and informal contacts. Indeed, the results suggest that formal ties foster more extensive primary contacts within the local community. Third, increased population size and density does not lead to the weakening of community attachments. But there is support for the notion of "community of limited liability" in that community attachments are not incompatible with desire to avoid the negative and undesirable features of local community life.

This analysis emphasizes the importance of length of residence, supported by the impact of associational life in accounting for community attachments. We are in this respect dealing with a process of "socialization" so to speak. In the contemporary setting length of residence requires careful analytical appraisal. Of course, length of residence is influenced by population growth. But we are making use of length of residence as an indicator of ecological, social organizational and normative processes. Length of residence is a reflection of the impact of large scale organizations on the life chances and values of the residents of the massive metropolitan concentrations which advanced industrial society has created. Length of residence of a citizen is not to be thought of primarily or even essentially as an individualistic or voluntaristic act. It is in good measure the impact of the industrial order in the allocation and reallocation of employment and transportation opportunities. There is merit in speaking of this process as the social construction of community – a term offered by Gerald Suttles in elaborating the older notion of the social world of the metropolis.[14]

Those who are concerned with the design of an appropriate system of local government need to take into consideration the relationship between residential mobility and community participation in the contemporary industrial order. These data and the theoretical perspective which we have employed reject the simple-minded notion that population density and residential mobility weaken community participation and attachment; for at a minimum that assumes some desired prior state of community participation. Instead it is more appropriate to emphasize that geographical mobility limits the capacity of a person and his family to develop effective patterns of community participation and attachment. Local voluntary associations assist in the formation of such attachments but they are at best secondary to the degree of residential stability. Of course, a modern industrial society could not operate on the basis of pervasive and all-powerful localistic attachments, but that is not the dominant dilemma in Britain. Nevertheless it is striking that Britain has a lower rate of residential mobility than most advanced industrial societies and that economic growth probably requires a higher rate of labour mobility than has been the case in the past.

The body of data to which these findings contribute does not indicate that the industrial order produces a "doomsday" machine in which, for the society as a whole or for each person and his family, the degree of residential stability is progressively declining. It does not indicate an evolutionary process in which social networks and communal attachments are destined to atrophy. It would be an equally gross error to think of the social organization of the local community as destined to develop a natural and effective equilibrium reflecting the transportation and communication system of the period.

The organization of the local community is a social and in turn a political construction which reflects not only the impact of large scale institutional factors, but the consequence of cultural tradition and the response of administrative agencies and voluntary associations which have a base in the local community. Comparisons between Great Britain and the United States are suggestive, even in the absence of adequate data. Great Britain is a society in which the rate of residential movement is much lower than in the United States, in part reflecting cultural tradition and in part reflecting industrial practices as well as the structure of local government. The results would indicate more extensive patterns of local social networks and stronger community affiliations. These social networks and community affiliations appear to contribute to the restraints and civility which operate in the British political system. However, it would be a grave error to assert that local community adhesion automatically contributes to political effectiveness and socio-political change. When local community attachments are reinforced by primordial sentiments — particularly of a racial and religious nature — they obviously become highly disruptive of democratic political systems. There is an optimum — but difficult to define — balance between localist attachments and a sense of participation in the larger society.

Thus, the patterns of community participation and sentiment need to be assessed in the context of the relative capacity and tenacity of the administrative organs of government and the political institutions to aggregate these local elements into a national policy. Again a comparison between the United States and Great Britain suggests that the system of local government in Britain is more adequately integrated into the national polity.

The contemporary extensive reorganization of local government will have a strong impact on the balance between local attachments and national integration. The trend toward larger units for the goals of efficiency and political consolidation complicate the tasks of local government. They make the tasks of articulating administrative agencies and elected bodies with the social structure and social networks of the local community more difficult. Each step toward consolidation of administrative and political units requires counter efforts to maintain and extend contact and interaction with an urban population whose persistent patterns of geographical mobility inhibit participation and integration into their home area.

NOTES

1. Robert E. Park and Ernest W. Burgess, *The City*, University of Chicago Press, Chicago, 1925; Roderick D. McKenzie, *The Metropolitan Community*, McGraw Hill, New York, 1933; E. Franklin Frazier, *The Negro Family in the United States*, The University of Chicago Press, Chicago, 1939; Amos Hawley, *Human Ecology: A Theory of Community Structure*, Ronald Press, New York, 1950; Ernest W. Burgess and H.J. Locke, *The Family: From Institution to Companionship*, American Book Co., New York, 1953; Michael Young and Peter Willmott, *Family and Kinship in East London*, Routledge and Kegan Paul, London, 1957; Peter Willmott and Michael Young, *Family and Class in a London Suburb*, Routledge and Kegan Paul, London, 1960; Leonard Reissman, *The Urban Process*, The Free Press, Glencoe, 1964; Philip M. Hauser, "The Chaotic Society: Product of the Social Morphological Revolution," *American Sociological Review*, Vol. 34, 1969, pp. 1-18; Amos Hawley, *Urban Society: An Ecological Approach*, Ronald Press, New York, 1971.

2. Louis Wirth, "Urbanism as a Way of Life", *American Journal of Sociology*, Vol. 44, 1938, pp. 3-24; O.A. Olsen and S.B. Hammond (eds.), *Social Structure and Personality in a City*, Routledge and Kegan Paul, London, 1954; R. Firth (ed.), *Two Studies of Kinship in London*, London School of Economics Monograph on Social Anthropology, 15, Athlone Press, London, 1956; J.M. Mogey, *Family and Neighbourhood*, Oxford University Press, London, 1956; Elizabeth Bott, *Family and Social Network: Roles, Norms and External Relationships in Ordinary Urban Families*, Tavistock Publications, London, 1957; C.S. Wilson, "The Family and Neighbourhood in a British Community," Unpublished Manuscript Thesis, University of Cambridge; Philip M. Hauser, "Urbanization: An Overview," in Philip M. Hauser and Leo F. Schnore (eds.), *The Study of Urbanization*, John Wiley, New York, 1965; Jennifer Platt, *Social Research in Bethal Green: An Evaluation of the Work of the Institute of Community Studies*, MacMillan, New York, 1971. Claude S. Fischer, "On Urban Alienations and Anomie: Powerlessness and Social Isolation," *American Sociological Review*, Vol. 38, 1973, pp. 311-326.

3. Ferdinand Toennies, *Gemeinschaft und Gesellschaft*, Fues's Verlag: Leipzig, 1887.

4. Louis Wirth, *op. cit.*

5. Robert E. Park and Ernest W. Burgess, *Introduction to the Science of Sociology*, University of Chicago Press, Chicago, 1921 and *The City*, University of Chicago Press, 1925; Morris Janowitz (Ed.), *W.I. Thomas on Social Organization and Social Personality*, University of Chicago Press, Chicago, 1967.

6. Morris Janowitz, *The Community Press in an Urban Setting* (University of Chicago Press, Chicago, 1951, 1967).

7. Morris Axelrod, "Urban Structure and Social Participation," *American Sociological Review*, Vol. 21, 1956, pp. 13-18; Basil G. Zimmer, "Participation of Migrants in Urban Structures," *American Sociological Review*, Vol. 20, 1955, pp.218-224; Basil G. Zimmer and Amos H. Hawley, "The Significance of Memberships in Associations," *American Journal of Sociology*, Vol. 64, 1959, pp. 196-201; Eugene Litwak, "Voluntary Associations and Neighborhood Cohesion," *American Sociological Review*, Vol. 26, 1961, pp. 258-271; Nicholas Babchuck and John Edwards, "Voluntary Associations and the Integration Hypothesis," *Sociological Inquiry*, Vol. 2, 1965, pp. 149-162; John Edwards and Alan Booth, (Eds.), *Social Participation in Urban Society*, Schenkman Publishing Company, Cambridge, 1973.

8. We wish to acknowledge the assistance of Dr. Mark Abrams, Director, Survey Unit, British Social Science Research Council for arranging access to the basic survey materials collected for the Royal Commission on Local Government in England. This survey was conducted by Research Services, Ltd., in March, 1967, and was published under the title, *Community Attitudes Survey: England* (London: HMSO, 1969).

9. F. Zweig, *Women's Life and Labour*, Gollancz, London, 1952; Peter Townsend, *The Family Life of Old People*, Routledge and Kegan Paul, 1957; Wendell Bell and Marion D. Boat, "Urban Neighborhoods and Informal Social Relations," *American Journal of Sociology*, Vol. 62, 1957, pp. 391-398; Harold L. Wilensky, "Orderly Careers and Social Participation: The Impact of Work History on Social Integration in the Middle Mass," *American Sociological Review*, Vol. 26, 1961, pp.521-539. Herbert J. Gans, "Urbanism and Suburbanism as Ways of Life: A Re-evaluation of Definitions," in Arnold Rose (Ed.), *Human Behavior and Social Processes*, Houghton-Mifflin Company, 1962, pp. 625-648, and Gans, *The Urban Villagers*, The Free Press, New York, 1962; Bernard Lazerwitz, "Membership in Voluntary Associations and Frequency of Church Attendance," *Journal for the Scientific Study of Religion*, Vol. 2, 1962, pp. 74-84.

10. In the survey five response categories were utilized for the two questions regarding proportion of adult friends and relatives residing in the local community. The first four categories included: none of them; half or less of them; most of them; and all of them. An additional category was added to each respective question for those who claimed they didn't have any friends and/or relatives or only had one or two relatives. These respondents were not included in the first four categories because the relative proportions would not have been meaningful and were, therefore, scored as missing data for those questions.

A number of people also failed to respond to other items on the questionnaire, which served to reduce the sample size for those particular items.

11. For ease of presentation, the intervening networks variables are given in terms of (1) per cent knowing many or very many people in their local community; (2) per cent having at least six friends within 10 minutes' walk of their home; (3) per cent having three or more relatives (excluding nuclear family) living within 10 minutes' walk of their home; (4) per cent responding that more than one-half of their friends live in their local community; (5) per cent responding that more than one-half of their relatives reside in their local community; (6) per cent belonging to two or more formal associations (organizations) in the local community; and (7) per cent participating in two or more informal social activities in the local community.

12. That is, number of people known in the local community was dichotomized into (1) none, one or two, a few and (2) many, very many; number of friends into (1) five or less and (2) over five; number of relatives into (1) two or less and (2) over two; proportion of friends into (1) none, half or less and (2) most, all; proportion of relatives into (1) none, half or less and (2) most, all; membership in formal organizations into (1) less than two and (2) two or more; informal social activities into (1) less than two, and (2) two or more; sense of belonging to community into (1) no and (2) yes; sorriness to leave into (1) very pleased, quite pleased, neither sorry nor pleased and (2) quite sorry, very sorry to leave; interest in community into (1) not at all interested, only a little interested and (2) quite interested, very interested.

13. When computing standardized partial regression coefficients, it is important to insure that multicollinearity is not seriously affecting the regression coefficients. If very high degrees of statistical interdependence exist among independent variables, measurement errors can seriously distort the regression coefficients (cf. Gordon, 1967; Blalock, 1964). Zero-order correlations (Pearsonian r's) were therefore computed among each set of exogenous and intervening variables. Among the exogenous variables, only population size and density ($r = .52$) exhibited a correlation above .10. Among the intervening variables, number of people known correlated +.33 with number of friends, +.30 with percent of friends in the local community, +.24 with number of relatives, +.21 with percent of relatives in the local community, +.21 with participation in formal associations, and +.16 with participation in informal social activities. Number of friends correlated +.23 with percent of friends in the local community, +.11 with number of relatives, +.11 with percent of relatives in the local community, +.13 with formal ties, and +.08 with informal social activities. Number of relatives correlated +.46 with percent of relatives in the local community and +.07 with both formal associational ties and informal social activities. Percent of relatives residing in the local community correlated +.09 with formal ties and +.13 with informal social activities, while formal associational ties and participation in informal social activities had a +.26 correlation. These correlations, though all statistically significant, are not large enough to make multicollinearity a problem in examining the model.

In computing the zero-order correlations and standardized regression coefficients between all variables in the model, we chose listwise deletion rather than pairwise deletion of cases that contained missing information on any of the 15 variables. Though this had the effect of reducing our final sample to 1,648, it is the only way to insure that all coefficients derived from the regression analysis are based on the same sample. A listing of those cases deleted from the original sample exhibited no systematic characteristics that we believed would have altered the final results.

14. Gerald Suttles, *The Social Construction of Communities,* University of Chicago Press, Chicago, 1973.

Chapter 8

CORRELATES OF RACIAL PREJUDICE

Richard T. Schaefer

In 1966 an extensive social survey (Rose, 1969) was undertaken to chart the extent and patterns of prejudice toward immigrants from the New Commonwalth countries (the West Indies, India, and Pakistan) to Great Britain. This paper seeks to present a reanalysis of the data from the 1966-1967 Survey of Race Relations.[1] The objective of this reanalysis is to place in a systematic framework those social variables that are indicated as crucial in accounting for differences in the extent and pattern of prejudice. The approach employed is explicitly sociological, although it is clearly recognized that psychological analysis can also be utilized whether as an alternative frame of reference or to reinforce the type of approach used in this reanalysis.

Prejudice is one aspect of social attitudes and can be described by means of a survey such as that which was undertaken in 1966. Attitudes are a part of the social reality which policy makers must take into consideration and are worthy of analysis both for policy and theoretical purposes. There is little point in developing a specialized theory of racial prejudice. On the cognitive level, prejudice may be seen as one part of the attitude formation process. On the behavioural level, prejudice and resulting discrimination and avoidance are aspects of intergroup relations. Although use will be made of multivariate analysis, the relevant variables can be grouped on the basis of existing sociological theory into two sets of variables.

A person's racial attitudes are strongly conditioned by his position in the social structure and are also deeply influenced by a situational component reflecting the extent and nature of his interaction with minority group members. Position in the social structure is seen as the basic or independent factor. It is assumed that the variables of contact and interaction, the situational correlates, act as intervening variables between prejudice and the independent variables that reflect an individual's position in the social structure of society.

Explanations based on position in the social structure make use of variables such as social class position (as well as income and education), age, mobility, membership in voluntary associations, and political party orientations. These explanations rest on the belief that an individual's position in the social structure serves both to indicate his group interest and to reflect his patterns of socialization. On the basis of group interest and socialization experience it is possible to make inferences about the level of prejudice that one would expect. It is hypothesized that a higher position in the social structure as measured by social class and education would lead to lower levels of racial prejudice. From the point of view of group interests, individuals in the middle class rather than those in the working class would be expected to have less conflict of interests with New Commonwealth immigrants. The affluent, or at least those relatively high in social class as measured by occupation, are insulated from the threat posed by foreign competition for scarce resources such as well-paying jobs. This insulation would suggest a greater tolerance for the immigrants who offer little challenge to those with a middle class background. In addition, the educational experience of middle class individuals reinforces their socialization experience and their cultural milieu, thus contributing to the diminishing of prejudice.[2] The very fact of being highly educated in a technological society serves as an advantage over aliens so that trained people can afford to be tolerant without sacrificing their group interests.[3] Nonetheless, social class could not be taken as a comprehensive explanation without relationship to other social structural variables.

Age is a second measure of position in a society's social structure and provides further clarification as to level of prejudice. The hypothesis that young people would be less prejudiced than older individuals in part reflects the impact of both increased and more recent education which is oriented toward a stronger emphasis on universalistic standards and norms. But it is asserted that age independent of education would have an effect on race prejudice in that the young have little to gain by applying and having applied particularistic criteria that would only serve to emphasize seniority and other accumulated rewards. These same privileges that generally work to the detriment of youth also serve to be barriers to qualified immigrants. Furthermore each successive age cohort tends to be more liberal and flexible.[4] The apparent conservatism of older generations partly reflects a frame of reference once possibly liberal that now tends to be closer to the moderate or conservative position.[5]

Other relevant factors placing one in a society's social structure that were available in this analysis are political party orientation, social mobility, and trade union membership. Tolerance is a part of "liberalism" and the followers of the more liberal national political parties might be expected to be more tolerant toward nonwhite immigrants. One would expect supporters, as indicated by the willingness to make financial contributions, to be more likely to embrace the approach of their respective parties; though it should be noted that since Labour's 1965 White Paper, the differences among the parties on issues affecting immigrants have narrowed and perhaps disappeared.

Social mobility supplies one form of summary measure of social change and would be expected to have its impact on an individual's social attitudes. The pressures and strains due to intergenerational and intragenerational mobility may be associated with the creation of ill-feelings toward minority group members. Feelings of insecurity and hence antagonism would be greater among people who have been frustrated in seeking higher status. Such individuals would resort to and promote particularistic values to secure themselves from further downward mobility. The creation of an underclass, such as a minority group, reassures one of one's social worth and guarantees a certain measure of economic security and social comfort. Similarly the increasing number of nonwhite immigrants and the likelihood of yet more despite restrictive laws is frequently seen to be a direct threat to semi-skilled trade unionists. Trade union membership should serve to amplify and extend the relative vulnerability of different social classes to outside pressures. As has been noted, the immigrant presents a very different threat to the labourer than to the manager or employer.

From the preceding discussion it is seen as possible to identify a series of sociological variables which may be presumed to be linked to an individual's racial prejudice. Furthermore, by means of multivariate statistical analysis one can calculate the relative contributions of these variables, and determine in what combinations they interact to account for different levels of prejudice.

The second stage in the analysis was to explore the extent to which the situational component, namely patterns of interaction and contact with nonwhite immigrants, conditions racial prejudice. The social structural variables would not adequately account alone for individual differences in patterns of prejudice. Individuals with similar social stratification or structural characteristics may display some important variation in their level of racial intolerance due to the situational component of contact and interaction. In the recent literature there has been a strong emphasis on the hypothesis that increased majority-minority group contact may under certain circumstances reduce racial prejudice.[6] The material on interpersonal relationships reflects the importance of the nature of the circumstances under which contact takes place.[7]

The consequences of interaction and contact are very problematic and there are conditions under which they would actually increase racial prejudice. It was hypothesized that the positive or negative consequences of the situational factors depended not only on the frequency, but also on the quality of the contact, the context of the social contact, and the status of those in contact. One can readily identify specific patterns of contact which would be expected not to conform to the general hypothesis that increased contact reduces prejudice. A white Englishman who continued to observe a West Indian in an unskilled factory job would probably not modify his preconceived notions. Such a situation would only strengthen stereotyped conceptions and would certainly not weaken the already learned belief that immigrants from the Caribbean are inferior. Likewise a second pattern of contact was implied earlier in discussing the low socio-economic status of Englishmen who are in competition with Commonwealth immigrants for jobs. Under the circumstances of competitive, involuntary association, there may be little likelihood of a decrease in hostility and a lessening of tensions. The available data from the Survey made possible the exploration of a variety of aspects of the situational component. It was hypothesized that equal status contacts in noncompetitive situations would lead to an increase in tolerance and mitigate the higher levels of prejudice.

METHODOLOGY

The data re-analyzed in this research were drawn from the Survey of Race Relations, conducted by Research Services Ltd. for the Institute of Race Relations in London and financed by the Nuffield Foundation. The Survey resulted in a principal publication, *Colour*

and Citizenship: A Report on British Race Relations, edited by E.J.B.
Rose. The survey itself consisted of two parts: an extensive schedule
in five boroughs preselected for their high concentrations of nonwhite
population and a shorter schedule administered to a national sample
of white adults.

The basis of the borough sample, that part of the Survey on which
this paper concentrates, was the Register of Electors from which each
n-th name was drawn where "n" was predetermined to achieve
a completed sample of approximately 500 for each borough. From
the original list of 4,500 names drawn, 11.5 per cent refused to be
interviewed, 8.6 per cent could not be contacted after four attempts,
and 7.2 per cent of respondents were nonwhite and thus eliminated.
This produced a final sample of 2,494 after incomplete interviews
were eliminated. The field work was conducted by Research Services
Ltd. from December 1966 to February 1967. The final sample
reflects the total population as indicated by the 1966 Census in
terms of social class. The sample slightly over-represents women (55
per cent in the Census) and the elderly (19 per cent over the age
65 as compared with 17 per cent in the Census) (Rose, 1969: 785).
The white adult interviewers introduced themselves as from Research
Services Limited and indicated that they were conducting a "public
opinion survey on how people feel about different countries and
their own neighbourhood." (In the national sample the explanation
was, "the survey was of people's attitudes to people who come to
Britain from abroad").

The sample for the national survey consisting of 2,260 white
adults was interviewed in March and April 1967 and was based on
a quota sample in terms of four age groups within four social grades
controlled by sex. The over 70 quota districts were arranged into
13 larger districts (e.g. Midland, East Riding, Scotland, Wales, etc.)
corresponding generally to census boundaries. Because of the
detailed interview schedule used in the borough sample, most of
the analysis to follow will rely on this sample.

The experience of the British with aliens and indigenous nonwhites
reflects a mixture of sympathetic acceptance and open hostility. To
find the relative balance between these two extremes in contemporary
times, it is necessary to turn to the 1966-1967 Survey of Race
Relations. The Survey remains the most comprehensive and rigorous
assessment of attitudes toward nonwhites in Britain. A necessary
step in a more adequate analysis of this Survey was the development
of a scale which allowed one to make distinctions concerning degrees

of prejudice rather than simply to make observations that differences do exist. Hypotheses concerning the relationships between the prejudice and certain social background and situational variables can be subjected to empirical test only when it is possible to measure each separate variable. Merely being able to note the presence of differences does not fulfil this requirement.

The immediate problem becomes which of several items should be combined to measure patterns of prejudice. Once this selection is completed, careful note must be made concerning the assumptions about either the character of the data subsumed under a given concept or the items themselves which are used as data. The interview schedule used in the five borough sample offers nearly 500 potential scale items relevant to the relations between nonwhite Commonwealth immigrants and white Englishmen. Four items were selected from the borough interview schedule as the least ambiguous and the most relevant to assessing hostility to nonwhites. The items were:

(1) Special Entry Regulations. Do you think coloured people should be let into Britain to settle on the same basis as other people from abroad, or should there be special regulations for coloured people?
(2) Who Fired? Suppose there are two workers, one coloured and one white, who do exactly the same work. If one, and one only, has to be declared redundant (fired or released), should it be the coloured or the white worker?
(3) Who Promoted? Suppose there are two workers, one coloured and one white, who do exactly the same work. If one, and one only, has to be promoted, should it be the coloured or the white worker?
(4) Sympathetic Feelings. Do you feel more or less sympathetic towards coloured immigrants than about white people who live in similar conditions?

The mean level of association (Goodman-Kruskal Gamma) of the above four items with one another was .56. Including any additional item brought the mean below the predetermined level of .50. Also each additional item further reduced the sample in the scale since a "don't know" response to one or more items eliminated the respondent from the sample. A special scale was constructed to determine whether "don't know" responses represented some middle ground between being prejudiced and unprejudiced. It was found that to include "don't knows" would not have increased the reliability of the scale and only increased the number of assumptions employed in constructing the scale. The scale used is a summative or Likert-type scale. Any given respondent's position on the scale of prejudice-unprejudice toward Commonwealth immigrants was

represented by the algebraic summation of the individual's responses
to the four items. The summative scale has the value of indicating
a respondent's level of prejudice by placing the subject along
a continuum, one end of which has been defined as prejudiced, the
other less prejudiced. On a summative scale the maximum score is
easily interpreted as a consistently prejudiced response to all four
items. Similarly a minimum score on a summative scale represents
a consistently unprejudiced response. Once constructed the scale
produced a distribution in which there was a declining rate from no
prejudice shown to strongly prejudiced. Based upon this summative
scale, responses to the four prejudice items were arranged as
indicated in Table 1.

TABLE 1

PREJUDICE SCALE VALUES (BOROUGH SAMPLE)

Value	Category	Responses	Frequency
0	No Prejudice Shown	4 Not Prejudiced	23.9 (501)
1	Weak Prejudice	3 Not Prejudiced, 1 Prejudiced	24.0 (502)
2	Slight Prejudice	2 Not Prejudiced, 2 Prejudiced	21.6 (451)
3	Moderate Prejudice	1 Not Prejudiced, 3 Prejudiced	17.7 (370)
4	Strong Prejudice	4 Prejudiced	12.6 (263)

N = 2,087

NOTE: An additional 407 respondents offered a "don't know" response to 1 of the
4 prejudice items and were eliminated from the sample. Percentages do not sum to 100 per
cent due to rounding error.
SOURCE: 1966-1967 Survey of Race Relations.

Some reference is made in this paper to the national sample and
the relative levels of prejudice displayed among its 2,260 respondents.
The problem of constructing a prejudice scale for the national sample
is simplified by the lack of items even remotely reflecting a
respondent's prejudicial attitudes. There are only two items that
consider prejudice and they both relate to the area of employment —
who should be promoted and who should be declared redundant.
The development of a scale using only two items is rather simple but
also rather questionable. The general tendency to respond to both

questions in the same manner suggests that in practice the scale is defined by the response to one item. Table 2 indicates the summative scale using two items. Less than 20 per cent of the sample responded differently (that is, prejudiced to one and unprejudiced to the other) to the two items. On a scale of 0 to 2, the mean level for the entire sample was .79.

TABLE 2

NATIONAL PREJUDICE SCALE

Level of Prejudice (Number of Prejudiced Responses)	Number (Per cent)	
None (0)	48.9	
		(1,105)
Moderate (1)	19.3	
		(437)
Strong (2)	27.5	
		(621)
D.K. (to either item)	4.3	
		(97)

N = 2,260 (2,163)

Most of the subsequent analysis will employ the prejudice scale based on the five borough sample. Great detail has been given concerning the construction of the prejudice scale because the measuring device is so crucial to the subsequent findings. Since conclusions based upon the scale can be no stronger than the scale itself, care was taken to reduce the number of assumptions made in the development of a prejudice scale for use in this study.

CORRELATES OF RACIAL PREJUDICE: SOCIAL STRUCTURAL CORRELATES

The re-analysis of the Survey provided the opportunity to determine the impact of various background characteristics on an individual's racial prejudice. Table 3 summarizes the relationship between several social background variables and prejudice by presenting the basic cross-tabulations. The data indicated that certain characteristics were associated with different levels of intolerance toward Commonwalth immigrants. Respondents who have

TABLE 3

SUMMARY OF RELATIONSHIPS BETWEEN SOCIAL BACKGROUND
VARIABLES AND PREJUDICE

Background Variable	Number of Prejudiced Responses		
	0–1	*2*	*3–4*
Respondent's Social Class (self-designated)			
Upper Middle	51%	15%	33%
Lower Middle	46	24	31
Skilled Working	46	21	32
Semi-skilled	49	23	28
Unskilled	44	27	28
Party Orientation (among those making a contribution)			
Conservative	41	19	40
Labour	66	19	14
Liberal	54	18	27
Terminal Education Age			
Under 16	45	22	33
16 to 18	56	21	22
19 or over	73	15	11
Sex			
Male	50	20	29
Female	46	23	30
Respondent's Age			
21-24	57	22	21
25-34	61	19	20
35-44	53	21	26
45-54	46	23	31
55-64	39	21	39
over 65	38	24	37
Type of Occupational Mobility (intergenerational)			
Upward	50	23	27
Stationary	45	21	34
Downward	49	23	27

contributed financially to the Labour and Liberal parties were less
likely to respond in a prejudiced manner than were contributors to
the Conservative party. The better educated were also shown to be
more tolerant. It has been maintained that more education is
conducive to a more universalistic outlook and tends to make one

less likely to endorse myths that sustain racial prejudice. It would also appear from the table that there was a trend for older respondents to be more likely than younger cohorts to offer prejudiced responses to the scale items. A respondent's sex, was shown to have little conclusive bearing on his racial prejudice.

Social mobility was less definite in its relationship with prejudice. The differences were rather small among the three types of mobility but in so far as differences were present, they indicated that respondents who have experienced mobility were less prejudiced than those who have not experienced any intergenerational mobility. Bettelheim and Janowitz (1949, 1964) observed that upward mobility was associated with tolerance of Jews and blacks but also found downward mobility to be related to more intolerant feelings, rather than less as indicated in this reanalysis.

There are several possible explanations for this departure from previous studies. Past researchers (Hodge and Treiman: 1966: 95-97, Marsh 1970:323) have suggested that such discrepancies in mobility data may represent a failure to consider the importance of class of origin and destination. An examination was made of prejudice and intergenerational mobility holding the respondent's present class, the class of destination, constant. The relationship remained the same in all social classes except for the skilled working class. In other categories the upwardly mobile were the most tolerant, the stationary more prejudiced and the downwardly mobile at an intermediate level. This control for class of destination still supported the finding that those who had experienced downward mobility were actually less prejudiced than those who were stationary in terms of social class. Although the upwardly mobile individuals in the lower middle or skilled working class did tend to be less tolerant than the other classes, the differences were rather small.

The second explanation may lie in the effect of other social factors found to be significant such as age and formal schooling independent of the mobility experience of the respondent. An analysis was made of the mean levels of prejudice for mobility holding education and age constant, separately and both at once. Controlling for either age or terminal education age, the relationship generally remained where the downwardly mobile were less prejudiced than the respondents who belonged to the same social class as their fathers. When both age and education were held constant, the relationship became less clear. Among the post-war educated the differences did tend to confirm earlier mobility studies although the differences were neither striking nor statistically significant. The upwardly mobile were the least prejudiced and the downwardly mobile were more prejudiced in this one case.

Clearly the various social correlates are not independent of one another. For example, both education and age were found to be associated with prejudice, but they were also closely associated with each other in that younger cohorts are better educated. In the five borough sample the relationship between increased formal schooling and tolerance was greater among those receiving their education since World War II. Table 4 presents the borough data and indicates that

TABLE 4

RELATIONSHIP OF EDUCATION TO PREJUDICE HOLDING
AGE CONSTANT

Terminal Education Age	Level of Prejudice Shown Under 35					
	None 0	Weak 1	Slight 2	Moderate 3	Strong 4	D.K.
Under 16	27.6 (90)	27.3 (89)	21.1 (69)	15.3 (50)	8.5 (28)	(62)
16 to 18	43.4 (56)	25.5 (33)	19.3 (25)	7.7 (10)	3.8 (5)	(20)
19 or Over[a]	54.8 (17)	25.8 (8)	3.2 (1)	16.1 (5)	—	(5)

N = 572 $\gamma = -.30$ $x^2 = 25.50$, d.f. = 8, significant at .01 level

	Age 35 and Over					
Under 16	19.8 (266)	22.7 (305)	22.1 (296)	20.1 (270)	15.0 (202)	(263)
16 to 18	24.8 (52)	24.4 (51)	22.4 (47)	15.3 (32)	12.9 (27)	(41)
19 or Over[a]	37.5 (18)	31.2 (15)	22.9 (11)	6.2 (3)	2.0 (1)	(16)
N.A.		(1)				(4)

N = 1,921 $\gamma = -.18$ $x^2 = 22.39$, d.f. = 8, significant at .01 level

NOTE: Row percentages exclude "don't knows." Statistics exclude N.A. and D.K. cells and are therefore computed on the basis of N = 486 and N = 1,596.

[a] includes those in school at the time of the Survey.

when the control for age was introduced the gamma for the prejudice scale and those under 35 increased in power to −.30 while the gamma for those over 35 decreased in power to −.18. The level of association was −.25 between education and the prejudice scale when the age of the respondent was not controlled.[8] The effect of the school's curriculum on attitudes could be the result of a change in orientation toward the inhabitants of the Commonwealth in British schools since World War II. The empirical evidence insofar as it exists was difficult to evaluate given the problems of curriculum analysis and hazards of advancing causality. The evidence was clear that racial hostility was greater among the less educated and the effect of formal schooling was increased when age was controlled. This close interplay among the independent variables would suggest that greater attention needs to be given to all the components rather than measuring the impact of each one individually and thereby disregarding the effects of the other factors.

SOCIAL CORRELATES AND PREJUDICE: SITUATIONAL CORRELATES

The Survey provided information on two aspects of the situational component of racial prejudice: the individual level or the type and amount of personal interaction and second, the context or social environment in which he is operating. As to the former, the Survey indicated that mere contact does not necessarily reduce intergroup hostility, nor does prejudice always mean avoidance of contact. The data on residential proximity indicated that the more prejudiced respondents were more likely to live near immigrants than the less prejudiced respondents. This relationship continued when respondent's social class, age and terminal education age were held constant. There was evidence that the older settlements of immigrants, that is, those which predated the controversy surrounding entry privileges, were associated with lower feelings of prejudice. Although contact with immigrants in work situations, as a bus conductor, or in a bar, were associated with reduced hostility, it was clearly important to know the nature of the interaction. Whenever the respondent had assessed the immigrants' conduct to be correct or found the experience to be favourable, there was greater expression of tolerant feelings toward the nonwhite Commonwealth immigrants.

Some variations were found when the effect of the independent variables on contact between white Englishmen and New Commonwealth immigrants was examined. It was noted that working with immigrants tended to be associated with higher levels of prejudice among the more educated respondents. This may have reflected the difficulties some employers have had in working with non-English speaking immigrants. Furthermore work experience with Pakistanis among those under 35 tended to be related with higher levels of hostility. This suggested that Pakistanis more than West Indians may be entering work situations which tend to be more competitive and place them in contact with younger Englishmen. The complexity of the relationship was also reflected in the data concerning school children. Having a few school children in contact with immigrants was related to low hostility, while feelings of prejudice increased as the concentration of immigrants increased. The survey confirmed the importance of intergroup contact in reducing or increasing prejudice. It is also evident that for such contact to be actually associated with a lessening of prejudice it must occur under conditions of equal status, and be assessed by the participants as positive and favourable.

The second aspect deals with regional differences in prejudice and the impact these may have on individual attitudes. It is hypothesized that a given community or region may inhibit or stimulate racial antipathy (c.f. Marsh, 1973). Naturally the opportunity for contact with New Commonwealth immigrants is not equally available to all Englishmen. While about 3.6 per cent of the British came from foreign countries at the time of the Survey, the proportion in the five boroughs ranged from 5.3 to 12.5 per cent. In Lambeth where one out of every eight people was "coloured," the opportunities for intergroup interaction were greater than in those areas having few if any nonwhite Englishmen. Opportunities do not insure interaction. Banton (1959:11) argues that "British behaviour towards coloured people is characterized not by aggressiveness but by avoidance of them in relationships which might get out of hand." The presence of intergroup contact in a given town or region, it is hypothesized, will serve to encourage or discourage ill-feelings toward minority group people. This situational component serves to determine prejudice toward nonwhites.

Although little attention has been given in social research to the differences in social attitudes throughout Britain, the national sample was divided into twelve quota districts. The location and mean level of prejudice for each of the districts is presented in Figure 1 with the

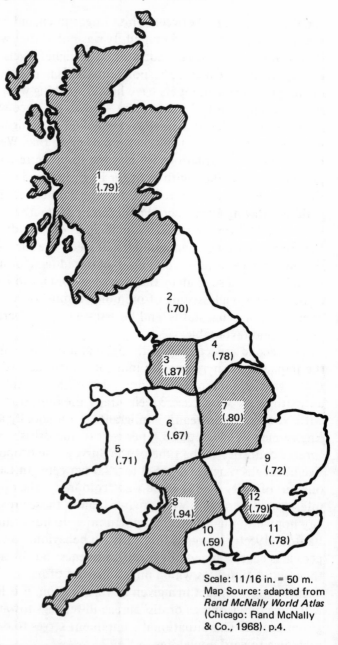

Scale: 11/16 in. = 50 m.
Map Source: adapted from
Rand McNally World Atlas
(Chicago: Rand McNally
& Co., 1968). p.4.

Figure 1: MEAN LEVEL OF PREJUDICE BY QUOTA DISTRICTS
Key: 1. Scotland   2. North   3. Northwest   4. East and West Riding   5. Wales
6. Midlands   7. North Midlands   8. Southwest   9. East   10. Southeast
11. South   12. London.
Hatched quota districts are those areas with a mean level of prejudice equal to
or greater than that of the entire sample (.79).

high prejudice areas designated. The national prejudice scale ranged from 0 to 2, reflecting the number of prejudiced responses, with a mean of .79 for the entire sample. The average level of prejudice within a district ranged from a high of .94 in the Southwest to a low of .59 in the Southeast. Both London and Scotland had a mean of .79, the same mean as that for the entire sample. Generally there was little association between the level of prejudice in a given quota district and the amount of white-nonwhite contact in a region. For example both Scotland and London, which had the same levels of prejudice, have vastly different levels of experience with nonwhites. A similar contrast occurred between the Southeast and the Midlands which had the lowest levels of prejudice, the former having levels of interaction with immigrants at or below the national average with the latter well above the national average. In an effort to explain the relatively high level of intolerance in the Southwest, one may observe that the "West Country" has undergone little change in its rural nature and is relatively immune from urban change. The Northwest, on the other hand, has a large working class population and a history of anti-Irish resentment and conflict. Consequently, the two areas reflecting the greatest amount of prejudice are those which have undergone the extremes, the most and the least, in the amount and direction of social change.

A second comparison that can be made from the re-analysis of the Survey data is the examination of the levels of prejudice in the five boroughs or towns sampled. As indicated in Table 5, the three boroughs having the smaller mean prejudice scores are Bradford, with 1.59; Ealing, with 1.63; and Nottingham, with 1.66. At the higher level, the Lambeth sample had a mean prejudice score of 1.85 and Wolverhampton of 1.88 in comparison to 1.71 for the entire borough sample. It was in those boroughs, Lambeth and Wolverhampton, where the concentration of nonwhites was the greatest and the residents' personal experience with them was the most extensive, that racial prejudice was the highest. Similarly, in comparison with the boroughs where racial hostility was less, the respondents indicated in other questions that they were more concerned about the presence of nonwhites in Lambeth and Wolverhampton and were more likely to feel that their neighbourhood was changing for the worse. Significantly, it was in the two boroughs of Wolverhampton and Lambeth that the immigrants tended to be more unskilled and were competing with white Englishmen for housing.

TABLE 5

BOROUGH RESIDENTS AND PREJUDICE SCALE

		Level of Prejudice Shown					
Borough	*Mean Score*	*None* 0	*Weak* 1	*Slight* 2	*Moderate* 3	*Strong* 4	*DK value*
Bradford	1.59	23.8	26.3	24.2	18.2	7.3	
		(127)	(140)	(129)	(97)	(39)	(67)
Ealing	1.63	25.6	25.9	20.4	15.9	11.9	
		(103)	(104)	(82)	(64)	(48)	(90)
Lambeth	1.85	22.0	22.2	21.2	15.5	16.9	
		(83)	(84)	(80)	(66)	(64)	(40)
Nottingham	1.66	23.4	26.0	23.6	14.8	11.9	
		(88)	(98)	(89)	(56)	(45)	(86)
Wolverhampton	1.88	24.3	19.0	17.8	21.8	16.8	
		(97)	(76)	(71)	(87)	(67)	(124)
N.A.	–	(3)	–	–	–	–	–
Entire Sample	1.76	23.9	24.0	21.6	17.7	12.6	
		(501)	(502)	(451)	(370)	(263)	(407)

N =2,494 x^2 = 42.96, df. = 16, significant at .001

NOTE: Row percentages exclude "don't know" values. The statistic excludes N.A.s and D.K.s and is based on a sample of 2,084.

From the 1966-1967 Survey of Race Relations, the past minimization of geographical peculiarities in social research in Britain appears unjustified with regard to racial attitudes. The social fabric of the region or town offers further explanation as to relative differences in individuals' racial attitudes. Further statistical analysis is necessary before one can maintain how important are such explanations relative to the other factors already discussed.

MULTIPLE REGRESSION SOLUTIONS TO RACIAL PREJUDICE

The complexity of social behaviour and the absence of controlled social environments require care to be taken in assigning relative levels of importance to a series of independent variables from cross-tabulations alone. The first step in the further statistical analysis consisted of producing a correlation analysis of the seventeen variables which have been the focus of attention in the five borough

TABLE 6

MATRIX OF MEASURES EXAMINED

| | | Variables – Intergroup Contact Measures | | | | | | | |
| | | Prejudice | | | | | | | |
Vari-able No.	Measure	1	2	3	4	5	6	7	8
2	Borough	-.088**							
3	Lviwi	-.036***	.268**						
4	Livind	.055***	.114***	.460**					
5	Livpak	.040*	-.023	.423***	.593**				
6	Wkwi	.096***	.062**	.118***	.014	.017			
7	Wkind	.087***	-.004	.069***	.084**	.058	.045**		
8	Wkpak	.060*	-.128***	.008	.013	.095**	.446***	.626**	
9	Classr	-.004	.026	-.024	.010	-.017	-.115***	-.064***	-.090**
10	Socgr	.116***	-.006	.007	.054*	.023	-.005	.056*	-.004
11	Party	-.103***	.073***	.020	.044*	.025	-.148***	-.099***	-.092**
12	Cont	.017	-.001	.028	-.005	.001	.032	.026	.004
13	Educ	.155***	-.019	-.007	.024	.005	.001	.096***	.008
14	Union	-.058*	-.058*	-.065*	-.026	-.012	-.143***	-.140***	-.117**
15	Sex	.033	-.014	.071**	.086***	.097**	-.252***	.258***	.242**
16	Age	.187***	0.042*	.077***	.039*	.030	.174***	.137**	.105
17	Mob	.027	-.018	-.000	.030	.016	.020	-.005	-.004

TABLE 6 CONTINUED

Respondent's Social Background Measures

		9	10	11	12	13	14	15	16
10	Socgr	.439							
11	Party	.213**	.171**						
12	Cont	.101**	.153**	.061*					
13	Educ	.316**	.397**	.113**	.153**				
14	Union	.109**	.104**	.162**	−.214**	.018			
15	Sex	.101**	.061**	−.083**	.086**	.011	−.281**		
16	Age	.041*	.205**	−.068**	−.070**	.171**	.002	.032	
17	Mob	.316**	.162**	.012	.022	.025	.007	.024	.063**

NOTES: Statistical significance: * indicates significant at .05 level, onetailed test; ** indicates significant at the .001 level, one-tailed test. All Pearson correlation coefficients are rounded off to three decimal places which accounts for −.000 correlations. *Variable Directory*: 1. Prejudice scale, higher values indicate greater amounts of prejudice. 2. Borough: Borough of respondents, higher numbers assigned to boroughs shown to have the lowest levels of prejudice (1 = Wolverhampton, 2 = Lambeth, 3 = Nottingham, 4 = Ealing, and 5 = Bradford). 3. Livwi: Living near West Indians, dichotomized with low value indicating yes. 4. Livind: Living near Indians, dichotomized with low value indicating yes. 5. Livpak: Living near Pakistanis, dichotomized with low value indicating yes. 6. Wkwi: Working near West Indians, dichotomized with low value indicating yes. 7. Wkind: Working near Indians, dichotomized with low value indicating yes. 8. Wkpak: Working near Pakistanis, dichotomized with low value indicating yes. 9. Classr: Respondent's social class, higher values indicate higher self-designated social class. 10. Socgr: Household head's social grade, higher values indicate higher self-designated social class. 11. Party: Political party preference: the three parties have been arranged in the alleged order of increasing liberality (1 = Conservative, 2 = Labour, 3 = Liberal). 12. Cont: Party contribution, dichotomized with low value indicating yes. 13. Educ: Terminal education age, low values indicate higher amounts of formal schooling. 14. Union: Trade union membership, dichotomized with low value indicating yes. 15. Sex: Respondent's sex, dichotomized with low value indicating males. 16. Age: Respondent's age, older respondents indicated by higher values. 17. Mob: Direction of mobility, the types of mobility have been arranged in the order of the hypothesized relationship with tolerance (1 = upward, 2 = stationary, 3 = downward).

survey. The brevity of the national survey does not allow its results to receive the same amount of scrutiny. Table 6 presents a matrix of the measures examined and offers a single summary statistic — the Pearson correlation. The coefficient varies from −1.0 to +1.0 with a coefficient of 0 always indicating no linear relationship while a +1.0 coefficient implies a "perfect" positive relationship. The correlation analysis assumes continuous data for reasons of economy and the ease of interpretation despite the nonparametric nature of the independent variables. The use of these measures as dummy variables is essential to the regression analysis that follows.[9]

The matrix reaffirms the significant association of age (.187) and education (.153) with prejudice. There is also a relatively high correlation (.171) compared to the other Pearson coefficients between the two independent variables of education and age, as has been previously noted. Other associations with the prejudice scale significant at the .001 level include the household head's social position (.116), party preference (−.103), working with West Indians (.096), and respondent's borough (−.088). Many of these social characteristics and measures of intergroup contact have strong interassociations, a number of which are significant at the .001 level. Therefore, one wishes to take into account the interrelationships among the independent variables and hostility toward nonwhite immigrants. To accomplish this multiple regression analysis will be introduced to this restudy of the 1966-1967 Survey of Race Relations.

The first step in exploring the multicollinearity of the independent variables is to produce a regression equation which would predict a given respondent's racial prejudice based upon his response to a number of items in the five borough survey.[10] Table 7 presents the multiple regression solution for estimating prejudice from the 16 independent variables previously noted in the correlation matrix. The multiple R gives the multiple correlation coefficient of determination; it explains 12 per cent of the total variance in racial attitudes in Britain.

For the purpose of evaluating racial prejudice, the more crucial question is not how much of the total variation can be explained, but how much by each selective subgroup of the independent variables in a regression equation. Three additional equations were computed; one based entirely on measures of the situational component, a second based on the position of the respondents in the social structure, and a third combining the most significant of both types of measures.

TABLE 7

MULTIPLE REGRESSION SOLUTION FOR ESTIMATING PREJUDICE
FROM ALL INDEPENDENT VARIABLES

No.	Independent Variable Measure	Partial Regression Coefficient	Path Coefficient or Beta-Weight
2	Borough	−.08083* (.02860)	−.08802
3	Living with West Indians	−.07479 (.09490)	−.02744
4	Living with Indians	−.15925 (.10544)	−.05669
5	Living with Pakistanis	.07733 (.10948)	.02680
6	Working with West Indians	.24284* (.09356)	.08860
7	Working with Indians	.07316 (.11659)	.02377
8	Working with Pakistanis	−.05924 (.12249)	−.01870
9	Respondent's Social Class	−.13364* (.04872)	−.09776
10	Household Head's Social Position	.20209** (.04471)	.15877
11	Political Party Preference	−.23977** (.06734)	−.10802
12	Party Contribution	.04204 (.12462)	.01026
13	Education	.27489** (.08829)	.10581
14	Trade Union Membership	−.09514 (.09121)	−.03320
15	Respondent's Sex	.01765 (.08882)	.00628
16	Respondent's Age	.18630** (.03176)	.17561
17	Direction of Mobility	.07767 (.06417)	.03744
Constant Term		1.2961	
Multiple R		.34765	
Multiple R^2		.12086	

* Significant at .05 level, coefficient greater than twice standard error.
** Significant at .01 level, coefficient greater than three times standard error. Figures in parenthesis are standard errors.

Table 8 presents the multiple regression solution for estimating prejudice from the seven situational variables. All the factors when combined are unable to provide an explanation for even 1 per cent of the variance. Among the seven situational variables, the respondents' borough and whether they have ever worked with West Indians clearly stand out as the most significant. The second statistically significant measure provides a more interesting dimension to the explanation of prejudice. The respondent's borough has a negative association with tolerance. The independent variable of borough of residence was arranged with the lower values assigned to the least tolerant boroughs as measured by the mean level of prejudice. This may suggest the relative importance of the social environment of a respondent which may either encourage or discourage the overt expression of prejudices as determined by position in the social structure. The fact that a respondent resided in a high prejudice borough makes a significant contribution to the predictability of a respondent's prejudice.

TABLE 8

MULTIPLE REGRESSION SOLUTION FOR ESTIMATING PREJUDICE
FROM INTERGROUP CONTACT VARIABLES

No.	Independent Variable Measure	Partial Regression Coefficient	Path Coefficient or Beta-Weight
6	Working with West Indians	−.34372** (.09566)	.12541
2	Borough	−.10561 (.02952)	−.11501
7	Working with Indians	.21525 (.11938)	.06995
8	Working with Pakistanis	−.17656 (.12715)	−.05572
4	Living with Indians	−.12825 (.10916)	−.04565
5	Living with Pakistanis	.06411 (.11402)	.02222
3	Living with West Indians	−.05324 (.09865)	−.01953
Constant Term		2.62714	
Multiple R		.18083	
Multiple R^2		.03270	

NOTES: ** Significant at .01 level, coefficient greater than three times standard error.
Variables are arranged in order of decreasing significance of the partial regression coefficient. Figures in parenthesis are standard errors.

TABLE 9

MULTIPLE REGRESSION SOLUTION FOR ESTIMATING PREJUDICE
FROM SOCIAL BACKGROUND VARIABLES

No.	Independent Variable Measure	Partial Regression Coefficient	Path Coefficient or Beta-Weight
16	Respondent's Age	.20031** (.03159)	.18882
10	Household Head's Social Position	.19109** (.04484)	.15012
11	Political Party Preference	−.28243** (:06712)	−.12724
13	Education	.22821* (.08808)	.11102
9	Respondent's Social Class	−.14197 (.04884)	−.10385
17	Direction of Mobility	.07539 (.06446)	.03634
14	Trade Union Membership	−.09159 (.09115)	−.03196
15	Respondent's Sex	.05073 (.08772)	.01804
12	Party Contribution	.04273 (.12488)	.01042
Constant Terms		1.20381	
Multiple R		.31913	
Multiple R^2		.10184	

NOTES: * Significant at .05 level, coefficient greater than twice standard error.
** Significant at .01 level, coefficient greater than three times standard error; figures in parenthesis are standard errors. Variables are arranged in order of decreasing significance of the partial regression coefficient.

In contrast to the previous equation, the regression solution (Table 9) comprised of only social background variables explains 10 per cent of the variance. Age, social position (or social class) of the household head, and political party orientation are all significant at the .01 level, with terminal education age significant at the .05 level. One relationship that may appear to depart from earlier analysis is the apparent relative unimportance of education. The respondent's extent of formal schooling is less important than the social position of the head of the household and the respondent's party allegiance. It appears that there is substantial "redundancy" or high intercorrelation among certain independent variables such as age, social position, and education. For example, the bivariate correlation between education and social grade is almost 0.4, significant at the .001 level. These three factors can be seen as part of the same subset. A respondent's political party may represent a different dimension of an individual's background which leads it to have little indirect effect. One may note that party preference has a relatively weaker association with prejudice, as measured by the Pearson correlation coefficient than does education; yet party plays a more vital role in the regression solution.[11] Apparently much of what a respondent's education serves to explain about prejudice is already described by age and the social position of the household head while political affiliation taps an independent aspect of the prejudiced person's position in the social structure.

TABLE 10

MULTIPLE REGRESSION SOLUTION FOR ESTIMATING PREJUDICE
FROM THE MOST SIGNIFICANT INDEPENDENT VARIABLES

No.	Independent Variable Measure	Partial Regression Coefficient	Path Coefficient of Beta-Weight
16	Respondent's Age	.18577** (.03130)	.17511
10	Household Head's Social Position	.20303** (.04342)	.15951
11	Political Party Preference	−.26525** (.06639)	−.11950
2	Borough	−.08960 (.02684)	−.09757
6	Working with West Indians	.25869** (.08100)	.09438
13	Education	.26976** (.08680)	.10391
9	Respondent's Social Class	−.11714* (.04590)	−.08569
Constant Term		1.20570	
Multiple R		.33893	
Multiple R²		.11487	

NOTES: Figures in parenthesis are standard errors. Variables are arraged in order of decreasing significance of the partial regression coefficient.
  * Significant at .05 level, coefficient greater than twice standard error.
** Significant at .01 level, coefficient greater than three times standard error.

The final regression solution (Table 10) brings together the most significant and important of the independent variables. One notes that the two measures representing intergroup contact and the situational aspect of prejudice formation are more important than education, again suggesting that much of what education can serve to explain is already indicated in a more direct fashion by age, social position, and political party. This equation explains about 11 per cent of the variance. One will note that the seven selected factors explain nearly as much variance as all sixteen situational and structural variables. The social position of the household head, rather than the social class of the respondent himself, also appears to be more important. The direct effect of social position serves to include the indirect contribution of the respondent's social class (c.f. Land, 1969:22-4).

CONCLUSION

In examining patterns of prejudice, attention was given to the importance of the situational character of racial antipathy. It was hypothesized that the social context in which a person finds himself conditions his attitudes toward minority groups as determined and predicted on the basis of his social position. The relative interdependence and multicollinearity of the independent variables was studied in order to determine the relative importance of each measure. No single condition explains the differences in the levels of prejudice among the white British surveyed. Racial intolerance results from the threat perceived, while certain features in the English educational system serve to mitigate the expression of intolerance. Yet certain aspects of position in the social structure deeply condition a person's racial attitudes. Age, social class, and the political party to which he gives allegiance, all have a substantial effect. Formal education, although somewhat less important, is the factor which social policy may be able to influence and thus may be seen as a crucial factor.

This social structural component is, in turn, strongly influenced by the situational component reflecting the extent and nature of a person's interaction with minority group members. A given situation may cause hostile attitudes to develop, but such development of prejudice is not necessarily irreversible. The respondent's borough, although of relative importance, does not provide a powerful indicator of an individual's hostility toward nonwhite immigrants. This finding should caution one from expecting certain failure or certain success on the basis of what is assumed to be the prevailing climate within a given community. One may expect that in societies such as Great Britain (and unlike the United States), where intergroup relations are not yet fully institutionalized, the situational nature of social interaction becomes crucial both in lessening and heightening levels of prejudice. In nations with large minorities, attitudes toward racial and ethnic minorities have evolved over several hundred years into what has been termed recently "racial etiquette." Although Britain has the legacy of the Empire, the British have only begun to experience racially different peoples in sizeable numbers in England since World War II. Consequently in Great Britain as against the United States one may expect intergroup relations to be more pliable and less institutionalized. The rising racial consciousness of the New Commonwealth immigrants and their descendants may serve to crystallize the attitudes of white Britons as they increasingly feel their hostilities returned by the minority. The no longer silent reaction on the part of the immigrants to their treatment may become an added factor in the situational component of white individuals' prejudice in the future. Not only will the individual white Briton be encouraged or discouraged to be tolerant by those around him most like himself, but increasingly he will be rebuked by the blacks or Asians themselves either personally or through the media. Differences in the intensity of prejudice toward the immigrants among the British appear to be a function of the various situational and structural factors that have been outlined. The overall level of intolerance may well be increased if "racial etiquette" becomes so commonplace as to be institutionalized and if racial consciousness leads to even more frequent and stronger expressions of hostility.

NOTES

1. The Survey included respondents' reactions to black Africans and to Caribbean immigrants. A fourth immigrant group, Cypriots, was introduced as a control. For reasons of clarity this analysis does not differentiate except where necessary between black West Indians and Africans, and Cypriots are not considered. Throughout this paper the term nonwhite will be used despite the fact that the word is disagreeable to some of the people to whom it is applied. The alternative term "coloured" is being rebuked by the younger generation and the other term, "black," has not been fully accepted, especially by Asian immigrants. A similar position is taken by Deakin (1969:385). The author

acknowledges the assistance of Morris Janowtiz, John Kasarda, Alan Marsh, and Gerald Suttles. Invaluable in carrying out this research was the financial and technical assistance of the Center for Social Organization Studies, University of Chicago. The author acknowledges the permission of the Survey of Race Relations and its director, E.J.B. Rose, which allowed the use of the data.

2. One should note that formal education may simply instruct individuals as to the "proper responses" (Schwartz, 1967:119; Tollet, 1970:13).

3. Goffman (1963:4) identifies low class status in Britain as a "tribal stigma, the sins of the parents, or at least their milieu, being visited on the child should the child rise improperly far above his initial station." Finer (1968:56) maintains that in an otherwise homogeneous society such as Britain, class distinctions take on greater importance in social analyses.

4. Lipset and Ladd (1971:654) noted ". . . individuals gain a frame of reference from the decisive events of a period when they first came to political consciousness — usually in their late teens or early twenties — which then shapes their subsequent values and actions. This, the prevailing climate in which a cohort comes of age politically, tends to frame its later political orientation."

5. Two forces may well be operating in the observed tendency for conservatism to be concomitant with age. First, an individual as he ages tends to be rewarded if he reaffirms the status quo. Second, in recent years, each successive cohort in Western, as well as developing, societies may tend to be more liberal and flexible than earlier generations. This research, as with most surveys, provides information on what can be termed the cohort phenomenon. Little information exists on whether a given individual becomes more conservative with age.

6. Homans (1958:260) has outlined the close relationship of sentiment, interaction, and activity. Suchman and Dean (1963:279) in summarizing the research on the effect of interaction on prejudice concluded that "prejudice reduction is an almost invariant concomitant of interaction." Similarly Williams (1964:160) concluded on the basis of his surveys, the comprehensive Cornell studies, "Out of hundreds of tabulations there emerges the major finding that in all the surveys in all communities and for all groups, major and minor, the greater the frequency of interaction the lower the prevalence of ethnic prejudice."

7. Ford's (1973:1443) research reaffirmed "the necessity for careful description of the specific conditions" under which inter-racial contacts occurred.

8. The data from the Survey confirm in part for England the research conducted for the National Advisory Commission on Civil Disorders in the United States (1968:35; Campbell, 1971:54-66). The American research found a positive relationship between education and racial attitudes only among those under the age of 40.

9. It should be noted for the regression analysis that follows that dichotomous variables are allowable in path models. The assumption made, valid where it is to be employed here, is that "the variable actually behaves in an all-or nothing fashion" (Land, 1969).

10. The assumption is made that prejudice toward nonwhite immigrants, a dependent or endogenous variable, is linearly dependent on a remaining subset of independent or exogenous variables that have already been shown to be

correlated among themselves to a certain degree (Land, 1969:6ff).

11. Political party and the prejudice scale had a negative Pearson's correlation of −.103, significant at .001. Since the parties were arranged in the order of increasing "liberality," this suggests that respondents do tend to embrace the restrictiveness or tolerant heritage of their respective parties.

REFERENCES

ALLPORT, Gordon M. (1958). *The Nature of Prejudice*. Garden City, New York: Doubleday.

BANTON, Michael (1959). *White and Coloured: The Behaviour of the British People Toward Coloured Immigrants*. London: Jonathan Cape.

BETTELHEIM, Bruno and JANOWITZ, Morris (1949). "Ethnic Intolerance: A Function of Social and Personal Control." *American Journal of Sociology*. Vol. 55 (September): 137-145.

———— (1964). *Social Change and Prejudice*. New York: The Free Press.

CAMPBELL, Angus (1971). *White Attitudes Toward Black People*. Ann Arbor: Institute of Social Research.

DEAKIN, Nicholas (1969). "Race and Human Rights in the City." *Urban Studies* Vol. 6 (November): 385-407.

FINER, Samuel (1968). "Great Britain", in MACREDE, Roy C. and WARD, Robert E. (eds.), *Modern Political Systems*. Englewood Cliffs, N.J.: Prentice-Hall.

FORD, W. Scott (1973). "Interracial Public Housing in a Border City: Another Look at the Contact Hypothesis." *American Journal of Sociology*, Vol. 78 (May): 1426-1447.

GOFFMAN, Erving (1963). *Stigma: Notes on the Management of Spoiled Identity*. Englewood Cliffs, N.J.: Prentice-Hall.

HODGE, Robert M. and TREIMAN, Donald J. (1966) "Occupational Mobility and Attitudes Toward Negroes." *American Sociological Review*, Vol. 31 (February): 93-102.

HOMANS, George (1958). *The Human Group*. New York: Harcourt, Brace, and Company.

LAND, Kenneth (1969). "Principles of Path Analysis," in BORGATTA, Edgar (ed.), *Sociological Methodology 1969*. San Francisco: Jossey-Bass.

LIPSET, Seymour Martin and LADD, Everett C., Jr. (1971). "College Generation and Their Politics." *New Society* (October): 654-657.

MARSH, Alan (1970). "The Incidence and Form of Racial Prejudice in Britain," in DEAKIN, Nicholas (ed.), *Colour, Citizenship and British Society*. London: Panther Books.

———— (1973). "Race, Community, and Anxiety." *New Society*, Vol. 23 (February): 406-408.

National Advisory Commission on Civil Disorders (1968). *Supplementary Studies*. Washington: Government Printing Office.

ROSE, E.J.B. (1969). *Colour and Citizenship: A Report on British Race Relations*. London: Oxford University Press.

SCHWARTZ, Mildred A. (1967). *Trends in White Attitudes Toward Negroes.* Chicago: National Opinion Research Center.

SUCHMAN, Edward and DEAN, John (1963). "Intergroup Contact and Prejudice." Unpublished Manuscript. Ithaca, New York: Cornell University.

TOLLETT, Kenneth S. (1970). "Feedback." *Transaction,* Vol. 7 (March): 13, 55.

WILLIAMS, Robin M., Jr. (1964). *Strangers Next Door: Ethnic Relations in American Communities.* Englewood Cliffs, N.J.: Prentice-Hall.

Chapter 9

COMMUNICATION AND VOTER TURNOUT IN BRITAIN[1]

Jay G. Blumler & Jack M. McLeod

After two decades in which a "limited effects" model has dominated the study of the mass media in politics, the tide of scholarly opinion is shifting towards the elaboration of a more important, though more differentiated role for communication factors in the political process. At this stage the empirical development of this "new look" is admittedly incomplete, for it still finds expression more often in critiques of past work, and in the generation of hypothetical frameworks to guide future studies, than in the production of supporting evidence. Nevertheless, its foundations are by no means merely speculative, and its evolution is sufficiently advanced to suggest that a definite turning point has now been reached in the field of political communication research.

Many features of the "limited effects" model, originating as a set of tentative inferences in the pioneering investigation of Lazarsfeld *et al.*, in the Presidential campaign of 1940, subsequently became reified into the status of virtual laws and at times were generalized into showing little or no effect at all.[2] Six major characteristics of the "limited effects" model can be discerned. First, political communication research was regarded as virtually coterminous with persuasion research; investigators were chiefly concerned with associations between communication and attitudes underlying the direction of vote decisions.[3] Second, a reinforcement of previous orientations was regarded as the typical consequence of exposure to political communications; even the so-called "mediating factors" through which communications operated were regarded as "such that they typically render mass communications a contributory agent in a process of reinforcing the existing conditions."[4] Third, these reinforcing tendencies were believed to derive largely from a mechanism of selective exposure whereby people "turn to the propaganda which affirms the validity and wisdom of their original decision."[5] Fourth, the model was part of an overall *weltanschauung* which put far more emphasis on the underlying stability of the world of politics than on its flux.[6] Fifth, although some individuals were unstable in outlook, their relative indifference to politics ensured that they monitored few of the potentially persuasive political messages. Finally, in many influential studies the conception of a communication effect was operationalized in relatively gross terms: associations were examined between no more than two or three variables; samples were dichotomized between "higher" and "lower" exposed audience members; and distinctions were rarely drawn between different individual media or patterns of content within a given medium.

THE "NEW LOOK" IN POLITICAL COMMUNICATION RESEARCH

The "new look" in political communication research has begun to question each of the traits of the "limited effects" model.[7] First, the world of politics no longer appears so stable to contemporary researchers as it did to their predecessors. Dreyer's analysis, published in 1971-1972, of a steady and steep downward trend across five successive Presidential elections since 1952 in the capacity of party identification to predict vote direction graphically illustrates this transformation.[8] It has been suggested that a prime source of this trend may have been the substantial increase in the exposure of voters through the coming of television to short-term information flows making for greater volatility. And as traditional party ties lose their salience for more people, the potential for mass communication to exert an influence correspondingly widens.

Second, it is no longer taken for granted that selective exposure is the "natural" mechanism that guides much of the consumption of mass media materials about political affairs. Reanalysis of past survey evidence has shown that the extent of such selectivity was much less than had been supposed, while a review of experimental evidence has failed to uncover the existence of a "general psychological preference for supportive information."[9] The implication is that selective exposure has been downgraded to the status of a variable from its previous elevation into the dignity of a supposed "law".

Third, a similar fate has partly overtaken the proposition that reinforcement is the dominant outcome of exposure to political communications. It is not denied that people with strongly held attitudes on a given topic are likely to emerge from communication exposure adhering to what they previously believed at least as tenaciously as before. Rather, more weight is now being given to the principle that when an individual's ego-involvement in a topic is low, then his defences against communication about it are likely to be thin and weak. "The combination of a low degree of loyalty and yet some exposure to election communications has become a more probable combination in the era of television than ever before."[10]

Thus, fourth, the assumption that the potentially unstable citizen is unlikely to be reached by political communications has also become more dubious. Three different samples studied by the University of Leeds Centre for Television Research have disclosed substantial proportions (up to a quarter of the electorate) who possessed each of four attributes: they followed campaign communications "to help make up my mind how to vote"; they were relatively knowledgeable about politics; they viewed news and political programmes on television relatively often; and yet they disclosed voting patterns, whether measured in the short-term period of an election campaign or in the longer span between campaign periods, of high volatility.

Fifth, there are some signs that more sophisticated methods are being introduced into political communication research. For example, there is more interest in tracing the influence of distinctive characteristics of specific media in the outlook of their heavy users. Wamsley and Pride have recently listed a formidable array of television traits that lend support to their belief that it may be "qualitatively different in its effect from other news media."[11] Other evidence suggests that the readiness of newspapers to support editorially particular parties or candidates may at one and the same time help to sustain the allegiances of readers with previously congruent preferences and to undermine those of readers with originally divergent loyalties.[12] Some political communication researchers are once again adopting panel designs in which communication can provide a dynamic element, campaign change can be isolated and effects of the local media can be assessed. An understanding of the dynamics of change is enhanced by using in these longitudinal studies more sophisticated techniques of measurement and analysis. Cross-lag correlation procedures have been used in an attempt to extricate us from the causation direction problem that arises when associations of communication with other variables must be interpreted. More studies are resorting to multivariate procedures to extract effects of communication from a host of associated third variables. Attempts to specify a wider and more sensitive range of independent variables of communication can be anticipated, including more graduated indices of exposure, the direction or bias of content received, and the amount, sources, heterogeneity or homogeneity of the politically relevant interpersonal communication engaged in. With the recent burst of empirical investigation of audience gratifications, possibilities have also arisen for injecting measures of needs sought in political communication behaviour as variables intervening between exposure and effects.[13]

Last, but by no means least, the "new look" has moved well beyond the earlier almost exclusive concern of political communication research with persuasion through attitude change to a consideration of other more likely, if often more subtle, dependent variables as effects. For voting behaviour, this involves a shift away from party direction as the main focus of interest and towards such possible criteria of effects as:

(1) Information gain.[14]
(2) Perceptions of the state of majority opinion in the community on topics of current controversy.[15]
(3) Cognitive shifts in the perceived importance of issues — the particularly active research front of "agenda setting".[16]
(4) Altered perceptions of political reality (for example, whether the U.S. is winning the war in Vietnam, what it is like to be a Black American residing in urban ghettos, the causes of strike behaviour).[17]
(5) Cognitions about the nature of one's political system or community (for example, whether it works well, its leaders are credible, etc.)[18]
(6) Turnout at the polls.

VOTER TURNOUT RESEARCH

Electoral turnout provides a particularly important criterion for investigating communication effects in the spirit of the new approach. The manifest function of campaigning is to furnish citizens with motives for casting a ballot and information on which to base their voting decisions. National campaigns invariably unleash a substantially stepped-up flood of political messages into the homes of the media-attending public. Especially where turnout levels tend to fall below near-universal participation rates, or fluctuate over time, communication could be expected to exert an influence. And in certain polities there has been evidence of a downward trend, in which communication factors may be implicated, towards lower turnout levels; in Britain, for example, participation declined steadily from 84% at the 1950 General Election to 72% in 1970. Finally, the relationship of communication to turnout has a bearing on the great divide between those authorities who regard the mass media as agents of political involvement and citizen mobilization [19] and those who see them as instruments of narcoticization and citizen apathy.[20]

The role of communication in turnout has received some attention in past research. Possibly for technical reasons, however, findings have been divergent and difficult to interpret. In these circumstances the "limited effects" thesis has tended to prevail — as in the recent statement of Dowse and Hughes that ". . . at best the nature of the electoral campaign . . . does not very significantly affect the turnout."[21]

It is true that in the 1948 Presidential election campaign Berelson *et al.* found higher voting rates among respondents with "high" rather than "low" media exposure when prior interest in the campaign was controlled.[22] Nevertheless, in conceptualizing the role of the campaign they referred to a process of "implementation", whereby early dispositions were subsequently translated into "a response to the demands of society for a vote in November."[23] This notion derived in turn from the Lazarsfeld *et al.* discussion of the impact of a campaign on voting in terms of "activation." In their words, "Political campaigns are important primarily because they *activate* latent predispositions." The process was likened to photographic developing, according to which the photograph exists on an exposed negative but does not appear until the developer acts to bring it out.[24] Of course the ultimate implication of this view is that full information about prior dispositions would reduce correlations between communication and turnout to near zero levels.

Subsequently, the coming of television prompted further efforts to identify its distinctive impact on voting — largely with negative results. Simon and Stern reported data from Iowa showing that in counties with a high density of television sets turnout in the Presidential election of 1952 was no greater than in those where television was less widely diffused.[25] Strictly speaking, however, this result merely indicated that aggregate turnout was not augmented by the addition of a new communication channel to those already in existence. Glaser's analysis of national survey data for the 1956 and 1960 Presidential elections did disclose some associations between mass media use and turnout – greater for newspaper reading than for television viewing or radio listening. But it proved difficult to resolve the conflict between two rival interpretations of those associations: that communication had boosted turnout; or simply that the different life-styles of voters and non-voters included different communication behaviours.[26]

A more recent study by Olsen did involve a multi-variate assessment of diverse influences on the voting rates of Indianapolis residents in the 1966 Congressional and 1964 and 1960 Presidential elections. This showed that eta correlations between mass media use and turnout rates in the three elections fell to low and only barely significant levels (a mean correlation of .13) when controls for age, education, degree of organizational participation and relevant political orientations (party identification and political interest) were applied. However, contacts with local party campaigners were mixed with mass media measures in the communication exposure index; and the dependent variable was not changed in respondents' participation intentions over a campaign period but whether in the end they had recalled voting or not.[27]

Even such a brief review of the literature shows how difficult it is to arrive at anything other than the ambiguous conclusion that communication may or may not affect turnout. The main obstacles to progress seem to include: the rarity of controls for the influence of other non-communication variables, despite the plausibility of the assumption that many situational and dispositional characteristics will determine any form of participation; lack of precision in defining communication variables; and a failure adequately to represent in study designs the dynamics of any processes that might be involved in the impact of communication on turnout.

INTRODUCTION TO A STUDY OF TURNOUT IN A BRITISH ELECTION

The British General Election of 1970 provided the focus for a study of "Political Communication and the Young Voter" conducted by the Centre for Television Research of the University of Leeds.[28] Interviews were held just before and immediately following the 18-day campaign with a main sample of 521 young adult electors (aged 18 to 24) and a control sample of 191 older adults drawn from names on the electoral registers of the six constituencies of the city of Leeds. In addition, those panel members who were still available were interviewed for a third time approximately eighteen months later. The investigation was based on the assumption that many youth-adult differences in political outlook and behaviour would be found, including an expectation that first entrants to the electorate would prove more malleable in their political views than their elders and more open to influence from campaign communications.

Along with the 1948 Presidential election in the United States, the 1970 British General Election has been a focus for heated controversy regarding the validity of public opinion polling. In each case, the winner was shown to be behind in most polls taken, even well into the campaign. Although post mortems have recommended modifications of polling practice, it is also considered that late voting shifts account for some portion of the apparent discrepancy.[29]

It is clear that signs in pre-campaign opinion polls of a considerable Labour Party lead over the Conservatives had much to do with the decision of the then Prime Minister, Harold Wilson, to call a snap election allowing the minimum period of a month between the announcement and Polling Day. However, the snap election strategy backfired, and the Labour government gave way to a Conservative administration under Edward Heath. Table 1 gives some support to the interpretation that Labour strength eroded during the campaign (at least in Leeds) as evidenced by 8 and 5 per cent Labour declines in the two samples. It is important to note, however, that Conservative Party support did not increase as a result of Labour's weakness. Instead the net direction of shift, when pre-campaign vote intentions were compared with Polling Day reported votes, was *away* from participation, the proportions abstaining having gone up from 15 to 26 per cent in the youth sample and from 9 to 19 per cent among older adults. Inspection of panel studies conducted in Britain since the war confirms this as an unprecedented result, most previous research having reported about as many would-be participants at the start of the campaign as actual voters at the end of it.[30]

The 10 and 11 per cent shifts in participation rates shown in Table 1 are, of course, net change proportions. The total amount of movement is better estimated in Table 2 which shows that 34 per cent of the young electors and 24 per cent of the older respondents had changed (switched parties, moved from abstention to voting, or the reverse) during the campaign. In both samples more than half

the changes were accounted for by a group whom we have termed
"contingent abstainers", those individuals who had a pre-campaign
intention but failed to vote on Polling Day.[31]

TABLE 1

PRE-CAMPAIGN VOTING INTENTION AND POST-ELECTION
VOTING REPORT IN THE 1970 GENERAL ELECTION,
LEEDS YOUNG ADULT AND OLDER ADULT SAMPLES

Party	Young Adults			Older Adults		
	Pre-campaign Intent %	Post-election Report %	Net Change	Pre-campaign Intent %	Post-election Report %	Net Change
Labour	48	40	−8	42	37	−5
Conservative	28	26	−2	40	40	0
Liberal	9	8	−1	9	4	−5
Don't know, no vote	15	26	+11	9	19	+10
Total	100	100		100	100	
(N)	(494)[a]			(176)[a]		

[a] Individuals unwilling to answer questions about vote intention and vote were omitted from these and subsequent tables.

TABLE 2

VOTING PATTERNS FORMED BY PRE-CAMPAIGN INTENT AND
POST-ELECTION REPORT IN THE 1970 GENERAL ELECTION,
LEEDS YOUNG ADULT AND OLDER ADULT SAMPLES

Pre-campaign Vote Intention?	Post-election Report as Voted?	Voting Pattern	Young Adults %	Older Adults %
Yes	Yes	Consistent Voters[a]	58	71
Yes	Yes	Switching Voters	8	6
No	Yes	Late Deciders	8	4
Yes	No	Contingent Abstainers	18	14
No	No	Consistent Abstainers	8	5
		Total	100	100
		(N)	(494)	(176)

[a] Both groups stated an intention in the pre-campaign interview and reported voting in the post-election survey; however Consistent Voters reported voting for the party originally chosen while the Switching Voters voted for a different party.

STUDY DESIGN

The study's panel design made it possible to classify variables in terms of time-dimension relationships. The key criterion for our analysis, turnout, was divided into two different dependent variables, depending on a comparison of the respondents' participation intentions at the outset of the campaign with their voting behaviour on Polling Day. One of these involved the distinction among pre-campaign intenders between those electors who subsequently did and did not vote.[32] Because of the large number of contingent abstainers in the samples and the lack of attention paid to disintegrating voting intentions in previous research, the first and most intensive analyses were devoted to this criterion. The results were then compared with those that emerged when "late decision", that is, movement from lack of a pre-campaign party preference to a Polling Day vote, was treated as an alternative measure of the incidence of the campaign on turnout. Here the dependent variable rested on the distinction, among pre-campaign "don't know's" and "won't vote's", between those respondents who ultimately voted and those who did not. All analyses were performed for the first-time young electors; the numbers available meant that in the older adult sample only a contingent abstention analysis could be conducted.

The analytic separation of respondents between those with and without voting intentions is analogous to the distinction made in cognitive consistency theory between the states of post-decisional dissonance and pre-decisional conflict. It also implies that to some extent the corresponding voting and abstaining groups which they produce on Polling Day should differ in various antecedent characteristics and behaviours; for example, contingent abstainers should differ from consistent abstainers and late deciders should differ from consistent voters. Table 3 shows data relevant to this supposition. While the two groups of Polling Day non-voters are similar on many characteristics, the contingent abstainers, as contrasted to the consistent abstainers, were more likely to come from working-class backgrounds, to be male, to have stronger political dispositions, and to show higher levels of mass media and interpersonal communication behaviour during the campaign. Late deciders, as contrasted with those having made their decisions prior to the campaign, were more likely to be occupationally mobile, unmarried, less highly politicized and more dependent upon friends as sources of information during the campaign. In short, there was some external evidence to justify separate analyses of voter turnout distinguished by pre-campaign intention. To put it another way, since contingent abstainers, for example, really *did* differ from consistent abstainers at the start of the campaign, it became meaningful to enquire in further analysis (a) why their original voting intentions had disintegrated and (b) whether campaign communication factors had played any part in this.

TABLE 3

LEVELS OF VARIOUS PREDICTOR VARIABLES BY VOTING PATTERNS, LEEDS YOUNG ADULT SAMPLE (%) [a]

	Voting Pattern				
Predictor Variable	*Consistent Voters*[b]	*Switching Voters*[b]	*Late Deciders*	*Contingent Abstainers*[b]	*Consistent Abstainers*
A. Parental Characteristics					
1. Parental political interest at least fairly	74	72	76	72	81
2. Parental party preference with party	83	79	54	77	58
B. Structural Variables					
1. Father's occupation non-manual	46	44	30	25	42
1. Own occupation non-manual	62	66	78	38	58
1. School-leaving age 16 or later	58	60	73	39	42
2. Sex men	48	33	46	58	39
2. Marital status married	32	42	14	28	25
2. Age over 21	42	40	32	50	38
C1. Political System Dispositions					
a. Duty to vote feel a duty	47	37	24	18	6
c. Interest in politics at least fairly	76	60	57	43	14
d. Caring about outcome at least somewhat	80	47	51	49	11
e. Motivation to follow campaign strong	43	48	32	21	6

TABLE 3 CONTINUED

Predictor Variable	*Voting Pattern*				
	Consis-tent Voters[b]	Switch-ing Voters[b]	Late De-ciders	Contin-gent Abstain-ers[b]	Consis-tent Ab-stainers
C1. Political System Dispositions cont.					
e. Altruism of politicans					
try to serve community	52	42	43	30	22
e. Efficacy of elections					
at least some	59	60	32	43	38
e. Effect of lowering voting age					
has effect on politicians	73	65	76	71	39
e. Attention to campaign arguments					
should pay at least some	85	88	81	82	78
C4. Customary Media Use					
a. Weight of viewing					
light or moderate	73	70	81	60	76
b. Frequency of newspaper					
reading					
daily	65	65	49	53	32
D. Cross-pressure Variables					
1. Press					
reads own party paper	85	73	c	73	c
2. Political contacts					
without dissent	51	16	c	34	c
3. Consistency					
living in own party const.	68	56	c	52	c
E. Campaign Exposure Variables					
1a.Party broadcasts seen					
at least one	80	81	62	70	46
1c.Television news					
4 or more days per week	49	40	27	24	11
2a.Family discussion					
at least occasionally	67	50	51	33	23
2b.Friends discussion					
at least occasionally	75	81	81	62	46
2c.Other discussion					
at least occasionally	78	79	83	64	49

TABLE 3 CONTINUED

	Voting Pattern				
Predictor Variable	*Consistent Voters*[b]	*Switching Voters*[b]	*Late Deciders*	*Contingent Abstainers*[b]	*Consisten Abstainers*
F. Campaign Issue Change					
1. Taxes					
net change (very important)	+7	+9	−5	+19	+11
2. Standard of living					
net change	−1	+9	+8	+19	0
3. Prices					
net change	+8	+5	+3	+15	+23
G. Campaign Reaction					
2. Noticing of promises by winner					
noticed	83	79	83	78	64
3. Strength of economy					
at least fairly strong	72	53	68	54	57
(N)	(262)	(26)	(36)	(84)	(39)

[a] Only those predictor variables capable of being represented in terms of percentages are shown here; nine other variables are included in subsequent analyses.

[b] These patterns include only those choosing the Labour and Conservative parties in the pre-campaign interviews; Liberal party intenders have been eliminated from this analysis because of the small numbers involved.

[c] Cross-pressure variables are not relevant to these respondents.

To answer such questions, a number of independent variables that might have influenced turnout had to be built into the analysis. These were also ordered by time sequence differences. Thus, a broad distinction was drawn between *pre-campaign measures,* the background and situational factors and the usual attitudes and behaviours that the person brings to the election; *campaign exposures,* how the individual followed the election in mass media and inter-personal channels; and *post-election reactions* to the campaign in various respects.

The choice of individual predictor variables was based on four criteria: previous research had shown them to be related to political participation (for example, stratification variables and various political dispositions); they represented potentially important differences in the situations occupied specifically by young people (for example, marital status, politicization of the parental home);

they measured exposure to various sources of communication about the campaign; or they stood for more specific orientations to party conflict. A total of 40 predictor variables was selected by these criteria, of which 28 were classified as pre-campaign factors and the remainder were evenly divided between campaign exposure and post-election reaction measures. Since our interest was in estimating the relative importance of types of variables rather than in the predictive powers of any individual variable, the 40 items were finally subsumed under 12 more general classes, which are specified below. (The letters and numbers beside the category headings correspond to designations used in all subsequent tables of this paper. Details of how each of the individual variables was measured are presented in the Appendix.)

PRE-CAMPAIGN MEASURES

A.	Parental characteristics	— interest in politics; having a party preference.
B1.	Stratification variables	— own occupation; father's occupation; school-leaving age.
B2.	Other structural variables	— sex; marital status; age.
C1.	Political system dispositions	— knowledge; interest; duty to vote; caring about election outcome; and eight other attitude items.
C2.	Party orientations	— attitudes to own party; to own party leader.
C3.	Issue salience	— importance of issues in three different clustered areas.
C4.	Customary media behaviours	— frequency of television viewing; newspaper reading;
D.	Cross-pressure variables[33]	— reading of opposition newspaper; political contacts with supporters of opposing party; living in constituency with predominance of opposing party.

CAMPAIGN EXPOSURE MEASURES

| E1 | Mass media exposure | — number of party broadcasts seen; TV news viewing during campaign; amount of election news reading in the press. |
| E2 | Interpersonal discussion | — frequency of campaign discussion with: friends; family members; others. |

MEASURES OF POST-ELECTION REACTION

F. Campaign change in issue salience — prices; taxes; standard of living.

G. Other post-election assessments — evaluations of specific features of the campaign ("campaign reaction score"); noticing campaign promises by the winning party; perceived strength of the economy.

A zero-order correlation matrix of the associations in the youth sample between these predictors and the retention or dissolution of original voting intentions confirmed the need to base the analysis on multivariate procedures. Nearly a half of the 40 independent variables produced statistically significant correlations with turnout. Some moderately high intercorrelations among some of the predictor variables themselves also called for multiple controls. It was decided, therefore, that the direct and independent contribution to turnout of each of the predictor variables, and of the classes into which they had been grouped, should be assessed by means of a multiple linear regression analysis.

This procedure entails a number of troublesome assumptions. One is that of a continuous distribution underlying the variable being measured. The criterion variable here, voter turnout, is measured as a dichotomy. That is, the person either voted or failed to vote in the 1970 election. It may be argued that the linear assumption of the regression model refers to an underlying propensity and hence to the conceptual definition of the dependent variable rather than to its measurement. Thus, a tendency to vote rather than abstain could still be thought of as a continuum on the conceptual plane. It is true that the AID (automatic interaction detector) approach, which was designed especially to work with dichotomous categories of variables and their interactions, could have been adopted as an alternative; but it has features which disqualified it for use in this case.[34] It functions on the principle of maximizing prediction among a given number of factors, without concern for the operation of particular sets of independent variables; this would have been at odds with our specific interest in understanding the role of communication influences *per se.* It also applies an iterative procedure, which extracts all variance from the strongest predictor and then selects subsequent predictors from the residual variance, whereas our goal required simultaneous rather than sequential control techniques.

A second assumption of regression analysis is that all relationships are linear and that no interaction effects have been generated by the joint operation of two or more predictor variables. To the extent that the regression model can account for substantial proportions of variance (as shown in the data below), the extra variance likely to stem from interactions may be considered negligible. In any case, the regression analyses presented here should be regarded as provisional linear estimates; more precise interaction effects will be examined in future cross-tabular analyses of two and three predictor variables in their relations to voter turnout.

A final assumption of concern is that of independence among the predictor variables. When there are high inter-correlations among a combination of predictor variables, a condition of multicollinearity occurs in which the estimate of the variance accounted for by any one of the variables involved may prove unreliable. This difficulty can be dealt with either by combining the inter-correlated variables into a single index or by treating them as a block or group in the analysis.[35] The latter course has been followed here. Were such correlations to be found across blocks (say between a communication and a political predisposition variable) a serious problem would arise. Fortunately, all cross-group correlations in our analysis fell well within acceptable limits. The lone within-group correlation of sizeable magnitude appeared in the set of stratification variables, where occupational status was highly correlated with school-leaving age. These should be considered as a common status variable, and no attention should be paid in the results to which of the two contributes to the turnout variance and which disappears.

Our regression analyses were solely designed to estimate the independent power of a given variable to predict voter turnout directly. From the standpoint of communication theory, however, we were also interested in developing an understanding of *indirect* paths to turnout — such as the factors that give rise to those communication behaviours that may in turn affect voting rates, or the way in which communication behaviours may lead to other consequences which have a direct connection to turnout. Such indirect paths were examined by conducting a further series of regression analyses centring on all variables found to have sizeable direct paths to turnout. The implied time order sequence of our predictor variables, starting with earlier parental influences and ending with campaign reactions, allowed some systematization of our approach. We began with the direct path latest in the time order and used all logically prior variables as predictors. We then worked our way back through the model attempting to identify the antecedents of all key variables. Standardized regression coefficients (beta weights) were used to index the resultant paths.

TURNOUT REGRESSION ANALYSES:
YOUNG PRE-CAMPAIGN VOTE INTENDERS

The first regression analyses of the study sought to explore the sources of contingent abstention in the youth sample. The dependent variable distinguished among original vote intenders between those who had eventually voted and those who had abstained. The numbers available in the sample permitted separate analyses to be performed for original Labour and Conservative supporters, respectively, thereby allowing for the possibility that different influences had played on young voters depending on their party of initial preference. The function of the regression analyses is to show the association of each predictor variable with turnout when the effects of the 39 other predictors are removed. The results are expressed in Table 4 as proportions of the variance accounted for by each variable singly and by the classes of variables into which they were grouped.

TABLE 4

PROPORTION OF TOTAL VARIANCE IN VOTE TURNOUT
ACCOUNTED FOR BY GROUPED AND INDIVIDUAL VARIABLES BY
PRE-CAMPAIGN VOTE INTENTION, LEEDS YOUNG ADULT SAMPLE

	Pre-campaign Vote Intention[a]			
	Labour		*Conservative*	
Predictor Variable Type	%	%	%	%
A. Parental Political Characteristics (2)[b]		0.6		0.0
B. Structural Variables (6)		4.7		19.3**
1. Stratification (3)	3.2		17.4	
2. Other: sex, marital status, age (3)	1.5		1.9	
C. Dispositional Variables				
1. Political System Dispositions (10)		11.8**		16.8**
a. Duty to vote (1)	2.5		3.2	
b. Political knowledge (1)	1.3		5.7	
c. Interest in politics (1)	1.4		1.2	
d. Caring about election outcome (1)	4.3		2.4	
e. Other political dispositions (6)	2.3		4.3	

TABLE 4 CONTINUED

| | Pre-campaign Vote Intention[a] | | | |
| | Labour | | Conservative | |
Predictor Variable Type	%	%	%	%
C. Dispositional Variables cont.				
2. Party Variables (2)		0.2		1.4
3. Prior Issue Orientations (3)		–		0.7
4. Customary Media Use (2)		0.9		3.8
a. Weight of TV viewing[a] (1)	0.3		2.4	
b. Frequency of newspaper reading (1)	0.6		1.4	
D. Cross-pressure Variables (3)		2.7		6.0*
1. Press: opposition paper (1)	–		6.0	
2. Political contacts: dissenting (1)	2.6		–	
3. Constituency: opposition (1)	0.1		–	
E. Campaign Exposure Variables				
1. Mass Media (3)		3.2		4.5
a. Party broadcasts seen (1)	2.8		0.3	
b. Press election reading (1)	0.4		–	
c. Television news (1)	–		4.2	
2. Interpersonal (3)		6.2**		13.3**
a. Family (1)	4.1		11.6	
b. Friends (1)	–		1.0	
c. Other (1)	2.1		0.7	
F. Campaign Issue Change (3)		2.0		1.2
G. Post-election Assessments (3)		5.4**		0.4
1. Campaign reaction score (1)	2.3		–	
2. Noted Conservative promises (1)	0.2		0.3	
3. Strength of the economy (1)	2.9		0.1	
Total Accounted For		37.7		67.4
(N)		(215)		(128)

[a] Table includes only young adult respondents choosing Labour or Conservative Parties in the pre-campaign interview. Liberal Party intenders were excluded because of the small numbers involved.

[b] Numbers in brackets indicate how many individual variables have been included in the particular category.

* proportion of variance accounted for is significant at the .05 level for this group of variables.

** proportion of variance accounted for is significant at the .01 level for this group of variables.

The inclusion of 40 predictor variables in a regression analysis obviously increases the likelihood that chance alone would have produced a substantial prediction of our turnout criterion. For that reason it was important to test the results against chance. The total proportions of variance accounted for (43 per cent for Labour and 77 per cent for Conservative young adults) were well in excess of chance in each case.[36]

Our first concern in examining the detailed regression results shown in Table 4 was to see whether the communication variables used as predictors would disappear when other factors were controlled. It is apparent that they did not disappear. The amount of exposure to certain sources of political communication seemingly acted, independently of other influences, to promote young voter turnout and/or reduce abstention among party identifiers.

When in Table 5 we treat as a block all ten variables in the analysis that measured some form of communication behaviour (including customary media use and communication cross-pressures as well as variables of exposure to the campaign through mass media and inter-personal sources), we find that the total variance accounted for (13 per cent for Labour and 28 per cent for Conservatives, both statistically significant at the .01 level) is on average well above that of the other 30 non-communication measures. Although on this reckoning a quarter of the variables are relevant to communication, they account for between a third and two fifths of the explanatory power of all 40 predictors in the two samples.

TABLE 5

PROPORTION OF TOTAL VARIANCE IN VOTE TURNOUT ACCOUNTED FOR BY COMMUNICATION VARIABLES BY PRE-CAMPAIGN VOTE INTENTION, LEEDS YOUNG ADULT SAMPLE

	Pre-Campaign Vote Intention	
	Labour %	*Conservative* %
C4. Media Predispositions (2)	0.9	3.8
D1. Press Cross-pressures (1)	–	6.0
D2. Political Contacts Cross-Pressures (1)	2.6	–
E1. Campaign Exposure Mass Media (3)	3.2	4.5
E2. Campaign Exposure Interpersonal (3)	6.2	13.3
	12.9	27.6

The relative power of communication factors appears yet more impressive when we consider some of the other variables in the analysis that did *not* predict voter turnout. Although attitudes toward the two major political parties and the images of their leaders were both highly related to *direction* of vote at both the pre-campaign and post-election interviews, these variables did not seem to produce the behavioural result of actually going to the polls. Similarly, the respondent's having grown up in a political or non-political home seems to have had little impact on turnout. Age, marital status and sex also seem to be relatively unimportant factors. So far as sex was concerned, it is worth noting, however, that somewhat more of the contingent abstainers were *men*. Although this may have been a chance result, it could also signify some diminution of sex-role related behaviour among young people.

Reflecting Britain's status-polarized political system, the Labour and Conservative direction of voting intention was rather strongly related to the stratification variables used in the analysis (father's occupation, own occupation, school-leaving age). These variables, however, played a different role in identifying the contingent abstainers, the three measures accounting for 17 per cent of the Conservative turnout variance but only three per cent among the Labour intenders. Erosion of the Conservative vote came heavily at the bottom of its status distribution whereas Labour's turnout problem was more evenly distributed. Thus the direct impact of stratification was mixed and certainly did not eliminate the communication variables when introduced as controls.

Whereas the specific partisan political attitudes added little to our understanding of "post-decision" young elector turnout, the more general political system dispositions appeared to play a much greater part. Political knowledge and interest, a feeling of an obligation to vote, and caring about the election, all were associated with turnout on Polling Day. For young people at least, electoral *turnout* seems to represent a quite different type of behaviour from voting *choice* even when the hard-core consistent abstainers have been excluded from consideration. Direction seems to be more a matter of specific ties to a particular party, while turnout is much more a function of diffuse attachment to the political system.

Up to this point we have established that the ten communication variables considered as a block have a direct and sizeable connection with voter turnout; however, we have not considered the role of the communication measures taken individually. In the zero-order correlation analyses conducted before turning to multivariate procedures, all ten communication variables had produced statistically significant associations with turnout for at least one party. The regression results, however, present a more selective and differentiated picture. Campaign exposure variables (Ela-c and E2a-c) account for considerably more variance than do pre-campaign communication behaviours (C4a, C4b); interpersonal communication assumes a greater direct role than do mass media measures, although the latter show some influence; and Labour turnout was predicted by a rather different subset of communication variables than was Conservative turnout.

One outstanding feature of the analysis is its emphasis on frequency of political discussion in the respondent's family as the most effective prop to participation among communication factors and as one of the two most powerful predictors among the total set of 40 variables. The primacy of family discussion implies not only that interpersonal communication is more influential than mass communication but also that it is more likely to provide an effective stimulus when communication takes place within a relatively homogeneous family circle (although alternative explanations of its superiority may also need to be entertained).

Despite the prominence of interpersonal communication, mass media variables also had some effect on turnout. The original Conservative supporters, for example, were exceptionally vulnerable to the detaching influence of what we have called "press cross-pressures" (D1). This variable was indexed by a conflict between the respondent's original vote intention and the editorial line followed by his morning newspaper. At this point, it is not clear whether the process underlying this apparent source of influence was "agenda setting" — the content salience of a particular set of issues — or some more direct form of persuasion through attitude change. Of course, it may also reflect the vote-sustaining influence of reading a consonant newspaper by those eventually going to the polls. Whatever the process, it appears that press cross-pressures did not affect young Labour supporters. The possible reasons for this will be discussed later.

Table 4 also indicates a very substantial difference in the origins of voter turnout between the supporters of the two major political parties. While almost three-fourths of the variance accounted for in Conservative turnout could be attributed to pre-campaign variables (A, B, C, D), Labour turnout was much more a function of the campaign itself with half the attributable variance going to forces exerting influence after the start of the election contest. As indicated especially by levels of post-election assessments (G), this meant that a sizeable number of young Labour intenders, having registered uniquely unfavourable impressions of the campaign, eventually failed to vote on Polling Day. In fact their campaign evaluations were not only more critical than those of the consistent Labour voters and of the consistent and contingent Conservatives; they were even more negative than those of the consistent abstainers. We will consider the significance of this point further in the discussion section of this chapter. But overall the results validate the original decision to look at influences on turnout in separate party sub-groups. A greater part of Conservative abstention could have been predicted in advance from knowledge of the sample members' pre-campaign situations and dispositions; Labour supporters were more affected by what, to some of them at least, had proved to be a disenchanting campaign.

TURNOUT PATH ANALYSES AMONG YOUNG PRE-CAMPAIGN INTENDERS

Our regression analyses sought to identify direct links between various groups of predictor variables and the criterion of electoral turnout. The purpose of our subsequent path analyses was to develop a tentative extension of these connections into a more elaborate causal network of various indirect paths to turnout. Although there is an almost infinite number of plausible causal sequences that could operate among the variables, we were fortunate in being able to reduce them to more manageable proportions by again ordering them in time-sequence terms.

In each party sub-sample regression analyses were performed on eight variables at three logical time points preceding the final turnout criterion. The sequence that was followed is set out below from left to right. First, all parental and structural variables in the analysis (A,B) were regressed on three dispositional variables that had predicted turnout directly (C1a, C1b, and C1d); then the dispositional measures were placed as predictors with the parental and structural variables and regressed on three different forms of exposure to the campaign (E1a, E1b and E2a); and finally all the above variables were regressed on two different measures of campaign assessment (G1 and G3) that had been implicated in the sample's turnout developments.

All parental and structural variables	Duty to vote Political knowledge Caring about the election outcome	Party election broadcasts seen Family discussion Election news-reading in the press	Campaign Reaction Score Assessment of the strength of the economy	Turnout

To index the strength of connection between two variables, standardized regression or path coefficients (beta weights) were used. Although many of the results were statistically significant at the .05 level, they were often of lower magnitude than would be required to make strong causal statements about the paths involved. Several reasons could account for this: some measures may have been less exact than they could have been; individual variables have not been combined to strengthen associations (for example, the three stratification measures might have been merged into one index); or young people in the process of change may in fact be subject to a diverse array of only moderately strong influences rather than to a small number of more potent ones.

Provisional path models for the Labour and Conservative sub-samples are presented in Figures 1 and 2. Lines of connection have been drawn where the path coefficients reached .15, but a few exceptions to this threshold are included for substantive interest. The results are best described by working our way "chronologically" through the models, commenting on the paths stemming from each set of variables of importance.

The parental political characteristics that had only negligible direct connections with turnout reveal indirect paths such that high parental interest leads to both caring about the election outcome and to family discussion. Both of these dispositions are associated in turn with higher turnout.

The stratification variables, already shown to have a direct path to Conservative turnout, also reveal indirect paths to political knowledge levels and caring about the election outcome in both parties. It is interesting to note, however, that no indirect path connected the stratification variables with any of the campaign exposure measures. In that sense the campaign communication effects on young elector turnout could be said to have been "democratically" based.

Among other structural variables, age is involved in the analysis largely through its connection with political knowledge in both

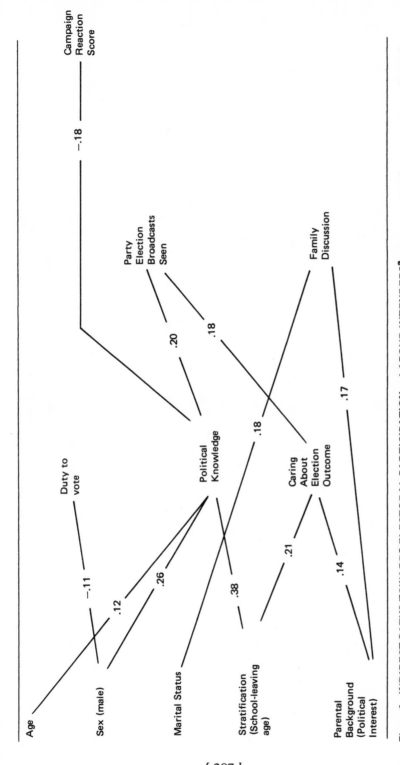

Figure 1 INDIRECT PATHS TOWARDS ELECTORAL PARTICIPATION – LABOUR INTENDERS[a]

[a]Among the variables depicted in this figure the main direct contributors to Labour turnout were: duty, knowledge, caring about the election, family discussion, party broadcasts seen and campaign reaction scores.

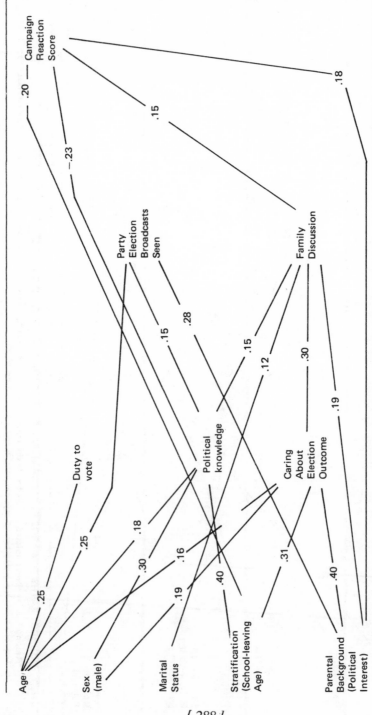

Figure 2 INDIRECT PATHS TOWARDS ELECTORAL PARTICIPATION – CONSERVATIVE INTENDERS[a]

[a] Among the variables depicted in this figure the main direct contributors to Conservative turnout were: stratification, duty, knowledge, caring about the election and family discussion.

sub-samples and, among Conservatives, through the fact that older respondents cared more about the election and felt a greater obligation to vote. Sex is interesting here for its connection with two seemingly contradictory paths; males are more likely to be politically knowledgeable, which encourages turnout, but are less likely to feel a duty to vote, which makes voting less likely. The chief indirect effect of marital status arises from the fact that the married respondents had entered into family discussions about the election more often than had the single respondents.

All three political system dispositions had provided at least moderate direct paths to voting. In terms of indirect paths, political knowledge encouraged party broadcast viewing, which in turn facilitated voting especially among the young Labour supporters. Among the young Conservatives, the better informed were also inclined to discuss the election more often with other family members. Caring about the election was also an indirect source of campaign communication effects on voting, being associated with party broadcast viewing in the Labour sub-sample and with family discussion among the Conservatives. Duty to vote, however, is an interestingly isolated dispositional variable. It is neither predicted by antecedent variables nor predicts any consequent variables. Its effect, then, is direct, and its sources remain an intriguing area for future investigation.

Although frequency of family discussion was associated with more positive assessments of the campaign among the young Conservatives, there were no indirect paths from the communication variables to post-election reactions in the crucial Labour sub-sample where such assessments had been related to turnout. In fact, two features of these evaluations are exceptionally interesting. First, our so-called "campaign reaction score" measure strikingly lacked association with most other variables in the analysis. The regression of 19 prior variables on campaign reaction scores managed to explain only 13 per cent of Labour and 15 per cent of Conservative variance. The circumstances which helped to determine the amount of exposure to campaign communications, then, were remarkably unconnected with judgments of how valuable the campaign had been. But second, the path analyses show that in both sub-samples it was actually the more knowledgeable respondents who had produced the more critical campaign reaction scores. As we have already seen, among the original Labour supporters, these negative assessments had led in turn to abstention from voting.

YOUNG VOTER VS. OLDER ADULT TURNOUT COMPARISON:
PRE-CAMPAIGN INTENDERS

All turnout analyses up to this point have dealt solely with first-time electors under age 25 who had indicated a party preference in the pre-campaign interview. From these data alone, we have no way of estimating the extent to which the findings are (a) a function of youth or (b) confined in application to the post-decision situation. External validity requires a comparison with older adults and with those who were undecided about party in the first round of interviews. Sample size restricts our ability to do this with only 161 adults with pre-campaign party intent and only 76 young and 15 older adults with no such intent. The small number of older respondents prevents analysis within the two major political parties; however we can make the necessary age comparisons by combining the pre-election adherents of the two major parties. The outcomes of the resulting "mixed" regression analyses of contingent abstention for the two age samples are presented in Table 6.

The merging of the party groups in the young adult sample produced a sharp decline in the predictive power of our 40 variables. The 36 per cent of the total variance accounted for is less than the explanatory power of these same variables for each party sub-sample examined separately. This confirms that pre-campaign party preference was itself a source of variance in the combined analysis that is removed when Labour and Conservative intenders are separated. It is another indication of the inference made earlier that somewhat different forces acted on the supporters of the two parties in affecting turnout. The decline was particularly noticeable for the stratification measures.

Table 6 provides a somewhat equivocal answer to the question of whether the importance of communication for young elector turnout would be replicated among older voters. Campaign exposure explained ten per cent of the variance in the merged young elector sample and four per cent in its older adult equivalent. For all ten communication variables, these figures rose to 14 per cent and 5 per cent, respectively, a level that was certainly not statistically significant in the adult case. It is not possible completely to dismiss the relevance of communication to the turnout of established voters on the basis of these data, however, since some part of its impact may have been suppressed by the necessary merging of prior party differences in a combined sample. Nevertheless, communication was

TABLE 6

PROPORTION OF VARIANCE IN TURNOUT OF PRE-CAMPAIGN
VOTE INTENDERS ACCOUNTED FOR BY GROUPED VARIABLES:
LEEDS YOUNG AND OLDER ADULT SAMPLES COMPARED

	Sample			
	Young Adults		Older Adults	
Predictor Variable Type	%	%	%	%
A. Parental Political Characteristics (2)		0.2		0.9
B. Structural Variables (6)		4.7		10.8
1. Stratification (3)	3.5		2.2	
2. Other: sex, marital status, age (3)	1.2		8.6	
C. Dispositional Variables				
1. Political System Dispositions (10)		13.0		3.6
2. Party Variables (2)		0.3		3.0
3. Prior Issue Orientations (3)		0.6		5.1
4. Customary Media Use (2)		1.5		0.1
D. Cross-pressure Variables (3)		2.4		1.3
E. Campaign Exposure Variables (6)		9.6		3.9
1. Mass Media (3)	2.9		1.6	
2. Interpersonal (3)	6.7		2.3	
F. Campaign Issue Change (3)		1.7		0.2
G. Post-election Assessments (3)		1.6		0.1
Total Accounted For		35.6		29.0
(N)		(343)		(130)

clearly less important for the electoral participation of older voters
than for those coming on to the voting register for the first time, an
outcome that is consistent with the investigation's original hypothesis
about the greater susceptibility of young people to influence from
campaign communication sources.

Two other age differences of some interest are evident in Table 6.
First, the relative importance of partisan and political system
dispositions is reversed such that the specific party attitudes account
for much more of the variance in turnout among the older adults; we
have already seen that the more general political system dispositions
were very important for young adults in contrast to the negligible
role of partisan concerns. Second, the non-stratification group of
structural variables proved relatively important in the older adult
analysis, whereas they were of little significance in the younger group.

In fact, much of the difference was due to marital status; in the older sample the widowed, divorced and single respondents were much less likely to vote than were the married.

TURNOUT REGRESSION ANALYSIS:
YOUNG PRE-CAMPAIGN NON-INTENDERS

Perhaps the most striking result of the analysis of young voters without a party preference at the start of the campaign is that their turnout on Polling Day was much better predicted than was that of the pre-campaign intenders. As shown in Table 7, about three fourths of the non-intenders' turnout variance was accounted for by the 37 predictor variables common to the two regression analyses; this compares with a figure of less than half that amount for those electors who had already chosen a party at the time of the first interview. Stated another way, we were more successful in measuring how pre-decision conflict had been resolved than we were in explaining post-decisional dissonance.

The previous finding of strong communication influences on young vote intenders is clearly replicated for the non-intenders in Table 7. The eight communication variables relevant to this group (cross-pressures having been omitted from the analysis for respondents without a prior party loyalty) accounted for a similar amount of the total variance: 14 per cent. However, involvement in interpersonal discussion of the election mattered less to the late deciders than to the contingent abstainers, while exposure to campaign communications in the mass media (especially in the press and to a lesser extent *via* televized party broadcasts) proved more influential. Insofar as interpersonal communication assumed a role in late decision it centred more on discussion with friends than with family members. It is also interesting to find some confirmation in Table 7 of the importance of evaluations of the campaign itself in prompting electoral participation. Just as critical reactions to the campaign had distinguished contingent Labour abstainers from consistent party supporters, so too were more favourable assessments associated with the ultimate readiness of some previously undecided electors to vote.

The biggest difference between the regression analyses for original intenders and non-intenders arises from the remarkably powerful effect of various political system dispositions on the latter group, accounting in all for 39 per cent of the variance. Three individual

TABLE 7

PRE-CAMPAIGN VOTE INTENDERS AND NON-INTENDERS COMPARISON:
PROPORTION OF VARIANCE ACCOUNTED FOR BY GROUPED AND
INDIVIDUAL VARIABLES, LEEDS YOUNG ADULT SAMPLE

| | Pre-Campaign Report [a] | | | |
| | Vote Intenders | | Non-Vote Intenders | |
Predictor Variable Type [b]	%	%	%	%
A. Parental Political Characteristics (2)[c]		0.2		1.1
B. Structural Variables (6)		4.7		0.8
1. Stratification (3)	3.5		0.8	
2. Other: sex, marital status, age (3)	1.2		—	
C. Dispositional Variables				
1. Political System Dispositions (10)		13.0		38.9
a. Duty to vote (1)	2.9		3.5	
b. Political knowledge (1)	2.3		—	
c. Interest in politics (1)	1.6		10.7	
d. Caring about election outcome (1)	3.7		9.0	
e. Other political dispositions (6)	2.5		15.7	
2. Party Variables (2)		0.2		6.9
3. Prior Issue Orientations (3)		0.6		1.1
4. Customary Media Use (2)		0.1		0.4
a. Weight of TV viewing (1)	—		0.2	
b. Frequency of newspaper reading (1)	0.1		0.2	
E. Campaign Exposure Variables				
1. Mass Media (3)		2.9		9.2
a. Party broadcasts seen (1)	1.6		3.7	
b. Press election reading (1)	—		5.2	
c. Television news (1)	1.3		0.3	
2. Interpersonal (3)		6.7		4.2
a. Family (1)	5.7		1.2	
b. Friends (1)	—		3.0	
c. Other (1)	1.0		—	
F. Campaign Issue Change (3)		1.7		6.6
G. Post-election Assessments (3)		1.9		4.8
1. Campaign reaction scores (1)	0.9		2.3	
2. Noted Conservative promises (1)	0.3		1.2	
3. Strength of the economy (1)	0.7		1.3	
Total Variance Accounted For		32.0		74.0
(N)	(343)		(73)	

TABLE 7 CONTINUED

a The vote intenders include those young adult respondents who chose either the Labour or Conservative parties in the pre-campaign interview; the vote turnout comparison for them is between those who remained voters and those who abstained on election day. Non-vote intenders are young respondents who had no party choice in the pre-campaign interview; for them the comparison is between the late deciders who voted on election day and the consistent abstainers.

b Since the cross-pressure variables were not relevant to the non-intenders, they have not been included in this table for either sub-sample.

c Numbers in brackets indicate how many individual variables have been included in the particular category.

measures stand out here: a feeling that the 18-year-old vote would make politicians pay more attention to young people (a variable unimportant in the contingent abstention analysis); an interest in politics; and caring about the outcome of the election. It may be important to note that political knowledge is no longer an effective predictor in this analysis, suggesting that motivation rather than cognitive competence is a key element in the behaviour of late deciding young voters. Despite the dominance of these general orientations, however, Table 7 also shows that party variables (chiefly differences.in assessing the party leaders) predicted turnout among the initially undecided more strongly than among those with a pre-campaign preference. A final area of difference from the vote intender analysis is the virtually complete elimination of stratification and other structural variables as factors in predicting turnout directly. It seems that late decision among previously uncommitted voters is not organised along traditional stratification or role-determined lines.

DISCUSSION

What conclusions may be reached from this study about the role of communication factors in voter turnout in the 1970 British General Election?

It is clear that communication variables bulked large in the main sample analysis of young first-time electors. Both interpersonal and mass communication influences had independently affected turnout when many other possible contaminating or confounding variables had been controlled. In the analysis of those young voters with a definite party preference at the start of the campaign, communication measures took up 13 per cent of the total variance for the turnout of original Labour supporters and 28 per cent of that for original

Conservatives. Among young electors without an initial party preference, communication factors also amounted to 14 per cent of the total. In fact the strength of communication variables in predicting turnout compared favourably with that of all other types of independent variables included in the investigation, being definitely exceeded only by measures of prior dispositions in the late decision analysis of young voters.

The inference to be drawn here is important in view of the insignificant part typically allotted to communication by the "limited effects" model. When election participation behaviours are examined dynamically, and especially for individuals eligible to vote for the first time, communication matters just as much as anything else does. What is more, it matters beyond what would be ascribed to it if it was merely involved in activating prior leanings and sentiments, whether rooted in social or psychological origins. This is not the place for a detailed analysis of where the "limited effects" model went wrong, but from other evidence at our disposal we suspect that it exaggerated in general the homogeneity of the world of political influences, communication and extra-communication, that play on the typical citizen and more specifically, the amount of selective exposure in which most people engage in order to reinforce their previous leanings.

In addition, however, the role of communication factors proved more complex than any single image of how they might be related to turnout could adequately convey. From this point of view an important lesson of the study is the need in communication research to identify and differentiate the several different processes that may simultaneously impinge on a dependent variable outcome. This need for discrimination may be illustrated by elaborating further conclusions of the analysis at three different levels.

One level concerns the group characteristics of the particular individuals who may be exposed to political messages. According to our evidence communication factors worked differently among young Conservative and Labour supporters, only the former having proved vulnerable to "press cross-pressures" while only the latter were apparently guided by their subjective reactions to the quality of the campaign. The complex of communication influences varied yet again according to whether the group under scrutiny had been in a pre-decisional or post-decisional frame of mind at the time of the pre-campaign interview, the former having responded more positively to the mobilizing influence of mass media sources and the latter to the participation-sustaining impact of family discussion (perhaps because only in the latter case was it logically possible for the family's party leanings to be congruent with the young voter's prior preference). In addition, the extent of communication influence varied as between members of the main youth sample and the adult controls, proving far more powerful in the former case.

This last result was to some extent expected. It may reflect certain features of the political outlook of young people — such as their relatively weak partisan sentiments and a loose internal structuring of their various political beliefs — which may stem in turn from such external factors in their situations as exposure to a diverse array of socialization agencies in preadult years and the recency and incompleteness of their occupancy of more adult statuses and roles. Even so the result may not be totally lacking in relevance for communication to older adults. As occupational and geographical mobility become more common, rates of social change accelerate, and public information flows increase, more and more adults may find themselves in circumstances not entirely dissimilar from those that made communication effects on young voters possible in the 1970 British General Election.

A second level where the study findings underline a need for discrimination concerns the direct impact of communication on turnout. Here we have been compelled to draw a distinction between three types of communication influence that may be exerted in a given situation. One form of such influence is directly *quantitative;* it manifests itself in a "more-the-more" relationship, with higher exposure rates independently producing higher turnout rates. Particularly interesting in this connection, perhaps, was the powerful effect of political discussion inside the family circles of the young original vote intenders. Yet even here a mass medium like television did not pale into insignificance, for it also transpired that in this group party broadcast viewing and frequency of family discussion were quite closely associated with each other (the beta weights connecting these variables were .20 and .26 in the Labour and Conservative sub-samples, respectively). The impression conveyed is that television is a medium which, because of its essentially domestic character, can inject into the home environment materials that may be taken up for further comment — presumably with consequences for sustaining political participation afterwards.

Another form of communication influence may be termed *relational;* it stems from congruent and incongruent relationships between the party leaning of an individual and that which is inherent in one of his regularly received sources of messages. According to our evidence this highlights a sense in which a party-aligned press may be politically important: it helps to hold firm those individuals whose party preferences were initially consistent with its point of view and to loosen the loyalties of those who originally diverged from its line. But why did the detaching influence of reading the opposition press make itself felt only among our young Conservative respondents? A likely explanation emerged when it was found that subjection to press cross-pressures was positively and moderately related to political knowledge in the Labour sub-group and inversely and powerfully related to information levels among the young Conservatives. In other words, the looser articulation of the political outlook of the average Tory reader of a Labour newspaper, as indexed by his limited stock of political information, made him exceptionally vulnerable to influence. Contrariwise, being better informed, the typical Labour reader of Conservative papers could also draw on stronger internal defences against their onslaughts on his convictions.

Perhaps the most novel and intriguing form of communication influence represented in our findings was *qualitative* in character – as shown by the fact that unfavourable "campaign reaction scores" had been significantly and independently associated with the eventual abstention of original young Labour supporters and that favourable ones had accompanied the conversion of some would-be abstainers into Polling Day voters. This suggests that at election time some voters may not only be receiving the discrete bits of information about issues, policies and candidates that happen to come their way; at the same time they may also be forming, sustaining or modifying impressions of politicians in their roles *as* campaigners and of the campaign itself as a typical example of the country's political processes. Obviously such perceptions may vary in favourability, and at some point the creation of a positive or negative impression may strengthen or weaken the individual's inclination to vote. The fact that it was the better informed youth sample members who were more critical of British politicians' conduct of the 1970 campaign is noteworthy in this connection. It has often been suggested, but rarely demonstrated, that, in addition to the more typical band of apathetic abstainers, there might be some citizens who will have taken a quite deliberate, and as it were informed, decision not to vote. In the Leeds youth sample of 1970 such an element apparently began to make its presence felt.

Interpretation of this point is additionally complicated by the fact that it was only Labour's ranks of would-be supporters that were thinned by unfavourable qualitative reactions to the campaign. We are not in a position to point to any particular feature of Labour propaganda, say, that could have provoked this result. Nevertheless, we were concerned to test further the related assumptions (a) that some original Labour supporters eventually became disenchanted with the 1970 campaign and (b) that they might well have voted if such disenchantment had not intervened.

The evidence in Table 8 is relevant to the first of these propositions. We reasoned that the disenchantment of the Labour contingent abstainers should have been reflected in declining rates of exposure to election propaganda as the 1970 campaign wore on in time. It so happened that one of our exposure variables did allow us to get inside the campaign, as it were, in terms of such a time dimension: our measure of the number of party broadcasts seen, which had been compiled from questions asked in the post-election interview about each programme individually. Table 8 shows that the rate of exposure of the contingent Labour supporters to the very first Labour broadcast of the campaign was nearly as high as that of the consistent Labour supporters; but thereafter, and quite against all the viewing trends prevalent in all other sample sub-groups, their viewing of Labour broadcasts declined steadily until at the end of the election period it had dropped to approximately half the level attained by the consistent Labour voters.

Then, as a further check on the voting propensities of various youth sample sub-groups, including the contingent Labour abstainers, we looked at the longer-term (18-month) development of their party preferences (drawing on follow-up interviews with the respondents in autumn 1971). The results, which are presented in Table 9, do tend to single out the contingent Labour electors as individuals who could have been more interested in participation throughout their political careers had not the 1970 campaign "put them off." It can be seen that many members of the contingent Labour sub-group had reverted to their original stands at the time of the third interview, only five per cent having been unable to declare a party preference. In contrast to this readiness to snap back to their first round loyalties, the ex-Conservatives proved quite unstable, only 29 per cent having returned to the Tory fold, and as many as 33 per cent having become "don't know's" when asked about their party affiliations.

TABLE 8

ORDER OF PARTY ELECTION BROADCASTS VIEWED DURING
CAMPAIGN BY CONSISTENT AND CONTINGENT MAJOR PARTY
SUPPORTERS, YOUNG ADULT SAMPLE

Broadcasts in Order of Transmission		Whole Sample %	Consistent Conservatives %	Contingent Conservatives %	Consistent Labour %	Contingent Labour %
Lab.	1	35	42	29	43	36
	2	25	27	10	29	24
	3	30	28	26	34	15
	4	32	36	16	40	22
	5	39	44	23	41	18
Con.	1	36	45	19	33	16
	2	17	30	3	18	9
	3	26	41	13	26	16
	4	38	48	19	44	20
	5	37	60	26	43	33
Lib.	1	24	26	6	33	26
	2	19	23	19	22	11
	3	35	34	29	40	24

The adoption of path analysis has opened up yet another level where researchers should be alert to the possible existence of distinctions between diverse communication roles. In fact the evidence from this part of the study, though not strong in the power of the reported associations and certainly needing much replication, seemed to identify three relatively distinct routes along which the forces making for participation or inactivity among young people might gather momentum.

One such path linked together some of the elements that could be said to favour a relatively informed and competent style of participation. It mainly develops cognitive orientations to politics, and its deepest roots originate in stratification distinctions, which correlate highly with knowledge, leading in turn to communication behaviours that stimulate participation. But stratification variables did not monopolize this avenue's point of departure; the tendency for men and the over-21s to be better informed also associated sex and age with it. The mass media may occupy more of the centre of

TABLE 9

PARTY PREFERENCES OF YOUTH SAMPLE MEMBERS, AUTUMN 1971,
BY 1970 CAMPAIGN DEVELOPMENTS FROM VOTING INTENT TO
REPORTED VOTE

| 1970 Campaign Developments | *1971 Party Preferences* [a] | | | | |
	Conservative %	Labour %	Liberal %	Don't know/ None %	N
Consistent Conservatives	73	15	3	9	78
Consistent Labour	5	87	2	7	131
Consistent Liberal	5	10	76	10	21
Contingent Conservatives	29	33	5	33	21
Contingent Labour	13	79	3	5	38
Contingent Liberal	—	25	25	50	4
Inter-party Switchers	25	44	25	6	32
Late Deciders	12	32	12	44	25
Consistent Abstainers	3	31	—	66	29

[a]   Percentages total 100% reading from left to right

this stream than do interpersonal communication sources.

A second type of path stemmed from situations where a circulation of political materials, leading seemingly to more affective attachments to the political system, is naturally encouraged. According to our evidence, the family circle plays a central part in blazing this particular trail. Thus, despite the irrelevance of the parental family's political background to turnout in a direct sense, it was found that the products of the more politically minded households had (a) engaged more often in family discussion about the election (itself a powerful force for participation) and (b) cared more about its outcome, a disposition which was also tied in, in turn, both with family discussion and with electoral turnout more directly. Also associated with this set of forces was marital status, which encouraged the married voters to talk about the election more often and so to go to the polls at the end of the campaign.

A third path towards political activity proved rather more obscure, for our results did little more than suggest its existence without identifying many of its components. Nevertheless, in addition to certain cognitive and affective avenues to participation, there seems to be a route which builds more on a sense of civic obligation.

Represented in our study by the influence on turnout of electors' acceptance of a duty to vote, this appeared to be almost a "free-floating" factor, neither strongly dependent on specific background variables inside the youth sample nor mediated in its impact on voting by communication variables. It was simply there in the outlook of some electors, and when it was present it favoured participation. There are some signs, however, that it develops strongly in association with advancing age[37] and that it appeals more often to women than to men.

In relation to all this an issue of external validity may be raised: how far can the outcomes of a study of one election in a particular nation, and in a single city of that nation at that, be generalized to other election situations in other countries? To this question three related responses seem appropriate. First, there is an impressive amount of in-study replication in the results. Communication factors, though differentially operative, were nevertheless definitely involved in turnout developments among several different sub-groups in the Leeds youth sample. Second, the significance of the findings inheres less in the details of their configuration than in the fact that they embraced so many different modes of communication influence. If turnout is not entirely determined by the operation of prior dispositions, then scope is afforded for quantitative, relational and qualitative communication forces to affect participation rates as well — in which case efforts to trace their influence in other situations should prove worthwhile. Thus, third, doubts about generalizability can in the end be resolved only by replications elsewhere. From this point of view we look forward to the eventual publication of findings from on-going studies of the reactions of young American voters to the 1972 Presidential election campaign currently being conducted at the Universities of Wisconsin and Denver.

What guidelines, if any, might be drawn from the results of the Leeds study for the conduct of future research in the political communication field?

Methodologically, the results support some of the tendencies that were associated in the opening section of this paper with the "new look" in political communication research. They illustrate the value of panel designs, in which campaign effects can be separated from pre-campaign influences, sensitive causal relationships between different types of variables can be traced, and key factors can be ordered by the passage of time. They confirm the need for multivariate analysis, so many variables having been initially related to turnout at the zero-order level of correlation. So far as the criterion of effect, the dependent variable of turnout, is concerned, the path analyses suggest that even this seemingly simple and readily identifiable act of going to the polls may be regarded as a form of multi-faceted behaviour: we may be dealing with "informed turnout," "concerned turnout" and "obligatory turnout," as it were. The results also underwrite the need to refine our independent variable measures of exposure to political communication. Gross measures of total amount of exposure, or of the number of media used, would certainly have been too crude to capture the many interacting forces that operated on our samples. In the future additional refinements could be sought along the lines of: examining the role of the gratifications that underlie political communication use; taking more account of the heterogeneity/homogeneity of interpersonal communication situations; and looking into the content of such forms of communication.

Some substantive implications of the Leeds research derive from three overall patterns in the findings. First, a developmental meaning inheres in the youth/adult difference over the relative importance for turnout of feelings about the political system at large and of attitudes to specific parties. Previous political behaviour research had already suggested that "adolescents and young adults have not yet acquired the relatively durable partisan attachments more characteristic of mature persons."[38] Perhaps a further implication of our evidence is that many young people may first develop a sufficiently positive attachment to the political system to feel that, for example, elections are worth bothering about and voting makes sense. Socialization to specific party loyalties , however, is more of a life-long process and may start to yield more entrenched attitudes after the individual has cast his first vote. As this process continues, then, and people grow older, party attitudes gradually take over from system dispositions as more effective determinants of electoral participation. However, we still know little about the communication forces that are involved in this developmental sequence.

Another pattern in the evidence sounds a warning against relying exclusively on stratification factors when explaining communication behaviour and its political consequences. Although social class distinctions undoubtedly distribute differential opportunities to citizens to become effectively active in politics, several other factors (marital status, sex, age, membership of a family circle in which some interest in politics is shown) may also favour attention to political communications and a readiness to become involved in civic affairs. If class horizontally stratifies people into graduated ranks according to the adequacy of their preparation for competent participation, , a number of other forces also impinges on the same individuals, as if from a vertical angle, somewhat diluting the effects of stratification on their relationships to the political system. Perhaps these other forces are most likely to be galvanized at election time.

This suggests that the rhythm of the political calendar has temporal implications of some importance. That is, election campaigns may be regarded not only as influential political events but also as distinctive communication events. Compared with the usual out-of-election period, the mass media transmit more political messages to their audiences at election time. More people are reached by political communications, in some cases against the grain of their initial dispositions. There are more stimuli to interpersonal discussion, and more numerous and purposive connections are forged between the mass media and face-to-face communication channels. It is as if an election campaign generates motivations, behaviours and processes of information acquisition that are less common at other times. It follows that the campaign is probably a particularly formative occasion for the politically less involved sector of the electorate.

Finally, the results of the Leeds study provoke many unanswered questions about political communication processes which could profitably be explored in detail as the field develops:

(1) Does interpersonal and mass communication *per se* lead to turnout, or is there an interaction with direction of content? The press cross-pressure result suggests the latter, but how far would this tendency be generalizable to other communication sources, such as television, the family environment and friendship circles? Is there, in fact, a mechanism of selective exposure which operates for certain individuals across diverse communication channels, and, if so, does a high degree of such selectivity have any bearing on participation?

(2) Communication sources at odds with the individual's prior party preference were conceptualized in this study as cross-pressures. How do such communication cross-pressures operate in relation to others to which the individual may be exposed? Are they uniquely effective regardless of other conditions, or does the presence of at least one congruent source render incongruent ones impotent?

(3) Why does family discussion act so powerfully to uphold election participation? Is the family the sort of group in which members develop a sense of joint responsibility and a shared decision to vote? Is it an arena of cognitive build-up leading to more participation? Does it offer a circle in which people can be more free to express their

political emotions, thus generating an affect for participation?[39] Or is its characteristic political homogeneity the trait that chiefly helps to sustain turnout?

(4) In the impact of mass communication on turnout what part is played, respectively, by exposure that is deliberately motivated by political concerns, and by more incidental exposure stemming largely from either usual media use habits or availability factors? Insofar as incidental exposure is involved, does it lead to more informed turnout (knowledge gain allied to voting) or just directly to voting of a possibly less competent kind? The question has policy implications, for in Britain, despite the dislike of many viewers and producers, the availability of party broadcasts is maximized by their simultaneous transmission on all available television channels.

(5) Why was there a surplus in the Leeds 1970 samples of shifts away from participation over shifts towards it? Viewed from the standpoint of this question, the results of this study are open to two interpretations. On the one hand, they may be regarded as a "one-off" outcome of the 1970 campaign as such. Some elections, it might be said, are more inspiring or more dispiriting than others; and Britain's 1970 exercise simply happened to be one of the more dreary ones. On the other hand, in light of the known movements of gross turnout rates since the end of World War II, it is tempting to discern the influence in the findings of some secular trends that may be helpint to restructure either the political communication system itself or the way in which political messages transmitted through it are received.[40]

Of course data from a single election study cannot resolve such an issue. Nevertheless, two factors have been identified in our analyses which might help to determine whether voters at one election would be prepared to go to the polls in the same numbers as on previous occasions. First, we can say that there is likely to be less participation when prior political system dispositions are less positive. This observation would hypothetically associate falling turnout rates with trend data suggesting that many political institutions in certain Western democracies are less esteemed by citizens nowadays than they used to be. Second, the discovery that "communication matters" for turnout suggests that election participation will falter if there is diminishing respect for political communication as such, diluting and inhibiting the mobilizing boost that it could otherwise administer. Table 10 presents some evidence on this point from British national samples contacted originally by the Audience Research Department of the BBC. This shows that over four successive General Elections between 1959 and 1970 there has been a distinct downward trend in popular appreciation of party broadcasts, possibly the prime vehicle of political propaganda in those campaigns.

TABLE 10[a]

AVERAGE REACTION INDICES[b] FOR PARTY ELECTION BROADCASTS
OF B.B.C. VIEWING PANELS IN FOUR BRITISH ELECTIONS

Party broad- casts by:	Ratings by:											
	Supporters				Opponents				Uncommitted			
	1959	1964	1966	1970	1959	1964	1966	1970	1959	1964	1966	1970
Labour	74	72	67	63	44	42	38	32	57	57	48	44
Conser- vative	73	66	65	65	45	38	38	34	55	53	48	41
Liberal	69	71	66	60	51	53	50	42	55	58	55	47

a These data have been abstracted from four separate reports, prepared after each election campaign by the Ausience Research Department of the BBC, on the basis of questionnaires completed by members of its Viewing Panel.
b Reaction indices are calculated from the panel members' use of a rating scale and range from 0 to 100.

In all this is it far-fetched to discern the emergent outlines of what might be termed a "post-industrial" political communication system?[41]

APPENDIX

SUMMARY OF MEASURES USED AS PREDICTORS OF TURNOUT, LEEDS YOUNG AND OLDER ADULT SAMPLES

Predictor Variable Type	How Measured
A. Parental Political Characteristics	
1. Parental interest in politics	Very, fairly, not much interested
2. Parents' parties	One parent with preference or not
B. Structural Variables	
1. Stratification	
a. Father's occupation	Non-manual or manual
b. Own occupation	Non-manual and student or manual
c. School leaving age	15, 16, 17+
2. Other	
a. Sex	Male or female
b. Marital status	Married or single/widowed/divorced
c. Age	Continuum: 18-24
C.1. Political System Dispositions	
a. Duty to vote	"You should vote only if you want to" or "Everybody has a duty to vote"

APPENDIX cont.

Predictor Variable Type	How Measured
C1. *Political System Dispositions cont.*	
b. Political knowledge	Score 0-9 for correct answers to questions on party politicians and policies and on political concepts
c. Interest in politics	Very, fairly, not much
d. Caring about election outcome	Care who wins great deal, somewhat, not very much
e. Altruism of politicians	"Most politicians are out to serve the community" or are "more out for themselves".
e. Motivation to follow campaign	Index of no. of reasons for watching party broadcasts endorsed to no. of reasons for avoiding them endorsed: strong, medium, weak.
e. Efficacy of elections	Give ordinary people big say, some say, little say in how country is run.
e. Effect of lowering voting age	Will make politicians pay more attention to young people's views or not.
e. Attention to campaign arguments	Voters should pay a lot, some or little/no attention
e. Issue sensitivity	Total number (out of 23) of issues endorsed as very important for next government to tackle.
2. Party Variables[a]	
a. Attitude to own party	Score +3 to −2 based on application of three positive and two negative statements as true/not true of party.
b. Attitude to own leader	Score +3 to +21 based on semantic differential ratings of three scales loading high in factor I (evaluation): straightforward, likeable, warm.
3. Prior Issue Orientations	
a. Bread and butter issues	Score +6 to +12 for regarding as very important issues associated in cluster analysis: prices, taxes, jobs, housing, welfare services, nuclear war.
b. Social welfare issues	Score +4 to +8 for clustered issues of: educational opportunity, hospital spending, improving race relations, educational spending.

APPENDIX cont.

Predictor Variable Type	*How Measured*
C1. Political System Dispositions cont.	
3. Prior Issue Orientations	
c. Law and order issues	Score +4 to +8 for clustered issues of: capital punishment, unofficial strikes, student demonstrations, coloured immigration.
4. Customary Media Use	
a. Weight of TV viewing	Heavy or not, based on number of nights per week and number of hours per night usually watch.
b. Frequency of newspaper reading	Heavy, some or none, based on number of days usually read.
D. Cross-pressure Variables	
1. Press	Only read opposition paper, read no party paper or read papers of both sides, and only read own paper.
2. Political contacts	0-3 cross-pressures if a parent or spouse support opposing party and if have opposition friend(s) without supporting one(s).
3. Constituency	Resides in constituency won by opposition.
E. Campaign Exposure Variables	
1. Mass Media	
a. Party broadcasts	No. of party broadcasts seen of 14.
b. Election news reading	Score 0-6 based on estimated frequency of reading of campaign stories and amount of attention paid.
c. Television news	Average no. of main evening news bulletins.
2. Interpersonal	
a. Family	Frequency of weekly talk about election with family members: quite often, 2-3 times, occasionally, none.
b. Friends	Frequency of weekly talk with friends.
c. Others	Score 0-2 for mentions of election discussion with workmates/school-mates or neighbours.
F. Campaign Issue Change	
1. Taxes	Regarded as important post/not pre, no change, or regarded important pre/not post.

APPENDIX cont.

Predictor Variable Type	How Measured
F. Campaign Issue Change cont.	
2. Standard of living	As above.
3. Prices	As above.
G. Post-election Assessments	
1. Campaign reaction score	Score 8-24 taking account of how felt about five negative and three positive statements about politicians' campaign behaviour: felt strongly, crossed mind, never occurred to me.
2. Noted Conservative promises	Consider winning party had made "firm promises during the campaign, which it is now commited to carrying out".
3. Strength of the economy	Very strong, fairly strong, DK, rather weak, very weak.

[a] For the late decision analysis, party variables were measured by subtracting the score for one side from that of the other.

NOTES

1. Dr. Blumler is Research Director of the Centre for Television Research, the University of Leeds, where Professor McLeod, Chairman of the Mass Communications Research Center of the University of Wisconsin, was a Senior Visiting Fellow for the first half of 1973. The data presented were collected in collaboration with Dr. Denis McQuail, Reader in Sociology, University of Southampton, and Dr. T.J. Nossiter, Lecturer in Government, London School of Economics, who have also contributed at many points to the interpretation of findings. The authors especially wish to acknowledge the invaluable guidance received at all stages of the analysis from Mr. Arthur Royse, Senior Lecturer in Social Statistics of the Department of Sociology, University of Leeds. They are also indebted to Mr. Roger Appleyard, Research Assistant in the Department of Sociology, who assumed responsibility for all computer programming and processing, and to Miss Alison J. Ewbank, Research Assistant in the Centre for Television Research, for help in the data analysis.

2. See Paul F. Lazarsfeld, Bernard R. Berelson and Hazel Gaudet, *The People's Choice: How the Voter Makes Up His Mind in a Presidential Campaign,* Revised Edition, Columbia University Press, New York, 1948, as well as Berelson, Lazarsfeld and William McPhee, *Voting: A Study of Opinion Formation in a Presidential Campaign,* University of Chicago Press, Chicago, 1954. The results were more firmly solidified in the literature review of Joseph Klapper, *The Effects of Mass Communication,* Free Press, Glencoe, 1960.

3. It is a striking fact that Part I of Klapper's book (*op. cit.*) was subtitled "The Effects of Persuasive Communication." Since the rest of the volume dealt, respectively, with the effects of crime and violence in the media, the effects of escapist media materials, the effects of adult TV fare on child audiences, and with audience passivity, it is clear how completely the author had identified the investigation of political communication phenomena with research into persuasion.

4. Lazarsfeld *et al., (op. cit.*) calculated that 53 per cent of their Erie County sample had been reinforced by the 1940 election campaign by virtue of the stability of their vote intentions across several interviews. Although the authors also entered the explicit *caveat* that, "We cannot say for sure whether all the constants were really reinforced by the campaign" (p.103), by Klapper's day the research was said to have "found" without qualification that "exposure to months of campaign propaganda . . . reinforced the original pre-campaining intentions of 53 per cent" (p.16).

5. Lazarsfeld *et al., op. cit.* p.90.

6. One of the first points made in the Preface to the Second Edition of *The People's Choice* (Lazarsfeld *et al., op. cit.*, p.xx) "concerns the stability of . attitudes", the authors going on to point out that, "The subjects in our study tended to vote as they always had, in fact as their families always had."

7. The authors do not wish to over-state the "novelty" of the position outlined below. Some examples of earlier writings in which a number of its elements appeared include:

Morris Janowitz, "Mass Communication", *International Encyclopedia of the Social Sciences*, Macmillan, New York, 1968.

Morris Janowitz and Dwaine Marvick, *Competitive Pressure and Democratic Consent*, University of Michigan, Ann Arbor, 1956.

Kurt and Gladys Engel Lang, "Mass Media and Voting," in Eugene Burdick and Arthur J. Brodbeck (Eds.), *American Voting Behaviour*, Free Press, Glencoe, 1959.

Harold D. Lasswell, "The Triple-Appeal Principle: A Contribution of Psychoanalysis to Political and Social Science," *American Journal of Sociology*, Vol. 37, 1932, pp.523-538.

Ithiel de Sola Pool, "TV: A New Dimension in Politics," in Burdick and Brodbeck.

For example, Janowitz and Marvick singled out for attention the strategic role of mass communication in mobilizing peripheral voters for electoral participation. And the Langs strongly underlined the capacity of the mass media to fashion a "second-hand reality" — to "provide perspectives, shape images of candidates and parties, help highlight issues around which a campaign will develop, and define the unique atmosphere and areas of sensitivity which mark any particular campaign." Nevertheless, the climate of political communication research is distinctly different today from that which prevailed a few years ago. The critique of the "limited effects" model has become more wide-ranging and insistent. Though still prominent in many summaries and reviews of the literature, that model is being displaced by other perspectives as a source of research guidance. And empirically minded investigators are devising new measures of political communication effects that do not involve a reversion to outdated mass persuasion models of media influence.

8. Edward C. Dreyer, "Media Use and Electoral Choices: Some Political Consequences of Information Exposure," *Public Opinion Quarterly*, Vol. 35, 1971-1972, pp. 545-553.

9. David O. Sears and Jonathan L. Freedman, "Selective Exposure to Information: A Critical Review," *Public Opinion Quarterly*, Vol. 31, 1967, pp. 194-213.

10. Elihu Katz, "Platforms and Windows: Broadcasting's Role in Election Campaigns," *Journalism Quarterly*, Vol. 48, 1971, pp. 304-314.

11. Gary L. Wamsley and Richard A. Pride, "Television Network News: Re-thinking the Iceberg Problem," *Western Political Quarterly*, Vol. 25, 1972, pp. 434-450.

12. David Butler and Donald Stokes, *Political Change in Britian: Forces Shaping Electoral Choice,* Macmillan, London, 1969; John P. Robinson, "Perceiving Media Bias and the 1968 Vote: Can the Media Affect Behavior After All?" *Journalism Quarterly,* Vol. 49, 1972, pp. 239-246.

13. Elihu Katz, Jay G. Blumler and Michael Gurevitch, "Utilization of Mass Communication by the Individual," Arden House Conference on Directions in Mass Communications Research, New York, 1973; *Public Opinion Quarterly*, Vol. 37, Winter, 1973-1974, pp. 509-523.

14. Steven H. Chaffee, L. Scott Ward and Leonard P. Tipton, "Mass Communication and Political Socialization," *Journalism Quarterly*, Vol. 47, 1970, pp. 647-659, 666.

15. E. Noelle-Neumann, "Return to the Concept of Powerful Mass Media," *Studies of Broadcasting*, No. 9, 1973, pp. 67-112.

16. See Maxwell E. McCombs and Donald L. Shaw, "The Agenda-Setting Function of the Mass Media," *Public Opinion Quarterly*, Vol. 36, 1972 pp. 176-187, and Jack M. McLeod, Lee B. Becker and James E. Byrnes, "Another Look at the Agenda-Setting Function of the Press," paper submitted to conference of the Association for Education in Journalism, Fort Collins, Colorado, August, 1973.

17. Wamsley and Pride, *op. cit.*

18. See Jay G. Blumler, J.R. Brown, A.J. Ewbank and T.J. Nossiter, "Attitudes to the Monarchy: Their Structure and Development during a Ceremonial Occasion," *Political Studies,* Vol. 19, 1971, pp. 149-171. See also the measure of "sense of community" used by Joseph Adelson and R. O'Neil, "Growth of Political Ideas in Adolescence," *Journal of Personality and Social Psychology*, Vol. 4, 1966, pp. 295-306. Subtle dimensions of cognition are scored from open-ended responses to hypothetical problem situations. These have also been used with success in studies of adolescent political socialization by researchers at the Mass Communications Research Center, University of Wisconsin.

19. For a recent statement see Paul Burstein, "Social Structure and Individual Political Participation in Five Countries," *American Journal of Sociology*, Vol. 77, 1972, pp. 1087-1110.

20. For the classic statement see Paul F. Lazarsfeld and Robert K. Merton, "Mass Communication, Popular Taste and Organized Social Action," in Lyman Bryson (Ed.), *The Communication of Ideas,* Harper & Bros., New York, 1948.

21. Robert E. Dowse and John A. Hughes, *Political Sociology*, John Wiley and Sons, London, 1972, p. 314.

22. Berelson *et al., op. cit.*, p.249.

23. *Ibid.*, pp. 277-280.

24. Lazarsfeld *et al, op. cit.*, p.75.

25. Herbert A. Simon and Frederick Stern, "The Effect of Television upon Voting Behavior in the 1952 Presidential Election," *American Political Science Review*, Vol. 49, 1955, pp. 470-477.

26. William A. Glaser, "Television and Voting Turnout," *Public Opinion Quarterly*, Vol. 29, 1965, pp. 71-86.

27. Marvin E. Olsen, "Social Participation and Voting Turnout: A Multivariate Analysis," *American Sociological Review*, Vol. 37, 1972, pp. 317-333.

28. The study was financed by a grant from the Social Science Research Council of Britain to the first author and to Dr. Denis McQuail, University of Southampton, and Dr. T.J. Nossiter, London School of Economics. The participation of the second author was made possible by grants from the same agency and from the Graduate School Research Committee of the University of Wisconsin.

29. See the report of the investigating Committee, *Public Opinion Polling on the 1970 Election*, Market Research Society, London, 1972.

30. The most strictly comparable studies were those conducted in Leeds during the 1959 and 1964 General Elections, for which findings were reported in Joseph Trenaman and Denis McQuail, *Television and the Political Image*, Methuen, London, 1971 and Jay G. Blumler and Denis McQuail, *Television in Politics: Its Uses and Influence*, Faber, London, 1968 and University of Chicago Press, Chicago, 1969.

31. The term "contingent abstainers" was first coined by Professor Hugh Berrington to refer to those individuals who expressed a definite intention to vote on Polling Day but failed to do so. See Appendix IV, "Voting Intention and Actual Vote," *Public Opinion Polling on the 1970 Election*.

32. Since the analysis was concerned with turnout rather than direction, inter-party switchers were merged with consistent party voters (after all, their original intention to participate in the election had been followed by the casting of a vote). They amounted, however, to only 10 per cent of the category of stable participants in the youth sample.

33. Cross-pressures constituted an ambiguous category in time-dimension terms. Though initially classified with the pre-campaign variables, their role in the analysis suggested a closer affinity with campaign influences.

34. See J. Sonquist, E. Baker and J. Morgan, *Searching for Structure*, Institute for Social Research, Ann Arbor, 1971.

35. N. Blalock, *Social Statistics*, Second Edition, McGraw-Hill, New York, 1972, p. 503.

36. Small proportions within these totals (six per cent and four per cent, respectively) represent aberrant results in the form of reverse outcomes for an individual variable within a cluster of related and consistent variables. This could be expected when so many interrelated variables are introduced as controls. To avoid confusion, we have eliminated such minor reversals from all regression analysis tables, treating them as if they had contributed nothing to the criterion variance.

37. Only 33 per cent of the Leeds young elector sample accepted a duty to vote compared with 66 per cent of the older adult controls.

38. David O. Sears, "Political Behavior," in *The Handbook of Social Psychology*, Second Edition, edited by Gardner Lindzey and Elliott Aronson, Vol. 5, Addisan-Wesley, Reading, 1969, p. 388.

39. This hypothesis is provoked by comments to be found in T.J. Scheff, "Inter-subjectivity and Emotion," *American Behavioral Scientist*, Vol. 16 1973, pp. 501-12.

40. For further discussion of recent developments affecting democratic political communication systems, see Harold Mendelsohn and Irving Crespi, *Polls, Television and the New Politics*, Chandler, Scranton, 1970.

41. The analysis presented in this chapter was completed before the British General Election of February 1974, at which the turnout rate rose to 78%. Although this increase over 1970 (72%) may have been due in part to such special factors as the up-to-date register in force, the crisis circumstances in which the election was held and the partisan spirit in which it was fought, it may also have been connected with the fact that the role of the media in the campaign proved "unexpectedly different from the conduct of previous elections in Britain" in a number of respects. In particular far more television time was devoted to campaign communication than ever before, especially in the main evening news, and ordinary electors and other non-party figures had greater access to political programming. See Jay G. Blumler, "The Media and the Election," *New Society*, March 7, 1974.

Chapter 10

TRENDS IN POLITICAL PARTICIPATION IN BRITAIN SINCE 1945

James Spence

INTRODUCTION

In the last thirty years Britain, in common with most European countries, has experienced a period of profound social and economic change. For example, women are playing a more significant role in economic life as family building and child care take up a smaller proportion of a woman's life. People in general have become materially better off, are educated for a longer time, and have more varied job opportunities. Service industries have proliferated at the expense of primary industries, and the population drift towards the prosperous South East of England has continued.

Political change seems to have occurred at the same time. In this essay, data will be examined that throw light on theories of political behaviour and on trends in political participation. The findings suggest the directions in which the British political system is now moving and the strains to which it is now exposed.

Poll, social survey and census data form the greater part of the evidence. Survey results in Britain tend to contain little continuous trend information beside the regular measures of support for the political parties and their leaders. Little political survey work has been conducted on a regular basis outside the polling organizations. The evidence is therefore limited, but its analysis may nonetheless throw light on issues of theoretical interest to sociologists and political scientists.

THEORETICAL BACKGROUND

Argument about the degree of political consensus in this country has continued since World War II. Mackenzie,[1] for instance, in the early 1960s maintained that there is fundamental consensus within Britain and British politics. He concluded: "the 'agreement on fundamentals' is very nearly as great as it ever has been in the modern history of British Parties . . . Two monolithic structures now face each other and conduct furious arguments about the comparatively minor issues that separate them." Beer,[2] however, considered that there was indeed a basic split between political parties that reached the heart of the democratic process. Also in the early 1960s he commented:

> Yet for all this agreement (on the basic legal structures, the basic parliamentary conventions, and the main contemporary practices of party government and functional representation), there was between Tory and Socialist a conflict over the meaning of the party system, the constitution, and democracy itself that one might call fundamental.

Both of these views described the conflict as seen by political analysts. However, when members of the public have been questioned about the difference between the two major parties, it appears that many people think of them as rather similar, and most think them less different than "ten years ago."[3] In certain respects the public detects differences; they identify the Labour party as the party of the working class and the Conservative party as the party of the business-man and the industrialist. But whether there is fundamental conflict in the electorate between the supporters of the two major parties must be examined from a different theoretical perspective and in the light of other kinds of evidence.

At this point we put forward Janowitz and Segal's thesis as being relevant to explain the effect of social developments on political party support.[4] They suggest that British political behaviour conforms to a "consensus and cleavage" model, which postulates:

> a more complicated pattern of social stratification in which political conflict is manifested by new and more differentiated social groupings which reflect economic, professional and bureaucratic interests. . . .
> Advanced industrialization produces a changing stratification system which alters older forms of political conflict and provides the basis for newer forms. These new conflicts are more delimited in scope, but they have deep consequences on collective problem-solving, and they may be so aggregated as to produce pervasive strains. Because there are built-in limitations in the trend toward greater social equality, in this view what is crucial is not only the persistence of the social-structural basis of cleavages but also the capacity

of the political institutions to adjust and to create the conditions for political consensus.[5]

Janowitz and Segal are suggesting that the political system is dependent to an extent on the ability of the structures to adjust, provided that the adjustment improves consensus within the system. But we may well find that the structural alterations increase cleavage. If we should find, for instance, that changes in the social structure are related to greater sophistication in the electorate and a greater heterogeneity of political demands, and that these demands have tended to be channelled through new political structures, then a development may be occurring that will create or reopen social and political divisions. Instead of a movement towards consensual politics, the structural innovations may be toward new or renewed forms of social and political conflict. The direction of the changes that are visible indicates the course of party development, and exposes the extent of the differences between parties and the extent to which the parties have been fulfilling their role as communication channels in the democratic process. To return to the electorate, the ways in which it takes part in the political process and accepts its structures, and the ways in which these change, may indicate the extent to which the British democratic process is under strain.

This paper is concerned, then, with political participation, and with its associated variable party affiliation. Since the early 1930s political scientists have discussed the relationship of apathy or alienation to political participation and hypothesized the effect that changes in the degree of apathy have on the political system.[6] In this essay I shall use the concept of political heterogeneity, as suggested by Janowitz and Segal's description of the consensus and cleavage model, to describe the manifestations previously associated with the psychological concepts of apathy and alienation: namely, an increase in the level of support for political parties other than the majority parties, Conservative and Labour, an increase in the level of non-participation in elections, an increase in what may be interpreted as anti-system political participation, such as direct action against political actors. The approach implies that apparently contradictory trends may be at work: increases in political apathy may be accompanied by increases in political heterogeneity. The object of the paper, then, is to examine the trends since 1945 in satisfaction with the system, its leaders, its effectiveness and with its alternatives in order to see how changes in political heterogeneity may affect the political system itself, both its "rules" and its structures.

THE SURVEY EVIDENCE

Preliminary Note *

British politics have been dominated by social class since the introduction of universal male adult suffrage in 1918. This continues to be the case, though there appear to have been some changes. Blondel, Durant, Janowitz and Segal, Butler and Stokes and the Nuffield studies of the British General Elections have all demonstrated the class basis of voting and political party support.[7]

Since 1945 the Conservative and Labour parties together have in all elections gained more than 85% of the total votes cast. The overall political situation of a two-party system has applied since World War II, and with the exception of a few years after World War I, has applied to British politics since towards the end of the nineteenth century.

But one major difference emerges when Britain's system is compared with the American two party system in this respect; in Britain's case the nineteenth century political parties achieved their dominating position before many people had the vote. And it was the extension of the suffrage in 1918 that established the Labour party as a major force. In the United States, however, universal suffrage was introduced while the parties were forming themselves. This may have an important impact on the role of the political parties and the development of politics in Britain.[8] Political scientists should recall in the ensuing discussion that it was not until 1928 that something approaching universal adult suffrage emerged in this country and it was not until 1948 that it finally applied to all parliamentary elections.

The Change in the Level of Voting

The first hypothesis for which we have sought evidence is that the level of formal political participation through voting has decreased since 1945. Given that Britain has only enjoyed universal suffrage since 1928 the important figures begin then, but all figures since the beginning of the century have been included for interest.

---

* The 1974 General Election is discussed in the postcript (p.335).

TABLE 1

ELECTORATE AND TURNOUT IN THE UNITED KINGDOM, 1900-1970

		% Turnout	Electorate	Winning Party
Male lodgers paying	1900	74.6	6,730,935	
£10 in rent per year	1906	82.6	7,264,604	
and all male house-	1910	86.6	7,694,741	
holders enfranchised	1911	81.1	7,709,981	
Voting age:	1918	58.9	21,392,322	
21 for men	1922	71.3	21,127,663	
31 for women	1923	70.8	21,281,232	
	1924	76.6	21,731,320	
Voting age:	1929	76.1	28,850,870	
21: Universal	1931	76.3	29,960,071	
suffrage	1935	71.2	31,379,050	
(some double	1945	72.7*	33,240,391	Labour
voting 1929-45)	1950	84.0	33,269,770	Labour
	1951	82.5	34,645,573	Conservative
	1955	76.7	34,858,263	Conservative
	1959	78.8	35,397,080	Conservative
	1964	77.1	35,894,054	Labour
	1966	75.8	35,957,245	Labour
Voting age:				
18: Universal	1970	72.0	39,342,013	Conservative
suffrage				

NOTE: *University seats are excluded: other 1945 figures are adjusted to eliminate the distortions introduced by voting in the 15 two-member seats then existing.

Turnout has remained relatively high throughout this century, despite the increasing electorate size. On one major indicator, then, this hypothesis appears to be true, with the exception of 1945 itself owing to the rather unusual circumstances surrounding that election. Since 1950 turnout has declined appreciably, though the drop between 1966 and 1970 is likely to have been sharpened by the inclusion of the 18-20 year old young voters. Yet there has been a 12 per cent drop. And the record in other countries is much better (see Tables 2 and 3).

For many middle-aged non-property owners (those aged about 45-50) and particularly for females, there had been few previous opportunities to vote. For those twenty years younger (that is, 25 in 1945) the act of voting was a right that everyone enjoyed. They would have been too young to remember the extension of the suffrage to women under 30. These people are now where their elders were in 1950, and they appear less likely to use their right to vote, despite never having experienced a time when they could not. Perhaps one reason for this is *because* they never have experienced not having the vote. A further reason may lie in the choice of alternatives for the vote.

TABLE 2

LEVEL OF TURNOUT IN GENERAL ELECTIONS OF INDUSTRIALISED DEMOCRACIES
(excluding those with compulsory voting)

	G.E. date	% Turnout		G.E. date	% Turnout
Austria	1970	92.9	Finland	1970	82.0
Italy	1963	92.9	France	1966	80.9
New Zealand	1969	89.4	Israel	1974	78.5
Denmark	1966	88.9	Ireland	1969	79.6
Sweden	1970	88.3	Canada	1968	75.7
Belgium	1968	90.0	S. Africa (whites only)	1974	75.0
W. Germany	1969	86.6	United Kingdom	1970	72.0
Iceland	1971	86.9	Japan	1969	65.0
Norway	1969	83.8	U.S.A.	1972	

TABLE 3

CHANGES IN THE LEVEL OF TURNOUT BETWEEN THE FIRST GENERAL ELECTION HELD IN THE 1950s AND THE MOST RECENT GENERAL ELECTION, IN WESTERN DEMOCRACIES

	%	%	% Change		%	%	% Change
Britain	84.0 (1950)	72.0 (1970)	−12	Belgium	89.1 (1950)	90.0 (1968)	+0.9
Austria	95.8 (1953)	92.9 (1970)	−2.9	Ireland	74.6 (1951)	79.6 (1969)	+5.0
France	80.2 (1951)	80.1 (1967)	−0.1	Finland	74.6 (1951)	82.0 (1970)	+7.4
W.Germany	86.0 (1953)	86.6 (1969)	+0.6	Canada	66.9 (1953)	75.7 (1968)	+8.8
Italy	92.2 (1953)	92.9 (1968)	+0.7	Sweden	79.1 (1952)	88.3 (1970)	+9.2

SOURCE: Kilbrandon Commission minority report p34.

If we accept elections as the major indicator of the degree of political participation within democratic countries, then Britain's political system is coming under strain. People are less willing to take part, for whatever reason, in the major democratic process, election of political representatives. This has implications for both the political alternatives available and the political structures.

The Change in Support for Political Parties

If turnout also provides an indicator of political heterogeneity, then political heterogeneity is on the increase in the United Kingdom. Indeed if the Northern Ireland figures are excluded, then the decline in turnout in Britain becomes more acute. People could be apathetic because they are satisfied, however. But other evidence suggests that people are not satisfied with the actions of more recent governments.

One indication is the changing level of support for parties other than the major ones, Conservative and Labour. Up to 1959 the major parties increased their share of the total votes cast at General Elections from 88.4 per cent in 1945 to 93.2 per cent in 1959. Since then their share has been 87.5 per cent in 1964, 89.8 per cent in 1966 and 89.4 per cent in 1970. But other findings show that voters are less likely now to have a stable voting pattern; they are more likely now to change their party support. This "volatility" is shown in the results of by-elections since 1945 in the results of panel surveys, and in the changes shown from one election to the next. One crude indicator of this change is "swing," which measures the difference between the two major parties at election 1 and compares this to the difference between them at election 2. The results of such analysis are shown in the chart. On this is plotted the swing since the previous General Election at all by-elections conducted since 1955 (the dots (o)) and the swing shown by the regular monthly voting figures derived from the Gallup poll, also compared to the previous General Election. The direction of the two measures, national poll and by-election swings, are remarkably consistent. But the extent of the swings alters appreciably; initially the swings appear relatively limited. Indeed between 1950 and 1955 this was especially true. But during the period 1967-1969 the extent of the swings was unprecedented.

"Swing" is a poor indicator of *all* the changes that occur from one election to another because by definition it looks at the shares of

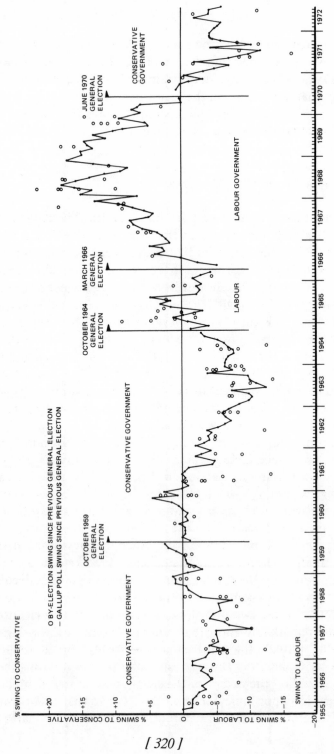

Chart 1: POLL AND BY-ELECTION SURVEYS 1955-1972
Source: F. Teer & J.D. Spence, Political Opinion Polls (Hutchinson University Libraries: London, 1973)

the vote of only the Conservative and Labour parties. The Liberals, the Nationalists and the Communists have also experienced dramatic changes in support over the period. Being minor parties, it may be argued that increasing support for them may illustrate the increasing disillusion that the electorate feels towards the present two major parties, but at least it will show an increasing degree of political heterogeneity. Has support for minor parties changed? At General Elections the answer must be no.* As we saw above, minor parties gained 11.9 per cent of all votes cast in 1945, 6.8 per cent in 1959, 12.5 per cent in 1964, 10.2 per cent in 1966 and 10.6 per cent in 1970. Third party support actually fell between 1945 and 1959, rose significantly between 1959 and 1964, fell marginally in 1966, and remained at that level in 1970. But the overall figures disguise some important trends, as the following table will show:

TABLE 4

LIBERAL PARTY SHARES OF THE VOTE AT GENERAL ELECTIONS
BETWEEN 1945 AND 1970

Election Date	*No. of MP's*	*Liberal Party*
1945	12	2,197,191 (9.1%)
1950	9	2,621,548 (9.1%)
1951	6	730,556 (2.5%)
1955	6	722,405 (2.7%)
1959	6	1,638,571 (5.9%)
1964	12	3,092,878 (11.2%)
1966	9	2,327,533 (8.5%)
1970	6	2,117,033 (7.5%)

From their position of strength in 1950 with over 2½ million votes but only 9 members, the Liberals' share was drastically cut and has only recently recovered its immediate post-war level. The lower share of the vote has not meant a proportionate drop in the number of Liberal MP's. They have never had fewer than six members over the period. Besides showing the vagaries of the electoral system in Britain when three times the number of votes can mean the same number of Liberal members elected, the pattern of ebb and flow changes with the majority governing party; the Labour win in 1964 saw the highest level of Liberal voting since 1950 when Labour was also in power. In 1970 the Liberal share of the vote dropped somewhat with the emergence of the Conservatives.

---

* But see the postscript on p335 for a discussion of the 1974 General Election.

This pattern is emphasised when by-election results are studied. During the 1961-1962 period the Conservative government of the day came under considerable popular criticism for its handling of Britain's affairs. Unemployment was high, prices were rising, relatively little economic growth occurred, and the protracted Common Market negotiations were winding to an unsatisfactory end. In many of the by-elections at that time the Liberals came close to winning where at the previous General Elections their share of the vote had been very small. At Orpington in March, 1962, the Liberals won the seat from the Conservative party. A "safe" Conservative majority of 14,760 votes was converted overnight into a "safe" Liberal seat with a majority of nearly 8,000 votes. Besides being quite unprecedented this remarkable result stands as the first of several electoral surprises. Subsequent to this result the Liberal party enjoyed a period of national popularity (according to the opinion polls) of the same level as the two major parties. Other by-elections also showed considerable increases in the Liberal share of the votes. From surveys conducted after these results it became clear that the new Liberals were in general disappointed major party supporters, who in many cases had not had a previous record of changing their votes. This level of Liberal revival was short-lived. In 1972-73, however, again during a Conservative Government's rule, the Liberal party has experienced a more sustained revival. In several by-elections they have gained the seat, in some cases with greater changes in party support than were witnessed at Orpington. National opinion polls have shown the three parties with similar shares of the vote for several months. Some of these surveys have indicated that the Liberals have drawn their support equally from Conservative and ex-Labour supporters.

But a major point to remember is that Liberal supporters are more evenly drawn from all social class groups (as defined by occupational group) than either Conservative or Labour supporters — and this has been true since 1945, as far as the evidence shows.

This pattern applies whether the Liberals have 7 per cent or 25 per cent of the national vote. The implication of this is that, as more people accept the possibility of voting Liberal, so the foundations of the two party system are weakened. The social class division is also weakened for props to it include the traditional patterns of political party support. A further general comment is that there is remarkable consistency between the patterns in 1964 and 1973: 16 per cent of

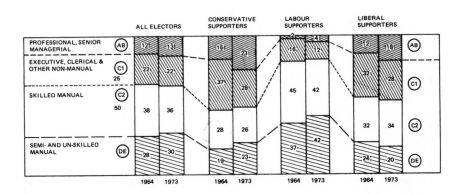

		ALL ELECTORS		CONSERVATIVE SUPPORTERS		LABOUR SUPPORTERS		LIBERAL SUPPORTERS		
PROFESSIONAL, SENIOR MANAGERIAL	(AB)	12	13	16	23	21 16	4 12	12	18	(AB)
EXECUTIVE, CLERICAL & OTHER NON-MANUAL	(C1) 25	22	22	37	28	45	42	32	28	(C1)
SKILLED MANUAL	(C2) 50	38	36	28	26			32	34	(C2)
SEMI- AND UN-SKILLED MANUAL	(DE)	28	30	19	23	37	42	24	20	(DE)
		1964	1973	1964	1973	1964	1973	1964	1973	

Figure 1: SOURCES OF SUPPORT FOR PARTIES BY SOCIAL CLASS 1964-1973 (NOP)

Labour supporters belong to the non-manual ABC1 socio-economic groups in 1973; 18 per cent did so in 1964. The overall patterns hide the more fundamental movements within the electorate that we have discussed.

The Liberals have traditionally been strong in the fringe areas of Britain, in Scotland and Wales. But since 1964 the Liberals in those areas have had to contend with increasing pressures from nationalist candidates and parties as pressure for political devolution has mounted. Neither the Scottish National Party nor the Welsh Nationalists are new political parties. Indeed the first was founded in 1934 and owes much of its thinking to the Scottish Home Rule Association formed in 1918 and to a number of like minded organizations, the Scottish Patriots and the Scottish Convention (1942). But its official formation occurred through the union of the Scottish Party and the National Party. SNP candidates have stood at all General Elections since 1945 and its paid-up membership has grown staggeringly since the beginning of the 1960s from 2,000 to 120,000 in 1968.[9]

In a by-election in April 1945, a SNP candidate, Dr. Robert

McIntyre, was elected though he was defeated in the General Election three months later. In the 1966 General Election, the SNP votes as a percentage of the total vote was more than twice that in 1964. In 1967 a second SNP candidate, Mrs. Winifred Ewing, was elected. In May 1968, in the municipal elections, with 20 per cent of the Scottish electorate involved, the SNP turned out to be the largest single party and improved by 50 per cent its 1966 General Election performance in absolute numbers.

In polls done between November 1967 and April 1968, an average of 24 per cent of those interviewed in Scotland favoured the SNP, almost as many as supported the Conservative Party and about three times the number supporting the Liberals (9 per cent). By June 1968, support for the SNP in Scotland had jumped to 32 per cent. This turned out to be a local phenomenon and in the 1970 General Election the SNP won only one seat. They also won 306,796 votes (1.1 per cent of the U.K. share). They gained, however, the third party position in Scotland, winning 11.4 per cent of the vote and putting up 65 candidates. This progress was maintained. In 1971 the SNP ran a close second to Labour in the Dundee East by-election winning 11,300 votes and being defeated by a small 1,000 majority by the Labour party. In late 1973 Glasgow Govan fell to the SNP at a by-election.

Certain major constitutional developments appear considerably more likely in view of the Kilbrandon Commission Report on the Constitution, suggesting a greater degree of government decentralization and devolution. These overturn Cook's proposition that the SNP has been a major political failure. Writing in 1972, he stated, "After the elation of Hamilton, the vessel of Scottish Nationalism had seemed set fair to sail. The 1970 election showed it to be a latter-day Marie Celeste."[10] In 1973 the Marie Celeste is crewed once more.

The Welsh Nationalist Party, Plaid Cymru, was founded in 1925 by the union of four Nationalist groups. Older than the SNP, having put up between one and twenty-four candidates at nine General Elections, with a membership of 30,000, it had a Nationalist candidate elected at a General Election before the SNP.

In 1955, Plaid Cymru won 11.4 per cent of the Welsh vote; in 1959, 12.7 per cent; in 1964 10.4 per cent; in 1966 it got 10.7 per cent of the vote and Gwynfor Evans became M.P. Since then, in March 1967, July 1968 and August 1968, Plaid Cymru candidates have been second in three by-elections.

In the 1970 General Election they won 11.5 per cent of the Welsh vote with candidates in all 36 constituencies, but lost the only seat they had held. Their local election results have been less spectacular than the SNP's in Scotland, and their support is clearly more narrowly confined to the rural areas of mid and North Wales.

The Communists have shown rather less electoral success, at both local and national levels, and indeed support of them has fallen away steeply since 1950, with a slight resurgence in the mid-1960s.[11]

TABLE 5

COMMUNIST SHARE OF THE VOTE AT
GENERAL ELECTIONS, 1945-1970

	Votes	*Share of total*	*Number of Candidates*
1945	102,780	0.4%	21
1950	91,765	0.3%	100
1951	21,640	0.1%	10
1955	33,144	0.1%	17
1959	30,897	0.1%	18
1964	45,932	0.2%	36
1966	62,112	0.2%	57
1970	37,970	0.1%	58

The levels of support for the nationalist and Communist parties may be taken as indicators of "anti-system" political support. Over time this shows that there has not been an increase except in Scotland. Yet at certain by-elections since 1970 "extreme" candidates do appear to have done rather better than they did in the 1950s and early 1960s. In the Rochdale by-election in October 1972 the Independent Jim Merrick won 4,074 votes, 8.9 per cent of the poll, while in the Kingston-upon-Thames by-election in May of that year the Independent Conservative Eric Scruby gained 5.4 per cent of the poll (1,705 votes). In neither of these cases was support significant though the growth or decline in this figure needs careful watching.

These data provide little evidence that there has been an increase in "anti-system" party support, with an exception perhaps in Scotland. Nevertheless there does appear to have been an increase in the heterogeneity of party support. More voters appear willing to vote for minor parties, at least between General Elections.

This finding is substantiated by examination of panel data derived from surveys conducted before General Elections in 1964, 1966 and 1970.[12] These panel surveys have shown increasing changes over the election campaign period. Whereas in 1964 only 12 per cent of all those interviewed changed their response to the question about party support between the first survey at the beginning of the campaign and the second just before the election, in 1966 18 per cent did so and in 1970 about 24 per cent did so. This does not mean that the overall situation has changed. In all but the last case it has not. Yet the changes beneath the apparently calm surface are both many and important.

Public Opinion about the Actors within the Political System

We still have not conclusively demonstrated that declining turnout and increasing political heterogeneity in the British electorate are caused by dissatisfaction. Some poll evidence throws light on this link. Public opinion on the leaders of the major parties has been monitored regularly since 1956. Besides being better known, the modern party leaders are on average less popular than their predecessors.

In an article in the Times in 1969 entitled, "Voters Show their Scepticism of Politicians," Rose concluded: "the significance of (the leaders) unpopularity (post 1966) does not rest in forecasting long term election trends, but in gauging immediate popular response to leaders' appeals to millions of individuals in their roles as workers and employers, . . . when public policies require more widespread popular support than at any time in 20 years, it is worrying to find that the men asking for this support enjoy decreasing public confidence." This table has been updated to include the years 1969-1973, and though the level of public support increased at the time of the 1970 General Election, a significant fall has occurred since then.

If one looks at the figures since 1970, the conclusion does seem justified that dissatisfaction with political leaders has recently been growing. Unfortunately, little direct evidence exists on other forms of dissatisfaction. One case study, however, throws light on the changes that have occurred. During the 1960s evidence suggests that electors judged the success or failure of political parties, to an extent according to the *economic* achievements of that party.[13] Certainly

TABLE 6

SATISFACTION WITH PARTY LEADERS, 1956-1970

Leaders	Period	PM %	Opposition %	Average %
Heath Wilson	July-October 1973	35½	42	39
Heath Wilson	January June 1973	39	41	40
Heath Wilson	July to December 1972	35½	47	41
Heath Wilson	January to June 1972	39	49	44
Heath Wilson	July to December 1971	35	55	45
Heath Wilson	January to June 1971	37½	59½	48½
Heath Wilson	July to December 1970	40	64½	51
Wilson Heath	January to May 1970	44	36	40
Wilson Heath	July to December 1969	39	33	36
Wilson Heath	January to June 1969	32½	30	31½
Wilson Heath	July to December 1968	32	29	30
Wilson Heath	January to June 1968	32	30	31
Wilson Heath	1967	46	33	39½
Wilson Heath	Apr. to Dec. 1966	55	37	46
Wilson Heath	Aug. 1965 to March 1966	60	47	53½
Wilson Douglas-Home	Oct. 1964 to July 1965	57	37	47
Douglas-Home Wilson	Nov. 1963 to Sept. 1964	45	62	53½

TABLE 6 CONTINUED

Leaders	Period	PM %	Opposition %	Average %
Macmillan Wilson	Feb. 1963 to Oct. 1963	38	54	46
Macmillan Gaitskell	Jan. 1962 to Jan. 1963	46	54	47½
Macmillan Gaitskell	1961	57	47	52
Macmillan Gaitskell	1960	68	46	57
Macmillan Gaitskell	Jan. to Aug. 1959	59	45	52
Macmillan Gaitskell	1958	48	40	44
Macmillan Gaitskell	1957	44	40	42
Eden Gaitskell	1956	50	41	45½

SOURCE: Gallup Political Index after Rose *op.cit.*

inflation, unemployment, wage rates and balance of payments have each been major public issues in the media, in Parliament and among the public. But government economic policy has seldom during this time tackled a problem similar to one previously experienced in a comparable way. One case appears similar; the wage freezes of July 1966 and of November 1972 though involving different measures in detail are similar enough for some comparison to be attempted.

During the 1966-1970 Labour administration certain counter-inflation measures were introduced. In July 1966 NOP asked questions in their monthly political poll at the time and a number of the same questions were asked in November 1972 and January 1973, at the time of the Conservative government's actions to stem inflation. Fewer electors in 1972/73 thought that the economic measures would work when compared to July 1966. Yet rather more thought the measures necessary than had thought so six years before. Forty per cent of the electors said they would not be affected by the freeze on wages and salaries at all, and a further 40 per cent considered it unlikely to affect them very much. In July 1966, rather fewer people said they would be relatively unaffected, rather more did not know what the effects would be.

To about a third of the electorate prices and the cost of living was the single most important problem facing Great Britain today (given a choice of 22 items). It was not surprising therefore to find almost all electors in November 1972 saying that the freeze on prices was necessary. But, like control of wages and salaries, control of prices was not thought likely to be effective by some 40 per cent of electors. About the same per cent (42 per cent) said it would be. Comparing 1966 to 1972 we may tentatively conclude that people now appear more sceptical about the effectiveness of this kind of political action. They are more likely to say that what has been done, though necessary, will not actually solve Britain's problems.

This evidence supports the view that the electorate is becoming more sceptical and more sophisticated, and by inference more heterogeneous. This implies that the electorate is becoming more responsive to political events, as the traditional political affiliations are weakened; and that future General Election and by-election results will be more difficult to forecast.

A variety of factors seem to be at work in accounting for increasing dissatisfaction and heterogeneity. Political education or civics was until recently deliberately excluded from school curricula, so we cannot look there for a direct link. Yet since 1945 Government spending on education in general has increased tremendously. From 1951-1952 to 1971-1972, total current expenditure by the government on education of all forms increased from £338 million to £2,625 million. Capital expenditure increased £70 million to £516 million over the same period. Even taking inflation into account, there has been a dramatic increase in expenditure on education. As mentioned earlier children are now staying at school longer, and proportionately more are going to university or other forms of further education. Spending on libraries has increased in a similar way. The impact of this increased expenditure may now be being felt in the political arena. Further evidence of increasing political heterogeneity is to be found in the increasing independence of women in general and the increase in their political independence. In the 1959, 1964, 1966 and 1970 General Elections a larger proportion of women than of men voted Conservative. This has become less so, particularly since the 1970 General Election. In 1945, for instance, 35 per cent of men and 43 per cent of women voters claimed to have voted Conservative.

In 1959, the proportions were 44 per cent and 52 per cent respectively. In 1970, 42 per cent and 50 per cent. In 1973, the claimed intentions to vote Conservative among men and women were 32 per cent and 36 per cent respectively.

If differentiation of the social structure has been occurring, we should expect people's social class association to become less definite. One piece of evidence is provided by a comparison of interviewers' assessed socio-economic grouping and respondent's self-assigned social class; using the common market research definition of socio-economic grouping:

TABLE 6

SOCIO-ECONOMIC GROUPING
(based on occupation of head of household)

	Professional managerial (AB)		*Junior executive, Clerical, non-manual (C1)*		*Skilled manual (C2)*		*Semi- & Unskilled manual (DE)*	
Self-assessed Class	*1966 %*	*1973 %*	*1966 %*	*1973 %*	*1966 %*	*1973 %*	*1966 %*	*1973 %*
Upper-middle/ middle	78	68	53	42	17	22	11	18
Lower middle	9	14	17	22	11	14	6	11
Skilled working	5	9	13	23	34	49	12	33
Ordinary working	8	1	17	4	38	9	70	32
No class/ d.k.	N.A.	8	N.A.	9	N.A.	5	N.A.	6

What appears to be happening is that the extreme socio-economic groups are less clearly identifiable; fewer members of the senior managerial and professional group identified themselves as upper, upper-middle, or middle class in 1973 than did so in 1966. The same applies to the DE group. In only one group has class-identification increased. While in 1966 only 34 per cent of the skilled manual (C2) group called themselves skilled workers, in 1973 almost half (49 per cent) did. A major survey on social class conducted for the "Daily

Mail" by NOP in 1972 concluded that, though most people recognized the existence of class groups, the distinguishing feature was not necessarily occupation, nor money, nor education. No one symbol appeared to be dominant, a sign of the gradual dissolution of the traditional division into social classes.

Parallel to these developments is the growth in the amount and the extent of government involvement in industry and commerce and other aspects of the social system, both national and local. Some attempt has been made to maintain public involvement. As if concerned that the pace of change and the increasing complexity and extent of government action would sever the political links between people and representatives, government commissions have been set up in the latter half of the 1960s to examine the problems of public participation and pressure group activities.

An implication of Janowitz and Segal's model of consensus and cleavage is that the public should be aware of major aspects of the political system and that these aspects, if institutional or structural, should adapt to changes in the system of party representation and in the patterns of party affiliation. Little research has been conducted into what the public know about the political process and its structures. Abrams[14] quotes the finding of a national survey in 1959 where 13 per cent classified themselves as very interested in politics. This low level of interest was no false modesty. Only 30 per cent of all respondents named at least five politicians correctly when asked to name three leaders of the Conservative party, three leaders of the Labour party and one leader of the Liberal party. Twenty per cent were unable to provide even one correct name. More recent surveys have tapped public knowledge of aspects of the political system and found a similarly low level of interest and knowledge. Recently the Boyle Commission on MPs' salaries commissioned a survey organization (ORC) to examine public knowledge about MPs' working conditions. The survey found that most people thought incorrectly that each MP had a secretary and an office to himself. The Redcliffe-Maud Commission on Local Government in England also conducted survey research among the general public which tried to discover *inter alia* the level of public knowledge of local government. Though this indicated a relatively low level of public knowledge, no recent comparative material exists. More recently still a survey commissioned by Granada Television examined public attitudes towards Parliament itself. All these surveys do demonstrate a relatively low level of public knowledge about certain political institutions. The Boyle Commission survey showed ignorance of details of how parliament runs. In the Granada survey, for instance, as many as 77 per cent said they knew nothing or "not very much" about parliament.

As Crewe and Spence[15] add, "perhaps the best evidence of public insulation from parliamentary debate came from the data on special groups within the sample. Thus only 13 per cent of trade unionists could recall any discussion of the Industrial Relations Act in the Commons, a figure which (considering it had provoked prolonged and bitter argument 2 months before), though twice the proportion of the national average, might be considered small. These figures hardly expose a nation of alert and attentive citizens." This survey also suggested that support for parliament and its perceived effectiveness were related *and* that parliament owed some of its popular support to its general legitimacy. It produced evidence that disgruntlement about the lack of political effectiveness is shown in people's resentment of the party political aspects of government rather than in their recognition that parliament itself has major shortcomings.

SUMMARY AND IMPLICATIONS

We have found that Britain's political system since 1945 appears to have been marked not so much by apathy as by an increased level of political heterogeneity, in parallel with a reduced level of satisfaction with the major political parties, their leaders and their problem-solving effectiveness. This has also coincided with an increased level of government involvement in all spheres of life, increased social differentiation and apparently an increase in the amount of pressure group activity. This has occurred despite a low level of public knowledge of the political process and interest in political activity.

What are the implications of these trends? We may ask whether the data justify a conclusion that the British democratic system is under greater strain now than it was thirty years ago. In one sense the answer must be 'no'. The change in political activity has not been to any marked extent anti-system, but rather to other legitimate political alternatives, such as supporting minor political parties, acting through the trade unions rather than the Labour party, acting through pressure groups, and calling for more public involvement in government rather than in politics.

In another sense, however, Britain's democracy is under greater strain. Though most people are relatively satisfied with the political structures that exist, there does exist, as the Kilbrandon Commission and others have found, a significant groundswell of dissatisfaction. Representatives of the two major parties appear to be considered a little too remote from the electors. The institution of Parliament is even more remote.[16] The two major parties have not shown sufficient flexibility in their problem-solving as the problems they are asked to solve diverge more and more from the traditional class-oriented problems encountered immediately after the World War II. Parliament's present solution of increasing the number of specialist committees has answered to an extent the problem of keeping pace with growing government involvement and complexity. It has not answered, and cannot answer, the problem of being unable to minister to the more varied and sophisticated needs of a changing electorate. The structural changes required to do this would seem to include a greater degree of local or regional government, more obvious and open channels of communication between representatives and the represented, and less class-oriented party groups. At a local level attempts are now being made to make planning a more public process. National institutions might attempt to offer a similar openness.

If some such structural changes do not occur, theoretical argument using the cleavage and consensus model would suggest that there will be an increase in anti-system political activity and considerable pressure for change upon the present structures. The durability of these structures has not yet been tested under these conditions.

POSTSCRIPT

The 1974 General Election held on February 28th in response, initially, to the miners' strike seems to have confirmed many of the trends discussed. However turnout at the election increased to 78.7%, against the turnout trend of the past 29 years. In other respects it was remarkable; though only capturing 14 seats, the Liberal party gained 19.3% of the popular vote, doing in a General Election what that party had been doing only at by-elections before. The two major parties only won 75.4% of the vote, and in Scotland only 69.5%. Both Scottish and Welsh Nationalists won seats (7 and 2 respectively).

The marked antipathy to the two major parties, the regional successes of the Nationalists, and the national success of the Liberals confirm that the public's demands were not being answered as satisfactorily as previously. But perhaps this is because sections of the public are learning to make their own distinct demands and expecting results, a situation to which the present structures are not fully adapted.

NOTES

1. R.A. Mackenzie, *British Political Parties* (London, 1963) 2nd edn.
2. S. Beer, *Modern British Politics* (London, 1965)
3. NOP Bulletin (June & July, 1971).
4. M. Janowitz & D.R. Segal, "Social Cleavage and Party Affiliation: Germany Great Britain and United States" *American Journal of Sociology,* vol. 70 (1965), pp. 601-608.
5. *Ibid.* p. 602
6. See, for example, M. Seeman, "On the Meaning of Alienation", *American Sociological Review,* Vol. 24 (Dec. 1959). M.B. Levin *The Alienated Voter,* (New York, 1962), B. Chapman, *British Government Observed,* (London, 1964).
7. See J. Blondel, *Voters, Parties and Leaders: The Social Fabric of British Politics* (London, 1963), H. Durant, "Voting Behaviour in Britain, 1945-1966" in R. Rose (ed.). *Studies in British Politics: A Reader in Political Sociology* (London, 1969) and M. Janowitz and D. Segal, *op. cit.*; D. Butler and D. Stokes *Political Change in Britain* (London, 1969).
8. For a fuller discussion of the development of universal suffrage in Britain see P. Pulzer *Political Representation and Elections in Britain* (London: George Allen and Unwin Ltd., 1967).
9. See also I. Budge and D. Urwin, *Scottish Political Behaviour: A Case Study in British Homogeneity* (London, 1966)
10. C. Cook, "The Liberal and Nationalist Revival" in D. McKie and C. Cook, (eds.) *The Decade of Disillusion: British Politics in the Sixties* (London: Macmillan, 1972).
11. See also H. Pelling, *The British Communist Party: A Historical Profile* (London, 1958) and G. Thayer, *The British Political Fringe: A Profile* (London, 1965).
12. F. Teer & J. Spence, *Public Opinion Polls* (London: Hutchinsons University Library, 1973), Chapter 8.
13. C.A. Goodhardt and R. Bhansali, "Political Economy," *Political Studies* (May, 1970).
14. M. Abrams, "Social Trends and Electoral Behaviour." Paper submitted to the British Sociological Association Conference, March 1962 (mimeo).
15. I. Crewe and J. Spence, "Parliament and Public," *New Society* (12th July, 1973), pp. 78-80.
16. For these findings see I. Crewe and J. Spence, *op. cit.*

DATE DUE

APR 23 '78			
NOV 30 '89			
GAYLORD			PRINTED IN U.S.A